Martin Blake
d. d.

Peter Blake.

St John the Baptist,
2000.

I dedicate this book
on the Collects of the greater Saints
to the memory of the lesser saints,
whom I have known as my friends
in the various Parishes in England and Zambia
in which I have been privileged to minister.

First published December 1999

ISBN 1 870781 10 4

Typeset by Tarragon Press
and printed by Antony Rowe Ltd, Chippenham

Published by Tarragon Press on behalf of Canon Peter Blake
Moss Park, Ravenstone, Whithorn, Scotland DG8 8DR

CONTENTS

ACKNOWLEDGEMENTS

I thank Bishop Alec Graham most sincerely for his Foreword.

I also thank Mrs Joan Baxter, Mrs Mary Donaldson, Mrs Elaine Waddell and, most particularly, Mrs Susan Palmer-Jones, all of whom have helped in the preparation of the text of this Commentary. Without their professional help and friendly encouragement it would not have been completed.

I am, further, most grateful to Mrs Gillian Sinclair and Miss Rosaleen Murdoch for carefully reading its final script.

Peter Blake
Tynron, 1999

Erratum
Page 176, 3rd line:
*'For our sakes he was made man,
who knew no sin...'*
should read:
*'For our sake he was made to be sin,
who knew no sin...'*

FOREWORD

by the Right Reverend A. A. K. Graham,
(formerly Bishop of Newcastle).

The writing of this book has, I sense, been a labour of love for Canon Peter Blake. His commentary on these Collects from the Book of Common Prayer expresses his deep love not only for the Collects, but also for the Scriptures, not least the Gospels and the Psalms, which in the translation familiar to traditional Churchpeople have become part of the fabric and fibre of his being.

This commentary will appeal to a wide range of thoughtful readers, to those who already know well the Saints' Day Collects from the Book of Common Prayer and to those who do not. It contains a mine of information about the origins of each Collect, together with much helpful insight which will enable the reader to pray the Collects with deeper understanding.

Most of all, Canon Blake has made his readers more aware of 'the riches of the glory of his [our Lord Jesus Christ's] inheritance in the Saints', that is to say of the immense and wonderful heritage which we have been given in our membership of the Communion of Saints, and in the encouragement and support to be found there on our pilgrimage to the heavenly city. At a time when Christian imagination, worship and piety run the risk of being starved by concentration on the Church militant here on earth, on the congregational expression of our Church membership, on social issues and on practical matters such as organization and fund-raising, it is all the more welcome to receive this commentary which will help us 'to comprehend with all saints what is the breadth, and length, and depth, and height'.

Alec Graham

O God of the spirits of all flesh, we praise and magnify thy holy Name for all thy servants who have finished their course in thy faith and fear, for the Blessed Virgin Mary, for the holy Patriarchs, Prophets, Apostles, and Martyrs, and for all other thy righteous servants, known to us or unknown;

And we beseech thee that, encouraged by their examples, strengthened by their fellowship, and aided by their prayers, we also may be found meet to be partakers of the inheritance of the Saints in light;

through the merits of thy Son Jesus Christ our Lord. Amen.

INTRODUCTION

In the Apostles' Creed we say that we believe in 'the Communion of Saints'. The Creeds link us with our ecclesiastical past, and so to the devotional lives of earlier Christians. However, what this particular article in the Creed means to ordinary Church of England worshippers today is very different from what it meant to the ordinary worshippers who used our ancient churches a thousand years ago.

Communion (common-union) means fellowship, and in this context for our imaginary ordinary present-day C of E worshippers it means simply 'fellowship of'. In this article they are declaring that they believe that in heaven there are holy people whom we call Saints, who share in the glory, peace and joy that characterises life there. Since Creeds are devotional documents and an integral part of our worship, we are supposed to respond to them devotionally. The word 'believe' in the context of the Creeds means 'put our whole trust in'; we are not just declaring that we think certain things are true when we say the Creeds. In so far as ordinary C of E worshippers today do respond devotionally to this article, they do so by rejoicing in the blessedness that now surrounds the lives of the Saints in heaven, and they look to them as examples to follow. All our Saints' Day Collects in the Book of Common Prayer encourage this response.

However, this is not at all the way this article in the Apostles' Creed would have been interpreted in mediaeval England by those other imaginary worshippers. To them the word 'communion' in this context would have meant 'fellowship with'. They did not simply believe that holy souls lived in heaven with God, enjoying fellowship with him and each other there; they also believed that they might have a close relationship with them, even while they lived here on earth. Moreover they believed that this fellowship was a vital part of both their spiritual and physical lives. Indeed they truly put their trust in this fellowship with the Saints. They did not just look up to them as examples to follow, but rather as patrons and friends on whom they could rely for help, as they made their perilous way through life towards that wonderful place in which these friends of theirs now dwelt.

In the mediaeval era, those in heaven and those on earth were close neighbours. As good neighbours should, they took the keenest interest in each other. Had not Jesus said that there is 'more joy in heaven' when we repent?[1] And in the Epistle to the Hebrews the writer, we notice, had likened those in heaven to spectators at the Games, 'a cloud of witnesses',[2] who from their heavenly vantage point look down on us as we run life's race with all its obstacles, eagerly concerned that we finish our course here and join them there. By implication there are cheers in heaven when we succeed, and groans of dismay when we fail. Naturally there is intense concern about the outcome, for after all what they are watching is a matter of ultimate importance for us and, by virtue of our mutual fellowship, of hardly less importance for them.

One consequence of this belief was to make the Saints the heroes of the masses and not just the interest of the few. Troubadours sang of them; strolling players portrayed their miracles and their heroism; their lives were the popular literature of the day. Ordinary Christians placed themselves under their patronage, choosing usually a Saint from their district, who would be sure to understand their language and the nature of their problems, when they prayed to them. The greatest Saints naturally received the grandest patronage, but there were many Saints and some were not, as it were, as busy as others. Several Saints were reckoned as specialists, being concerned for those in particular trades, or for those suffering from certain afflictions, or for those anxious to excel in scholarship or the arts. All aspects of life on earth were of interest to the Saints, and to succeed in any enterprise, it was deemed essential, not merely sensible, to seek their help. After all, were they not now intimate with God;

did they not now dwell in his Courts; did they not have special access to a knowledge of his will? If ordinary Christians made themselves open to their guidance, and by prayer they could, their patron Saints could help them know and obey God's will, and that, of course, was what truly mattered. Indeed, how could ordinary, sinful, ignorant people possibly manage without their supernatural help, especially since the Devil and his demons had been 'let loose upon the earth', eager to make them fail?[3] The complexities of life were so confusing, the consequences of their decisions so grave. Surely it was madness to go it alone.

The Church then, both in its exhortations from the pulpit, and also in its liturgy, strongly encouraged this belief in the vital importance of this intimate fellowship between earthly and heavenly Christians. Further, we can perceive that this was indeed the expected interpretation of this article in the Apostles' Creed by those who framed it. It is otherwise strangely placed. It comes after mention of the Church but before mention of our forgiveness, which is then followed by mention of our final resurrection to eternal life. The sequence indicates that, in ascribing trust in 'the Communion of Saints,' we are thinking of something that relates as much to our life here as it does to our life hereafter. Such, at all events, was the faith of the Church that gave us that Creed, and it is this faith that we see reflected in the Saints' Day Collects in the mediaeval Sacramentaries.

One of the main aims of the Reformers, however, as well as one of the main results of the Reformation, was to sweep away this mediaeval belief in a direct fellowship with the Saints. It is hard to exaggerate the significance of this aim and of the fact that it was so successfully accomplished. It has greatly changed the devotional lives of the imagined ordinary worshippers in our Church. Nowhere is this change made plainer than in the way in which the Collects for the Saints' Days in the B.C.P. differ from those in the mediaeval Sacramentaries. Whereas Cranmer made the fullest use of the mediaeval Collects for the Sundays and seasonal Festivals in his Prayer

Book of 1549, all the Saints' Day Collects there, except for those for the Purification, the Annunciation and Michaelmas Day, are new reformation prayers, even though in several echoes of the old mediaeval prayers remain. The reason for this is that all the other mediaeval Collects reflected this belief in the fellowship with the Saints that the Reformers both rejected and sought to suppress.

Why, we may ask, did the Reformation seek to sweep away this ancient and widely- held belief in our fellowship with the Saints? Here we need to recognise, first, how the Renaissance preceded the Reformation and how, in large measure, the latter grew out of the former. The independent-minded scholarship that we call the Renaissance originated from within the many new universities that sprang up throughout western Europe in the 12th-14th centuries. In our country, for instance, our first great universities of Oxford and Cambridge were founded at the end of the 12th and the beginning of the 13th centuries. Of decisive significance for the Renaissance was the rediscovery of the works of Aristotle and other ancient Greek philosophers and poets. This was the unexpected, and the most important, consequence of the Crusades, that had been the western Church's response to the overrunning of vast areas of her eastern sister Church by Mohammedans from the south and Mongols from the north. This ancient literature, ironically perhaps, brought a breath of fresh air into the tired scholasticism of the early mediaeval period. As a result of its study, a new scholasticism emerged, inspired by a devotion to pure reason and historical research, rather than to the narrower disciplines of defining ecclesiastical law and of continuous, and often fantastical, biblical exegesis. It created, among both tutors and students, a new critical spirit that became increasingly impatient of the dogmatic claims of the Church, and was rebelliously sympathetic to all demands for freedom of thought and, in due course, to other more political and nationalistic expressions of freedom as well.

Many scholars, like the great St Thomas Aquinas, who remained devoted sons of the Church and to whom the title Schoolmen has been given, sought to harmonise the new secular wisdom with the old ecclesiastical dogma. They were saintly and erudite men, 'the scribes trained for the Kingdom of heaven', foretold by Jesus, who were to 'bring out of their treasure what is new and what is old'.[4] But, as he also foretold, a satisfactory harmonisation of the old with the new is hard to achieve. New wine put into old skins destroys them, and those who enjoy drinking old wine are not likely to desire the new, for they will say, 'The old is best.'[5] Nonetheless, thanks largely to their labours and influence, the Church remained intact for the next 300 years. Yet we can recognise with hindsight that a fuse had been lit that was not snuffed out. There was , unfortunately, in the mediaeval Church so much to protest about, especially about the Papacy, which, although claiming to be the focus of all unity, became itself divided for a generation at the end of the 14th century. This critical spirit conceived by the Renaissance in due course grew into a rebellious, reforming giant that could not be restrained. In 1520 Luther set in motion the Reformation that finally destroyed the unity of western Christendom.

Among the several areas of doctrine that clearly required some reform was the ubiquitous cult of the Saints. Reason and research, those lode-stars of the new scholasticism, showed beyond doubt that all too many of the legends and myths that made the lives of the Saints so exciting and popular were gross exaggerations and obviously untrue. Had not the Church, who had so fully endorsed them, been therefore guilty of leading the faithful astray? Probably; but more importantly, those early protesting scholars, like our own John Wyclif, the first English Protestant, perceived that really much more was at stake than merely the encouragement of an unwise credulity about the Saints. That glorious 'cloud of witnesses' had been allowed to become a cloud of a different kind, one that tended to shut out 'the light of the glorious Gospel of Christ'[6] from the devotional lives of ordinary Christians. The cult of the Saints had not acted as something that, after the teaching of Hebrews, always pointed the faithful to Jesus, 'the author and finisher of our faith',[7] but rather as something that seemed to stand between the faithful and their Lord. Because of the strength of this cult, Jesus had become for so many of the faithful a distant monarch, approachable only through intermediaries, whether they be Saints in heaven or Priests on earth.

This, it was perceived, was not the spiritual experience of the faithful in New Testament times. St Peter could say of his early converts: 'Without having seen him you love him; though you do not now see him, you believe in him and rejoice with unutterable and exalted joy. As the outcome of your faith you obtain the salvation of your souls.'[8]   In contrast, despite the witness of such holy souls as St Francis, and many others, the generality of the flock of St Peter's mediaeval successors in the Papacy did not enjoy the same intimate love and joyous liberty and joy in their religion. The main message that they heard was not, "Jesus is your divine Saviour", but "there is no salvation for you outside the Church". Were they therefore being preached a false Gospel, no less destructive to their salvation than that of the Judaisers and Gnostics against whom the Apostles had fought so hard?[9]   Increasingly, this was the charge being levelled against the leaders of the Church by the reforming sons of the Renaissance who had found a fresh, personal basis for their own faith from their independent-minded study of the New Testament.

The custom of the times, however, played, as is always the case, an important part in the religious situation. The feudal system spanned Europe throughout the mediaeval era. Through it all were linked within a controlling chain of authority. All within it had their allotted place into which God, it was deemed, had been pleased to call them. Such a socio-religious strait-jacket inevitably did not encourage ordinary people, and especially those of the lower strata of society, to believe that they could personally approach 'the King of Kings and the Lord of Lords'.[10] On the other hand, the idea that the Saints, who occupied a privileged place near to the Father and his Son, could intercede for them if asked, fitted well with such an accepted pattern of behaviour. The Church, as part of that feudal world, in this way propagated its own religious feudal system. Such teaching, however, is not found in the New Testament. It has no place in 'the glorious liberty' that Jesus had won for 'the children of God.'[11] Increasingly this truth was being perceived and this liberty demanded. The Reformation sought, perhaps above all, to encourage faith in a personal Saviour, and to give to all the blessed assurance of knowing by faith that they are the accepted children of God.

So the lists became drawn, and among the targets for reform was the widespread, much loved and constantly used devotion to the Saints. Their shrines abounded and were constantly visited, and the great apostolic shrines, like those of St Peter in Rome and St James in Compostela, received pilgrims in their millions. In our own country, perhaps the most honoured and visited shrines were those of Our Lady at Walsingham, St Edward at Westminster, St Thomas à Becket at Canterbury and St Cuthbert at Durham. As the Reformation, however, became fully established in our country, all forms of devotion to the Saints were declared pernicious, 'fond [things] vainly invented and grounded upon no warranty of Scripture but rather repugnant to the Word of God.'[12] From now on, the Saints were to be our examples only. All reliance on their intercession was condemned and, as a consequence, the many shrines, great and small, up and down the country, were systematically closed. Since, however, they were usually linked with Religious Orders and often situated within monastic buildings, the desire to eradicate the cult of the Saints can be seen as a contributory factor in the eventual wholesale dissolution of our wonderful monasteries that was, surely, one of the most tragic features of the Reformation. How wretched it is to recognise that a desire to emphasise the scriptural truth that there is 'one mediator between God and man, the man Christ Jesus'[13] should have undoubtedly helped to bring about the destruction of beautiful places dedicated to his worship and service. (Henry VIII's desire for cash and to eradicate Papal support were, of course, the main cause of this vandalism.)

However, as far as this book is concerned, our Reformers' root and branch opposition to the cult of the Saints resulted, as has been said, in a rewriting of nearly all the mediaeval Saints' Day Collects. Except the three mentioned earlier, they all rejoiced in the intercessions of the Saints and stressed the value the Church placed upon their prayers. This made them, consequently, unacceptable in the Reformers' eyes.

In the New Testament the word Saint does not mean a hero or heroine of the Church. Rather it refers to an ordinary Christian. A glance at the way St Paul starts nearly all his Epistles makes this plain.[14] In them he is writing to those he calls 'Saints' who are nonetheless simply the Christians in those cities. The Greek word he uses is *hagios*, and, although that certainly means a holy person, the biblical meaning of 'holy' is 'dedicated to and accepted by God', not 'especially virtuous.' In Baptism the believer is described as baptised 'into Christ'[15] and, having been in this way 'dedicated to' God, he is also deemed to have been 'accepted by' God. He is therefore 'holy'. The title Saint in the New Testament, therefore, specifically refers to those who have been baptised, and it was only later that the word took on its current heroic meaning.

The earliest heroes of the Church, Saints in our usual understanding of the word, were martyrs. Yet here again there has been a change of meaning given to the word. The Greek word *martus*, from which our word comes, does not mean someone who is killed or persecuted, but one who is a 'witness' and, in particular, one called to give a public testimony in a trial. To be so called, however, was the regular grim experience of the earliest Christians, and one usually leading to their death or imprisonment. What anyone believed then was not simply their own business. To believe as a Christian was a very dangerous matter indeed, and all Christians had to be prepared to acknowledge their faith in Christ as 'their Lord and their God'[16] before a hostile court. In imperial Rome such words belonged to the Emperor, and to deny them to him was treason. Yet to do this was also reckoned to be all Christians' special injunction, and also privilege. 'If you are reproached for the name of Christ, you are blessed because the spirit of glory and of God rests upon you,'[17] wrote St Peter. Jesus, who had witnessed so boldly before both the Sanhedrin and Pontius Pilate, had given every Christian an unavoidable example.[18] As St Paul reminded St Timothy, to be called to follow him in this way was simply the surest way to 'take hold of eternal life'.[19] So it was that the word *martus* became, before long, a special Christian word for the Church's heroes and heroines, who had through suffering entered into the joys of eternal life, its 'noble army'.[20]

The history of the first 300 years of the Church is one of constant harassment that regularly flared up into terrifying persecution. All the Saints, whose Collects we shall be considering, were martyred, except the two St Marys and St John the Evangelist, and in those first centuries, many more thousands were 'called to be Saints' in the most heroic meaning of that phrase. In time, however, it was felt that the honour of Sainthood should be extended to include those who were clearly totally dedicated to our Lord, but who had not been called to prove their dedication 'to the point of shedding their blood'.[21] They too, surely, were part of 'the cloud of witnesses' that now lived in heaven and so were able to help us on earth, not only by their example but also by their intercession. The need particularly to include St John, the one member of the Twelve not to be martyred, was an important factor in establishing this recognition; and, of course, there was the special case of St Mary, who from the earliest times was acknowledged as the Queen of Heaven, being recognised as 'the woman clothed with the sun, the moon under her feet, and a crown of twelve stars on her head'[22] seen by St John the Divine.

Nevertheless, the horrors of the periodic persecutions, that were so dominant a feature of the first 300 years of the Church's history, left an indelible mark. The Church has consequently always considered martyrdom to be the surest route to Sainthood. In the earlier years of the Church every Bishop had the power to declare someone who had been martyred to be a Saint, and his or her Festival Day was that on which the Saint had died. The site of their martyrdom would then become the site of a shrine and, probably, a church, built both to commemorate the Saint's courage, to preserve their relics and to be the focus of pilgrimage for those seeking the Saint's intercessory prayers. So a new cult would begin. Usually these cults of the Saints in the first centuries of the Church's history remained entirely local in their influence, and only occasionally did they become of wider importance. At their shrines, however, legends gathered concerning the Saints' wonderful healings and mysterious appearances. There the heroic stories of their lives and deaths were constantly retold, and not infrequently, as one can easily understand, embroidered by their devotees. These in due course became the exciting material from which the Church created the popular and influential lives of the Saints that flourished in the mediaeval era after the early centuries of persecution were over. Hagiography and hagiology were activities of first importance for at least a thousand years from the 3rd Century.

However, as the Church in the West became increasingly centralised under the Papacy, it was not long before this earlier haphazard way in which Saints were declared by Bishops began to change, and canonisation became the recognised responsibility of Popes. Innocent III (1199-1216) finally made this the Church's official policy. Much later, Benedict XIV

(1734-38) created the lengthy and quite complex procedure for canonisation that pertains today in the Roman Church. Sadly, because of our Reformation, the Church of England lay outside this sensible development, and consequently it has now no official procedure for canonisation. As part of the revision of the B.C.P. in 1928, this matter was addressed, but not solved. Various committees were set up in the 1920s, but they all failed to establish an Anglican procedure whereby our Church might canonise; so the Calendar of 1928, like that of 1662, does not include any post-Reformation Saints. Now, however, through its newly formed General Synod, the Church of England has simply taken to itself the right to add names to its Calendar without attempting formal canonisation. Consequently, in the A.S.B., several holy and famous post-Reformation personalities have been added, including some like the Wesley brothers and William Law, the non-juror, who effectively ended their lives outside our Communion. We do well to reclaim them.

To tell the whole story, however, mention should be made of the ill-starred decision in 1662, as an after-thought, to add to our Calendar three Red-Letter Festivals (no less). These commemorated the death of Charles I, who was declared a martyr, the birth of Charles II, and the failure of the Gunpowder Plot. (January 30, May 29 and November 5.) A special supplement setting out the Prayers for these Festivals was annexed to the B.C.P. by Convocation in 1662, when it met to consider and approve what the Commons had passed in the Act of Uniformity the previous year. However, to keep them legally part of the B.C.P., since they had not been included in the 1661 Act of Uniformity, they needed to be approved both by Convocation and by each subsequent monarch on his or her accession. This continued until Queen Victoria, in 1859, on the advice of Convocation, rescinded her approval, and these commemorations ceased to be legally part of the B.C.P. The veneration of King Charles I as a martyr, however, has continued, and several Parishes still have him as their Patron Saint.

Guy Fawkes's Day is, of course, still remembered, but certainly no longer as a religious occasion. That the lusty King Charles II was once deemed worthy of a Red-Letter Festival, wisely tolerant though he was in a period of great intolerance, is understandably forgotten, but that he restored the monarchy and our established Church will rightly always stand to his lasting credit.

This book is concerned only with the Collects of the major Festivals in our B.C.P., commonly called Red-letter Days, as revised in 1928. There are 24 of these. They all have their own Proper (Collect, Epistle and Gospel) printed out in full. In the 1662 Calendar, however, 72 men and women are mentioned by name; in 1928 this number was raised to 87. Beside those named, groups of Saints are commemorated in such Festivals as All Saints and The Innocents, and there is also the corporate Festival of St Michael and All Angels. Some Saints share their Festivals, as in the case of St Simon and St Jude, and St Philip and St James. Some are allotted more than one Festival Day; St John the Evangelist and St John the Baptist both have two, and the Blessed Virgin Mary has five. Surprisingly in 1662 both St Martin of Tours and Edward, King of the West Saxons, were allotted two each; but in 1928 St Martin's commemorations were reduced to one and King Edward's were removed from the Calendar altogether. It was the policy of the Reformers not to allow any Saint more than one major Festival, with the exception of St Mary who was allowed two. This means that three of the Marian Festivals are designated minor or Black-Letter Festivals, and in the case of the two St Johns only one of their days is given Red-Letter status. In the 1928 revision, however, a valuable supplement, called the Common of Saints, was added, that gave Propers to cover the lesser or Black-letter Saints' Days. This enables Parishes who wish to keep the Festivals of the lesser Saints, one of whom may be their Patron, to do so with appropriate solemnity. Included, also, in the number of the B.C.P.'s 24 Red-Letter Festivals, and so considered in this commentary, are the two

Holy Days of Jesus, his Circumcision and his Transfiguration, the latter being given that honour only in 1928.

The choice of Saints in our 1662 Calendar is often surprising. For instance, although St Anne, the Blessed Virgin's mother, is there, St Joseph, her husband, is not! Nor, strangely, was so important a figure added to the Calendar in 1928. However in the A.S.B. he has very properly been given not only his traditional day, March 19, but also Red-Letter status. Then such famous New Testament figures as St Timothy and St Titus are omitted in both the 1662 and 1928 Calendars, but are honoured at last in the A.S.B. In 1662, comparatively obscure Saints like St Evurtius and St Machutus are mentioned, whereas such luminaries as St Francis of Assisi and St Bernard of Clairveux are not. In 1928, very properly, the first two are omitted and the latter two included. However we should recognise here the part custom and politics will have played in the choice of the Saints in 1662. In the case of St Evurtius, his day, September 7, was Queen Elizabeth I's birthday, which was still being kept as a national holiday, and St Machutus's inclusion was due to the special devotion in which he was held in our western Dioceses and especially in Wales. He was a Welshman, and all parts of the Church needed representation in the Calendar.

Saints' Days, despite the new attitude of the Reformers to them, continued for centuries to retain their social and economic associations. They were linked all over the country to the Fairs and Festivals that have always played such a vital role in the life of our towns and villages. The important Quarter Days were also all major Church Festivals, Lady Day, St John the Baptist's Day, Michaelmas Day, and Christmas Day. All trades continued to retain and honour their Patron Saints, and this consideration no doubt assured that St Crispin, St Dunstan and St Cecilia, for instance, were named in our Calendar, otherwise the Guilds for shoe-makers, jewellers and musicians would have been most upset. The reason why fewer major Saints' Days, which were all kept as public holidays, came in summer than in winter had much to do with the demands of agriculture. Why St Martin was given a second day of remembrance is, probably, because he had given his name to the period in July called Martinmas, which, like Lammastide in August, was a term used in legal documents. Consequently, despite the changes in the general attitude of worshippers to the Saints, many remained household names in our land long after their cults had ceased. Even the ravages of the Covenanters under Cromwell failed to eradicate the affection in which the Saints were held, especially in our country areas. In this matter, however, the arrival of the Industrial Revolution and the urbanisation of the majority of our population has, sadly, been more successful. Now it must be said that a genuine interest in the Saints, let alone a love of them, has become the concern of the few rather than the many. Ordinary C of E worshippers, let alone ordinary citizens, now very largely ignore them, and, if we may be allowed to say it, their spiritual lives are the poorer for doing so.

Every society needs its heroes, and the Church of England and the Anglican Communion have plenty of them. No doubt great care must be taken in adding names to our Calendar, but the faithful will always be greatly encouraged when this is done. The best means, obviously, is through a method of canonisation, but if this cannot now be established, the addition of new names to the Calendar, made official by an appropriate ceremony of recognition and celebration, should regularly take place. Some who have died comparatively recently should surely soon be added to our Calendar of Saints, holy people, whom Jesus has used to his glory, and whose story will awaken faith whenever it is told. 'Their memorial' must not be allowed 'to perish', for 'they were the glory of their times'.[23]

'Such honour have all his Saints',[24] said the Psalmist, and it is very important for the life of the Church that their honour is properly recognised, so that their heroic and beneficial influence may be fully extended. This, however, as we have seen, is a matter that, sadly, has bitterly divided Christians, and the way in which they should be properly honoured has been fiercely contested. Our Reformers swung the emphasis wholly onto our acknowledging them only as examples to follow. Although the faithful should rejoice in their memory, in effect they were to treat them no longer as alive and blessed, but rather as dead and departed, waiting in their graves for Judgement Day. Jesus alone, it was said, has (as yet) risen from the dead, and so is the only person to have passed through death into life. Consequently, he alone in heaven 'ever lives to make intercession for us.'[25] The Reformers' main point, however, was an important one; they believed that the ubiquitous cult of the Saints detracted from everyone's need to have a personal faith in Jesus. St John the Baptist had said, 'he must increase, but I must decrease.'[26] The mediaeval Church, they declared, had turned this Gospel truth upside down. Nothing must take the spiritual spot-light off Jesus, and this, they believed, is what the cult of the Saints had done. Moreover, it was claimed that we hear nothing of this fellowship with the Saints in heaven in the New Testament Church.

However, a different assessment of the New Testament's evidence and teaching can be made. Since in those earliest days of the Church it was generally hoped that Christ's Second Coming would be soon, even within the lifetime of some of Christ's first disciples, our fellowship with the Saints in heaven inevitably did not loom large. That does not mean that the concept of our fellowship with them is absent from the New Testament. St Paul in Philippians uses a particularly interesting phrase to describe it. In Greek it is *to politeuma en ouranois*.[27] This is variously translated, in the N.E.B as 'citizens of heaven', in the R.S.V. as '(our) commonwealth (is) in heaven', and in the A.V. as '(our) conversation (is) in heaven'. The word *politeuma*, which is linked to *polis*, a city, refers to the kind of citizenship that belongs to those who are expatriates, living in some foreign land but all the time nostalgically conscious of their real home. That is where their hearts are, though their work keeps them where, for the time being at least, they must remain. Many thousands of our countrymen in our imperial centuries knew the meaning of *politeuma*, and Philippi was a place where many such Roman imperial expatriates lived. *En ouranois* means 'in heaven', and that, said St Paul, is really where the hearts of the Philippian Christians belonged. So with us, our 'citizenship', our 'commonwealth', our 'conversation', our *politeuma*, is really in heaven, not on earth. We are to live looking up to the unseen world where the Saints we have known or heard of have gone, conscious of common 'citizenship' with them, having spiritual fellowship with them in worship, and intimate 'conversation' with them in prayer. St Paul to the Corinthians talked about the wonder of this heavenly citizenship, in which we are even now partakers by faith and hope, as 'an eternal weight of glory beyond all comparison'.[28] We are to look forward to its joy, eager to share it with those for whom it was now a reality and not just a hope. Not to recognise our 'fellowship with' the Saints in heaven, not to trust in this way in 'the Communion of Saints', is, therefore, it can be claimed, to fail to 'comprehend' with them what is 'the breath and length and height and depth' of the Gospel.[29]

It is surely relevant to notice that the eastern Orthodox Churches, which did not experience the impact of the Renaissance, and therefore were untouched by our western Reformation, retain to the full their ancient devotion to the Saints. There have been, it is true, iconoclastic controversies in their Churches, but they were the result of Jewish and Moslem influence rather that of rival Christian attitudes. In Orthodox churches, around the sanctuary where Christ is enthroned in his tabernacle, the Saints, depicted through their icons, stand in attendance on Jesus, ready and eager to join in our worship of him. All, both they and us, are 'looking to Jesus,'[30] and in no way does their presence in such numbers detract from him being the focus of the adoration of the faithful; on the contrary, it greatly stimulates it. In their Churches 'such honour have all his Saints'. It is neither narrowed nor exaggerated. Also, for them, as indeed it is for western Catholics, Christ's Mother plays a particularly vital part in all their spiritual lives and corporate fellowship. They take Jesus at his word, as reported by St John, loving and honouring St Mary as their Mother too. Further, they seek to honour Jesus by finding a special relationship with someone with whom he himself had a special relationship, and to claim that person as their Patron Saint. The inspiration to live a better Christian life that is experienced by those who do enjoy such a relationship, however, is not confined to their Church. Cardinal Newman's relationship with his Patron Saint, St Philip Neri, in this consideration, comes to mind, and, more generally, through just such a spiritual relationship, many, not least in our Church, can witness to being made better Christians by being Franciscans.

The power of the great lovers of Jesus to make disciples for him continues, and does not end with their death. Though dead, as so many can testify, they have not really departed. Like that of Abel, the blood of the martyrs still speaks to those who have ears to hear, but of him for whom they shed their blood and whose blood was shed for us all[31]. Indeed, if we seek to cut ourselves off from their fellowship, we find we cannot benefit so very much simply from their example. We may perceive a devotional truth here. Churches, and individual Christians, that really value the example of the Saints and seek fully to honour it, find themselves drawn, albeit unexpectedly, into a blessed experience of their fellowship. 'Such honour have all his Saints.' When it is given, 'fellowship with' them follows, and then we are enabled truly to benefit from their example.

These reformation Collects are splendid prayers, and in some instances, as we shall have occasion to show, they are an obvious improvement devotionally on the mediaeval Collects they replaced. In this one respect, however, they may be said to be deficient; they do not seek to encourage the sense of fellow-'citizenship' or spiritual 'conversation' that we may have with the Saints in heaven. In spite of their merit, this is a great pity. However, in the end they do not wholly deprive us of this ancient element of our faith. This is because 'the truth as it is in Jesus'[32] has a way of emerging whenever the Church, his new Body on earth, meets for worship. Then most definitely we are in living communion with all the company of heaven, a truth that Cranmer clearly recognised in the Sanctus that remains so important a part of the Holy Communion Service that he has given us. It is also a major concern of this commentary to emphasise this truth.

SAINT ANDREW'S DAY

November 30th

Almighty God, who didst give such grace unto thy holy Apostle Saint Andrew, that he readily obeyed the calling of thy Son Jesus Christ, and followed him without delay: Grant unto us all, that we, being called by thy holy Word, may forthwith give up ourselves obediently to fulfil thy holy commandments, through the same Jesus Christ our Lord. Amen.

St Andew's Day is the first of the Saints' Days. The liturgical year starts with Advent, and St Andrew's Day invariably falls within a day or two of Advent Sunday, if the two days do not coincide. This is, however, an appropriate honour for St Andrew for a more devotional reason. He was the first missionary. Having met Jesus with St John and having stayed and talked with him, he hurried back to tell his brother, St Peter, and to bring him to Jesus.[1] That story as told by St John indicates that like him and probably others of the Twelve, St Andrew had been a follower of St John the Baptist. In the Gospels St Andrew is always mentioned among the first four in all lists of the Twelve,[2] although he clearly ranked below the triumvirate of Sts Peter, James and John, who were marked out by Jesus for such special intimacy.[3] He probably had a particular friendship with St Philip. They came from the same town, Bethsaida, and their closeness is apparent in the story of the Greeks who wanted to see Jesus in Holy Week.[4]

St Andrew's later history is legendary. He is linked with Greece, where he is said to have evangelised Scythia and Epirus, and met his martyr's death in Patras in Achaia. He is, however, also said to have founded the Church in Constantinople whither his relics were later transferred from Patras. His connection with Constantinople had another consequence. From there Russia was evangelised in the 9th century by missionaries under his patronage, and for that reason he became the Patron Saint of Russia.

To the claim that his relics lie in Constantinople there is a rival claim that they, or perhaps more likely some of them, were taken by St Rule in the 4th century to Scotland. Guided by an angel, so the legend goes, St Rule travelled on until he came to Fife. There he buried his precious relics and built a church over them. This church soon became a centre for evangelism and later for pilgrimage, and the city that arose around it was called St Andrew's. He became in consequence the Patron Saint of Scotland also.

Among the most firmly held details of St Andrew's story is that he was crucified on an X-shaped cross, and one of that shape is commonly called a St Andrew's cross. The legend of his martyrdom is particularly moving. When he saw the cross that had been erected for his execution, he saluted it and kissed it. He rejoiced that he was going to die in similar fashion to his Lord, seeing in it the surest way to be forever united with him. He stripped himself willingly, gave his clothes politely to his executioners, and from the cross before he died preached the message of God's forgiveness and of our salvation through Jesus to those who had come to see him die.

This apocryphal story is especially relevant to our consideration of this Collect for an unusual reason. It was composed in 1552 to take the place of the one composed in 1549 that had been based upon this legend of St Andrew's death. A Collect consists of three elements: the invocation, the petition and the aspiration. The invocation is like the foundation of the prayer, and in the Saints' Day Collects, this always consists of some fact that is known about the Saint. The Reformers, we have stressed, were suspicious of all legends of the Saints, however edifying, and accepted as irrefutable only that which had the warranty of Scripture. This stirring story of St Andrew embracing his cross before he was crucified is not, of course, scriptural, yet Cranmer in 1549 had used it in the invocation of his first Collect. Then it read, 'Almighty God, who has given such grace to thy Apostle Saint Andrew, that he counted the sharp and painful death of the cross to be a high honour and a great glory...' On reflection, or perhaps after criticism, Cranmer rejected this earlier Collect in his revision of the B.C.P. in 1552 and substituted the one we now use. The Sarum Collect disqualified itself by praying that St Andrew might be for the Church ' a perpetual intercessor'.

In Cranmer's new invocation we recall the famous call of St Andrew and his brother, Peter. As it is told by St Matthew and St Mark it reads almost like a miracle. 'As Jesus walked by the Sea of Galilee he saw two brothers...He said to them, "Follow me"..Immediately they left their nets and followed him.'[5] This sort of thing does not happen in ordinary life! Perhaps we may believe that Jesus, the Son of God, could have wielded such authority, and extracted such obedience from strangers, and indeed the way that the first two Evangelists have told the story they probably sought to suggest this. However, St John reveals that in fact both St Andrew and St Peter had previously met Jesus, and they were already convinced that he was the Messiah.[6] Almost certainly, then, a more accurate description of what happened on that fateful day for those brothers would read: 'As Jesus walked by the sea of Galilee, he was looking for the two brothers who were fishermen, whom he had met earlier in Bethany beyond Jordan.' We may further suppose that when Jesus found them and called them, they were ready and eager to follow him, and not at all, as the account given in the first two Gospels would suggest, in a state of shocked bewilderment. No doubt neither brother could have guessed where their call would take them, but they both knew that to follow Jesus was above all else what they wanted to do. So, when the moment came, they 'immediately left their nets and followed him.'

An important truth is revealed here. No vocation ever comes to us completely out of the blue, however much it may seem as if it does. Always there has been a time of divine preparation, however mysterious or unperceived, which St Paul describes like this: 'Those whom he fore-knew he also predestined...and those whom he predestined he also called.'[7] God's ways with us may well be hidden from us; indeed, some are sure to be, for from our birth, and indeed earlier from our conception, we are to believe we are the objects of God's love. 'Before I formed you in the womb I knew you,' Jeremiah was told.[8] Vocations may seem, like falling in love, experiences that catch us totally unawares to change our lives, but that is because we are generally so unaware of 'God's hand that leads us and his right hand that holds us,' as the Psalmist long ago perceived.[9] Grace, however, is the name we give to this mysterious loving care of God for us, and his grace, we are assured, will always be 'sufficient for us' to achieve all that he wants us to do.[10] So we are to go forward in a spirit of 'ready obedience', like St Andrew, immediately it becomes clear that God is calling us in any way into his service.

A call from God, of whatever nature, is certain to alter the way we live our lives, and perhaps their whole direction. We must accept the realities of this, whatever the cost, without fear, because of our confidence in God's sufficient grace. Yet how hard this is for us, for we are so timid and know our weakness and sin so well! This, however, should not surprise us. After all it was even so, we know, for St Peter, who in the Lucan version of his call with his brother cried out to Jesus, 'Depart from me, for I am a sinful man';[11] and we can surely believe it was therefore the same for St Andrew. This story of their initial rejection of Christ's call (for we can confidently link the two brothers in both stories of their call), however much it may seem to be at variance with the other version, not only rings true, but is also just as we would expect. Indeed, we need both versions of their calls for the truth of them to be fully told.

As sinners, such inevitably will be our own initial response to a call from God. It has always been so, and always will be so. 'Who am I that I should go to Pharaoh?' said Moses.[12] 'I am a man of unclean lips,' said Isaiah.[13] 'I am only a youth. I do not know how I speak,' said Jeremiah.[14] 'Lord, I am not worthy,'[15] is, therefore, certain to be our own instinctive response too to the very idea of being called by God to his service. The Collect speaks of 'giving up ourselves', and in so doing it emphasises the element of sacrifice that will always be involved. Some fear , therefore, is only reasonable. But as it was for St Andrew, so it will be for us. 'Such grace' will be given us to enable us (if we may compare little with great) to overcome every obstacle to 'ready obedience', and for us, too, to 'follow without delay' wherever the call of God may lead. The words of the Collect also remind us of the Prayer Book's General Thanksgiving, where the dynamic that powers such 'giving up [of] ourselves to [God's] service' is visualised as a deep 'sense of all [his] mercies' such as will, despite the cost, make 'our hearts unfeignedly thankful.' This is because 'we know that everything works for good for those who love God and are called according to his purpose.'[16]

Before ending our thoughts on a prayer for St Andrew's Day, we must not forget the particular theme that the Church has given to it. Because St Andrew was the first missionary, his Festival has traditionally been kept as a day of prayer for missions and of thanksgiving for the lives of missionaries. The petition stresses the central role of God's 'holy Word' in the life of the Church. Although this Word is found in the pages of Scripture, our experience of hearing it is not restricted to our reading it there. It can be spoken to us formally by a preacher or, very simply, by someone, perhaps a friend, or even one of our own family, telling us of

Jesus. So it was when St Andrew told his brother, 'We have found the Messiah.'[17] In that scene we see how the missionary work of the Church began, and we get a picture, too, of how it may be continued by anyone, even by children, even by you and me.

The word 'mission' and 'missionary' derive from the Latin word *mittere* meaning 'to send'. 'How can men preach unless they are sent?' asked St Paul,[18] but before they are sent they must first be called. In this Collect we do not find the word 'mission' or 'send', but we do find the word 'called' twice. This is the order of events that we see in the story of St Andrew. 'Follow me,' said Jesus, and then, having made him his disciple, he said to him, 'I will make you a fisher of men.'[19] So it is for us, and in this Collect we pray that having been 'called' we may 'forthwith give up ourselves obediently to fulfil God's holy commandments.' We should not, however, restrict these to the general commandments that God lays upon everyone, because for each of us God has special commandments too. Just as he calls us one by one, so he gives to each of us our own personal vocation. 'There are varieties of gifts...and of service...and of working, but it is the same God who inspires them all in every one.'[20] What, however, will be a common element in God's loving purpose for each of us is that we become agents of the Gospel. All of us in our own situation are both called and sent to 'do the work of an evangelist'.[21] God 'apportions [a vocation] to each one individually as he wills'.[22] Whatever it is, it will be appropriate to our talents and circumstances, but for us to fulfil our vocation is as important for ourselves, as it will be for others. The famous saying of St Paul may be said to apply even to us, 'Woe to me if I do not preach the Gospel'.[23] Our experience of spiritual fulfilment depends upon it.

To fulfil our vocation, words are sure to be of some importance. 'Let your talking be of all his wondrous works.'[24] None of us should be unwilling to tell others of what we believe, if the opportunity should present itself. 'I believed and therefore will I speak,'[25] and did not Jesus say, 'He who hears you, hears me'?[26] But our conduct also will equally play its part, and it may well be the more crucial factor, or even the only means possible. Just as people 'watched' Jesus,[27] they will do the same to us. 'You are the salt of the earth' and 'you are the light of the world,' he said to his first disciples,[28] and we must accept that this truth will apply to us too. 'Your good deeds,' said St Peter to his converts, are so important because 'through them unbelievers may come to glorify God',[29] a teaching that echoes Jesus's 'let your light so shine before men that they may see your good works and give glory to your Father, who is in heaven.'[30] St Paul also stresses these principles of everyday evangelism in his homely admonition to the Colossians, 'Conduct yourself wisely towards outsiders, making the most of the time. Let your speech be gracious, seasoned with salt, so that you may know how you ought to answer everyone.'[31] Even in the most personal area of married and family life, he said, we remain 'under authority' 'to fulfil God's holy commandments'. 'Wife, how do you know whether you will save your husband? Husband, how do you know whether you will save your wife?'[32], and '[parents] bring up your children in the discipline and instruction of the Lord'.[33] Do not such challenging words of St Paul to ordinary Christians in Corinth have a particularly modern resonance about them?

Wherever we are, wherever we go, we live 'in Christ'.[34] We are always his representatives, always on duty. How hard this is for us, certainly, but we are to be like servants whose 'loins [remain] girded and their lamps burning'.[35] We are not, moreover, to let our sense of unworthiness cloud this truth for us, for Christ now has no other hands and feet and lips to act and speak through than ours.[36] Isaiah was overwhelmed at first by his sense of unworthiness, but then 'such grace' was given him that he could still say, 'Here am I! Send me.'[37] So with us. The Gospel story ends with the risen Christ saying, 'Go and make disciples.'[38] We are all to accept that each of us has a part to play in the continuing mission of the Church, and St Andrew's Day is the day on which the Church especially brings this truth before us.

SAINT THOMAS THE APOSTLE
December 21st

Almighty and everliving God, who for the more confirmation of the faith didst suffer thy holy Apostle Thomas to be doubtful in thy Son's Resurrection; Grant us so perfectly, and without all doubt, to believe in thy Son Jesus Christ, that our faith in thy sight may never be reproved. Hear us, O Lord, through the same Jesus Christ, to whom, with thee and the Holy Ghost, be all honour and glory, now and for evermore.

St Thomas was a twin. Even though family connections among the early disciples are often referred to by the Evangelists, his sibling is not mentioned. Nonetheless this fact about him seems to have marked him in some special way, since it is mentioned three times in St John's Gospel, in which he plays so prominent a part.[1]

After Pentecost the Church began to expand with remarkable rapidity. In the Acts of the Apostles we hear especially of St Peter, St Paul and St Barnabas with regard to this missionary outreach, but legend has it that, guided by the Holy Spirit, all Twelve went forth in various directions to evangelise and, in due course, to suffer martyrdom. This at all events perfectly fits the story of St Thomas, as it is told in the apocryphal book called the Acts of St Thomas. There we hear that St Thomas was sent to evangelise India, and it is an undoubted fact that the Mar Thoma Church in South India traces its origins to St Thomas. His story, as told in his Acts, is both charming and exciting, if, sadly, legendary. According to it, our hero does not, however, start too well! We are told that at first he flatly refuses to go to such a faraway place as India, because it would necessitate a dreaded sea journey. However, as in the Gospels, the risen Jesus had his eye upon him, and himself took a hand in seeing that he did not fail. It happened, so the story goes, that a courtier of King Gundaphorus of South India had arrived in Jerusalem at that time seeking a particularly skilled carpenter, for the King wanted to build himself a palace worthy of his kingdom. The risen Jesus then appeared to this courtier and told him that he was himself a master carpenter, and that, although he could not go himself, he had a slave, who was equally skilled, and exactly the man he needed. Moreover he was prepared to sell him to the man. Now St Thomas was indeed a carpenter, and when Jesus and the Indian courtier approached him the following conversation ensued. 'Is this your Master?' inquired the courtier. 'Indeed he is,' said the astonished St Thomas. 'Then I have bought you from him, and you must come with me.' So it was, we are told, that St Thomas, the slave of Jesus Christ, went to India to build, not only a palace for the Indian King, but also an Indian Church for Jesus! Whatever the truth may be of how St Thomas came to India, in the end we are told that St Thomas was killed at Mylapore, near Madras, where an ancient stone cross still stands, marking the place of his martyrdom.

This Collect was composed by Cranmer for the 1549 Book. Since the Sarum Collect 'sought' the Saint's 'assistance' and 'protection' as we 'sought' to 'follow in the steps of his faith', it was rejected by him as theologically objectionable. The faith of St Thomas referred to in it would, however, have been that which he declared in those immortal words, 'My Lord and my God',[2] when he finally met with the risen Jesus, and in Cranmer's new Collect the same occasion and the same faith are equally central, although now all reference to our seeking the Saint's assistance to share in it is omitted.

Cranmer made another significant change from the mediaeval Proper for this day; he included in the Gospel the last two verses, 30 and 31, of St John's Chapter 20, which had not been part of the mediaeval Gospel. These read: 'Now Jesus did many other signs in the presence of the disciples, which are not written in this book, but these are written that you may believe that Jesus is the Christ, the Son of God, and that believing you may have life in his name.' As his Collect is particularly about the purpose and importance of faith the addition of those two verses is especially appropriate. They are indeed among the most important verses in the Bible, and to be welcomed for that reason, but, since Chapter 21 is a later addition, they also constitute the original ending of St John's Gospel. Consequently what we should particularly notice because of this is that when St John finally lets the curtain fall on his marvellous Gospel drama, it is St Thomas, and not St Peter (as in the added ending), who is with Jesus holding centre stage.

Is this fact fortuitous? It is surely unexpected. We should remind ourselves, however, that in no book is every small detail more worthy of close and prayerful consideration than in St John's Gospel. Has it, therefore, some meaning besides telling us simply what happened? This is very likely, for hidden meanings and *doubles entendres* are found everywhere in this Gospel. The point perhaps is this; in his doubt St. Thomas is so typical a character; he is Mr. Everyman. In particular he personifies the 'you' that so suddenly and unexpectedly arrives in those two final verses which Cranmer included, 'these are written that you may believe', and that 'you may have life in his name'.[3] The one, then, who 'so perfectly and without all doubt' (at least in the end), expresses the true heart of the Christian faith is, consequently, someone just like us, like 'you' and me! Are we to believe that this final, comforting but powerful revelation, with which we are left by St John, was not intended? Surely not!

The Gospel can quite easily seem to us, the ordinary reader, very remote;

the story is so wonderful, the message so exalted, that even when we believe it to be true we can doubt that it really embraces us. Can we really know God? Can he really so love us personally that he gave his only begotten Son that we might not perish but have eternal life?[4] Can Jesus really be the Friend and Saviour of such as we know ourselves to be? The fact, however, that it is St. Thomas who in the end fills centre-stage in St John's Gospel, kneeling before Jesus and being accepted so personally and lovingly by him, is surely meant to contradict any such anxieties. On the contrary such a reaction is being shown up to be among those 'doubts' that Christ reproved, a wrong attitude towards him that we must not allow to grip our hearts and minds. So just as St Thomas in that scene expresses for us our faith in Jesus, so too he helps us fully to appreciate Jesus's acceptance of us, an equally important consideration. Cranmer may have been right, some would say, to object to the belief expressed in the Sarum Collect that St Thomas can 'assist us by his protection' to 'follow the steps of his faith', but nonetheless this story of him does most certainly 'assist us', who are so like him, to share his faith, as we meditate on all that happened to him, be it worthy of rebuke or praise, in that dramatic ending to St John's Gospel.

The Collect declares that God allowed St Thomas to doubt, and indeed that he did so for a good and sufficient reason. But does this truth also apply to us? For do we not all experience doubts? In this Collect, however, and in the Gospel, doubts are not considered in any way good things. We pray here that we may have a 'perfect' faith, one that is 'without all doubt', and Jesus, we know, said to St Thomas, 'Be not faithless'. Doubt may so easily harden into the sin of disbelieving in God altogether, to love and obey whom is the first and great Commandment. To allow doubt in our spiritual lives, therefore, as if it does not matter, cannot be right, and so cannot be what this prayer supports. How, then, are we to understand what it is saying of God, and of his dealing with us?

It is, however, a fact of the spiritual life that faith and doubt are inextricably linked. In practical terms they are not opposites. Rather they are like two sides of one coin, mysteriously part of each other. It is as if doubt contributes to the value of faith, and faith justifies doubt. Perhaps we can even say that faith that has never experienced and overcome doubt is not actually true faith at all! Yet we know that faith is good and doubt is bad, and that we must struggle to maintain faith and to suppress doubt. These words of Jesus to St Thomas, therefore, should probably be translated, 'Become not faithless.' A process, a struggle, is thereby implied, which can surge back and forth. Does this not describe our own experience? And, moreover, does it not seem probable that in this life we shall never be free from this most disturbing fact of the spiritual life? Fortunately, however, the Collect seems to assure us that this common spiritual experience may be for us a positive, and not just a negative one.

We are considering here an issue that is part of the wider mystery of temptation, to which there are also two sides. The Greek word *peirasmos,* which is usually translated a 'temptation' means also a 'testing' or a 'trial'. God, however, does not tempt us, but he does test us.[5] Just how close the connection is between these two truths is well illustrated by St Matthew's description of what happened to Jesus, 'Then Jesus was led up by the Spirit [of God] into the wilderness to be tempted by the Devil'.[6] Moreover, have not many wondered what to make of the petition that God should not 'lead us into temptation'? It certainly seems to need the following petition that he will instead deliver us from the power of evil, or the Evil One, to make sense. In life this is certainly our daily experience. We are tempted to do what is wrong, but in our temptation we are also being tested to do instead what is right. So out of our temptation, or our trial, we may be led up or down, we may experience defeat or victory, our relationship with God may be weakened or strengthened. Clearly this reality is 'suffered' by God (who can deny it?), but his purpose must be that we should be led up, experience victory, have our relationship with him strengthened, all 'for the more confirmation of our faith', even as it was for St Thomas.

It is to this vital end, we also believe, that God gives us his grace, and it is the Church's Word and Sacraments that are 'the means of grace'.[7] It is central to the story of St Thomas, both in respect of his doubts and of his rediscovery of faith, that for several days he left the fellowship of his fellow disciples, missing thereby their experience of Easter Day, and that the risen Jesus came to him only after he had returned to their fellowship. So with us. It is only as we remain within that fellowship that we can be sure to receive the grace that will enable us to be strengthened rather than weakened by our trials, or temptations, and to have our faith confirmed in spite of our doubts.

The Collect also speaks of a faith that is 'perfect', and that is 'without all doubt', and that may 'never be reproved'. How can we conceive of such a faith? No doubt we may conceive of it as a characteristic of the faith of Jesus himself. Perhaps we may conceive of it as characteristic of his greatest Saints. Perhaps now of St Thomas. But how can we conceive of it as something possible for such as ourselves?

We are, I believe, given the clue as to how we can in that famous declaration of St Thomas, 'My Lord and my God'. St Thomas was both a brave and a passionate man. One of the stories told of him by St John makes it clear that he at least fully accepted what Jesus had said about having to die, even if others among the Twelve refused to accept this awful truth. So, when Jesus finally decided to go to Jerusalem, St Thomas said, 'Let us also go, that we may die with him'.[8] Then, later, when the Twelve were in the Upper Room and Jesus was telling them that he was soon to go from them, but that they would follow him in due course, St Thomas spoke for them all, 'Lord, we do not know where you are going, [so] how can we know the way'?[9] Both stories show how much he loved and wanted to be with his Master. For St Thomas that was all that mattered, to be with his Master. His going away on his own cannot obviously be put down to fear, but it can perhaps be explained by his desperate sense of loss, and also by his wondering how he might yet follow Jesus through death. Here, perhaps, we may make a further observation. As we have noticed, we do not hear anything of St Thomas's twin. Had he or she died, and had the death of one so close to him left a very special mark upon his mind and spirit? Had this experience of such a special bereavement made his sense of loss at the death of Jesus more painful for him than for any of the Apostles? At all events, what we hear in that ecstatic exclamation, 'My Lord and my God', is surely joy, wonder and worship rather than simply faith.

Faith and hope are among the greatest virtues, but they are not as great as love.[10] They may be said to be love's foundations and so 'abide', but there is a sense in which they may be, and perhaps should be, swallowed up by love. It is love that banishes doubt, not faith! Whereas faith will be for ever badgered by doubt, love is proof against it. That there are no doubts in love, even love in the world can show us. After all, even the worldly can love 'for better, for worse, for richer, for poorer, in sickness and in health, till death us do part',[11] with a passion and sincerity that scorns all doubt and accepts any suffering. So it may be in our relationship with Jesus Christ, and indeed much more so in our relationship with him. When like St Thomas we can also say from our hearts, 'My Lord and my God', then we too will have left doubt behind. This Collect speaks of a relationship with God that is 'perfect and without all doubt', and not to be 'reproved'. That can only be one of love. Faith will still be part of it, of course, but something greater than faith will dominate it; and the lasting outcome of such a relationship is that to which St John points in those last words of his Gospel, 'life in his name'.[12]

SAINT STEPHEN'S DAY

December 26th

Grant, O Lord that, in all our sufferings here upon earth for the testimony of thy truth, we may steadfastly look up to heaven, and by faith behold the glory that shall be revealed; and, being filled with the Holy Ghost, may learn to love, and bless our persecutors by the example of thy first Martyr Saint Stephen, who prayed for his murderers to thee, O blessed Jesus, who standest at the right hand of God to succour all those that suffer for thee, our only Mediator and Advocate. Amen.

This Collect was composed by Bishop Cosin in 1662. Behind it lie the Collects in the Sarum Missal and the 1549 Book. Both stressed the teaching we particularly associate with St Stephen, that we should love even our enemies and pray for them, and this remains prominent in this Collect. However in marked contrast with Cranmer's Collect, which was extraordinarily brief, indeed consisting of just one sentence, Bishop Cosin's new Collect includes other allusions to St Stephen's story, a reference to the Holy Spirit, a reminder of our Lord's heavenly glory which we may hope to share, and the mention of his role as our Mediator and Advocate. All these new elements jostle together to make an unusually rich devotional mix that sets it apart from the other Saints' Day Collects. It is also unusual in that it is addressed to Jesus, not the Father, the only one of these Collects to be so.

All that we know about St Stephen is told us in the Acts of the Apostles.[1] As he is the first named of the Deacons, he was probably their leader. Even more to be noticed, however, is the manner in which St Luke praises his character. No one, not even St Peter and St Paul, the twin heroes of his narrative, are described in such glowing terms. 'A man full of faith and the Holy Spirit', one who was 'full of grace and power', so much so that his face shone 'like the face of an angel'. One is reminded of the Blessed Virgin, and even of Jesus himself at his Transfiguration.[2] Clearly, therefore, we must not remember St Stephen only for his defence before the Sanhedrin and his martyrdom, for it would appear that it was his holiness that made him most memorable to his contemporaries. Is not this quality in him particularly apparent in his dying prayer, which echoes so wonderfully that of Jesus on the Cross? The Old Testament lesson set for Evensong on St Stephen's Day recalls the stoning of Zechariah, a son of the famous High Priest Jehoiada. Judah then was being led back into the apostasy from which his father had saved it, and Zechariah bravely denounced the King and his courtiers for what they were doing. There, however, the similarity between those two equally brave and passionate men ceases. The dying prayer of Zechariah, 'May the Lord see and avenge,' is very different from St Stephen's sublime, 'Lord, lay not this sin to their charge'.[3]

One of the best known biblical texts is, 'Greater love has no man than this, that a man lay down his life for his friends'.[4] On every Remembrance Day the country stands remembering it, but nonetheless this inspiring text does not express the full demands of the Gospel. The love of enemies is obviously so much greater than the love of friends, and it is to this supreme love that the Gospel calls us. Perhaps the emphasis is meant to be laid in it on the word 'man', thereby stressing that a love that will die for those we love is the best that 'man' on his own can do. Jesus, however, has revealed what is possible if 'man' becomes 'full of the Holy Spirit'. Such a man was St Stephen. In the Crucifixion, and in St Stephen's martyrdom, we see 'man' loving with divine love. And is it not an astonishing sight?

The Collect, however, speaks of 'all our sufferings... for the testimony of thy truth'. Its implication, therefore, is that such a call may still come to any of us, and if it does, we will be expected to respond to it as Christ and St Stephen did. But could we? How could we possibly rise to such heights? Are we really expected to? From the concentration camp at Auschwitz, however, has come this amazing prayer: 'O Lord, remember not only the men of good-will, but also those of ill-will. And do not remember only the suffering they have inflicted on us; remember also the fruits we have borne thanks to this suffering, our comradeship, our loyalty, our humanity, our courage, our generosity, the greatness of heart which has grown out of it. And when they come to judgement, let all the fruits which we have borne be their forgiveness.' Surely such a prayer is a miracle of grace! From those mass graves the inspired words of that prayer speak to us so much 'more graciously than the blood of Abel'.[5] Who wrote it? No doubt we shall never know. All we can be sure about him is that he was such a man as is envisaged in this Collect. Surely he was 'filled with the Holy Ghost', and was one who points us to 'the glory that shall be revealed'. Could his name have been Stephen? Probably not, since Stephen is not a typically Jewish name, but certainly he was like him, 'full of grace'. We learn from him also both how this Collect is not out-dated, and never will be, and how even by ordinary people it can yet be fulfilled if they 'look up to heaven' and are 'filled with the Holy Ghost'.

The Collect's stress on 'the testimony of thy truth' points us to the work of evangelism as well as to the potential suffering of those who undertake it. Jesus claimed, 'I am the way and the truth and the life, and no one comes to the Father but by me.'[6] The Church's evangelistic 'testimony' therefore, can only be to 'the truth as it is in Jesus'.[7] However this truth, which is such a joy and wonder to believers, may be intolerable, even blasphemous, to those who are not. This, however, is how it has always been. In Christ's day many said to him, 'Who do you claim to be?...Your testimony is not true.'[8] We may still hear the echo of that hostile question and the angry and contemptuous rejection of his answer, even in our own country, today.

The Collect recalls the vision of St Stephen at his trial, where he saw Jesus 'standing at the right hand of God', a vision that reminds us of the warning Jesus gave the High Priest at his, that he who was there judging him, would one day see Jesus 'seated' there, this time acting as his Judge. The Sanhedrin reacted in the same way on each occasion. They 'ground their teeth' and 'stopped their ears' at St Stephen's testimony, even as they had 'spat' at Jesus and 'struck him with the palms of their hands'.[9] We do not expect such a violent reaction to the 'truth as it is in Jesus' today, at least in our country, but the Church in its wisdom never allows us to forget the reception that the Gospel and its evangelists may receive, and down the centuries have received. The arrangement whereby St Stephen's Day follows Christmas Day is not fortuitous. Having celebrated joyfully the arrival of 'the Prince of Peace',[10] we are immediately reminded how others may think of him.

That the Gospel will certainly be rejected, even fiercely, by many creates a specially sensitive dilemma for the Church in this Decade of Evangelism. Perhaps this can be best put in the form of a question. "Must preaching the Gospel inevitably lead to conflict rather than reconciliation with those of other faiths?" Significant changes have taken place in our country in recent years. Quite suddenly we are more an established multi-faith country than one with an Established Christian Church. The heir to the throne and our Church's next Governor wants to be 'the Defender of Faith' rather than 'the Defender of the Faith'. His reasons are understandable. He does not wish to seem unsympathetic to the deeply held religious views of many of his future subjects. There is also the unfortunate relationship between religion and race. Although a great many non-whites are Christians, the vast majority of non-Christians are non-white. Suddenly it seems that our country has become like a troubled sea in which it is very difficult, even politically incorrect, that most deadly of epithets, to 'fish for men'.[11] In consequence evangelism has increasingly been relabelled and given unfamiliar objectives, such as the promotion of the common good, social justice and honest behaviour. In this way evangelism may have been shorn of its sharper and potentially troublesome edges, but has it also been shorn of its purpose and its power?

Traditionally, however, evangelism is to do with 'fishing for men', with 'making disciples [for Jesus] of every nation'.[12] It is primarily to do with changing individual lives, and not, at least in the first instance, changing general attitudes in society or influencing Government policies. Certainly the Gospel has social, political and economic dimensions. To be a citizen of a Christian country is a great blessing,[13] unappreciated often enough until such a blessing is slowly or suddenly withdrawn. Indeed, it is the fear that this is what is happening in our day that worries many, and no doubt was one of the reasons why the Decade of Evangelism, ten years ago, was called into being. The main way, however, in which the generalities of life are changed for the better is for individuals inspired by Christ to be prepared to oppose current ways of life that contradict the Gospel, and to fashion their own lives in opposition to them.[14] It is when this happens, and only when it happens, that the Church becomes a powerful living force, acting as 'salt' in society, healing and transforming it. This Gospel 'salt', however, can be drained of its unique 'saltness'. Should the Church lose control of its evangelistic agenda, then, according to our Lord's warning, what it offers in the name of evangelism will quickly be 'trodden underfoot by men'.[15]

As the Established Church, the dangers of heretical Erastianism are inherent in our Church's privileged position. Always it must avoid both being subservient 'to Caesar', as it renders the proper 'respect' and 'honour' due to him,[16] and also being 'of' society as it ministers at all levels 'in' it.[17] Christ had the common touch, and loved, and was loved by, ordinary men and women, but 'he did not trust himself to them, because he knew what was in man.'[18] As Christ's Body, the Church is called to act with a similar wisdom. 'The testimony of [the] truth' of the Gospel cannot simply reflect society. If it does, it is a false testimony. Always the truth to which it bears its testimony is an offer of redemption and a word of judgement, and must by its hearers be received or, perhaps, rejected. But even though it may be rejected, if it is a truthful testimony, it cannot ever be deemed to have failed. As it was for Jesus, so it will be for the Church. His Crucifixion was not a sign that his 'testimony' had failed.

The story of St Stephen confirms this traditional understanding of evangelism, both in what it consists, of how it is done and its final outcome. St Stephen's claims for Christ failed hopelessly to impress the authorities to which they were addressed. Yet his 'testimony' was not a failure. Since it was a word of God that he spoke it did not 'return' unfulfilled.[19] It achieved in particular two things. It started to change the life of Saul the Pharisee, with ultimately astonishing consequences for the spread of the Gospel. It also inspired many ordinary Christians to 'go about preaching the word', taking the testimony that he had given to the truth with them, when, because of the persecution that followed his martyrdom, they were forced out of Jerusalem and Judaea.[20]

However difficult it may appear to preach the word and make disciples today, the Church must at all costs evangelise. If it should fail to do so, falling back into mere social activity, however praiseworthy and useful, it has failed. Here, grateful mention must be made of the Alpha Movement, which though Anglican in origin is now fully ecumenical in its evangelistic outreach. It has been this Decade of Evangelism's bright light. The point is this. All mankind needs Christ, and all other religions are without Christ. Their faiths contain no saving Gospel, for 'there is salvation in no other Name.'[21] Are we loving our neighbours if we hide this truth from them?

The example of St Stephen reminds us of the potential cost in this matter; yet it also enables us to see the mysterious way in which God always 'confirms the message of the Gospel by the signs that attend it.'[22] The Church must simply be faithful to its 'marching orders', the Iron Duke's famous description of the last words of Christ in St Matthew's Gospel. 'Go and make disciples of all nations, baptising them in the Name of the Father and the Son and the Holy Spirit.'[23] Those who set out to do this may not live to see its results. Often enough the seed may appear to 'yield no grain', but in the end a harvest is promised.[24] The Church today must neither let itself be side-tracked or bullied, nor become discouraged or impatient, as it does the necessary work of evangelism that no-one else can do.[25]

Finally, this Collect ends in a particularly meditative manner. It leaves us looking up to the heavenly Jesus, who is portrayed as 'standing at the right hand of God' interceding for all who suffer, and his heavenly role as 'our only Mediator and Advocate' is specially stressed. As has been said, the Reformers particularly rejected the teaching that we should seek the intercession of the Saints, which had been so marked an element in mediaeval spirituality. Hebrews was the Epistle to which they particularly appealed. Jesus is portrayed there as the great High Priest of the human race. Although he is one with God, as a man, nonetheless, he 'is able to sympathise with our weaknesses'[26] and to understand our sufferings. His sacrifice secures for us all 'an eternal redemption', and 'consequently he is able for all time to save those who draw near to God through him, since he always lives to make intercession for them'.[27] So they stressed that it is the intercession of Jesus, not that of the Saints, that has power with the Father.

As he is in that Epistle, Jesus is usually depicted as being seated at the right hand of God, the place of judgement.[28] Standing at the right hand of God, however, as St Stephen saw him, seems to portray Jesus fulfilling a different role to that of Judge, that of 'Mediator and Advocate', the one this Collect stresses. This, as we have said, was a role that the Reformers believed the mediaeval Church had allowed the Saints to take away from Jesus. A favourite text with them, therefore, was, 'For there is one God, and there is one mediator between God and man, the man Christ Jesus.'[29] In this Collect Bishop Cosin is clearly seeking to emphasise this by interpreting the vision of St Stephen in the light of it.

Jesus, however, is a person of many roles, and the mystery of his person is highlighted by the way in which his various roles may even appear to be incompatible. Indeed, the New Testament glories in the apparent incompatibility of them! They constitute an essential part of the Gospel. We may well ask, "How can one born like us of a human mother be in any true sense 'our Lord and our God'?"[30] Yet this 'truth as it is in Jesus' is the essential first element of the Gospel. We are being reminded here of another apparent incompatibility within that mysterious truth. The heavenly Jesus is not only our Judge, but also our Mediator and Advocate. As our Judge he condemns us for our sinfulness, but, even as he does so, as our Advocate he pleads for our forgiveness, and then as our Mediator he gives us the grace to approach our Judge with the necessary spirit of repentance, faith and hope to obtain that forgiveness. Is not this extraordinary? But is it not Good News? 'O the depth of the riches and wisdom and knowledge of God! How unsearchable are his judgements and how inscrutable his ways!'[31] These apparent opposing truths, however, are reconciled within 'the truth as it is in Jesus', and become central to the Gospel. Our judgement and our salvation are thereby essentially connected. They meet in Jesus.

There is, however, another more devotional way of interpreting what St Stephen saw. It is a much simpler, perhaps even childlike, way. Jesus, it is suggested, by standing up is getting ready to welcome the first martyr of his Church into that heavenly place where he lives with his Father, the holy Angels and the Saints! It is, surely, an appealing interpretation, and if accepted, then, as it were instinctively, other scriptural scenes, and the language in which they are described, come readily to mind. 'In my Father's house are many rooms; if it were not so, would I have told you that I go to prepare a place for you? And when I go and prepare a place for you, I will come again and take you to myself, that where I am you may be also.'[32] And then later, 'Mary turned round and saw Jesus standing there...He said to her, "Mary". She...said to him, "*Rabboni*".[33] Then later still, 'Jesus came and stood among them and said to them, "Peace be with you,"...Then were the disciples glad when they saw the Lord.' [34] That Jesus is really eager to welcome us into his eternal home with his Father, having gone to prepare a place for us there, is one of the most certain, yet amazing, aspects of the Gospel.[35] 'So we shall always be with the Lord. Therefore comfort one another with these words,'[36] said St Paul.

SAINT JOHN THE EVANGELIST'S DAY
December 27th

Merciful Lord, we beseech thee, to cast thy bright beams of light upon thy Church, that it being enlightened by the doctrine of thy blessed Apostle and Evangelist Saint John may so walk in the light of thy truth, that it may at length attain to the light of everlasting life; through Jesus Christ our Lord. Amen.

We know more about St John than any of the other Apostles except, perhaps, St Peter. The Gospels give us the names of his family; his parents were Zebedee and Salome and his elder brother James.[1] His family's fishing business was clearly successful, for men were 'hired' to work in it, and since it was run in partnership with Sts Peter and Andrew, we may presume that like them, his home town was Bethsaida.[2] The 2nd Century historian, Hegesippus, declares that Salome was St Mary's sister,[3] which makes Sts John and James our Lord's cousins. Not only was he among the first to be called, he was also one of the three picked out by Jesus to share several special moments with him, in which the other members of the Twelve were not included. The healing of Jairus' daughter, his Transfiguration and his last vigil in the garden of Gethsemane are mentioned in the Gospels,[4] but there may very well have been more. In his own Gospel, St John describes himself as 'the disciple whom Jesus loved.'[5] Does this imply for St John a particular, even unique, intimacy with Jesus, even among the three? Certainly it was he who lay next to Jesus at the Last Supper,[6] and only he of the Twelve who accompanied St Mary and her female companions to the Cross. It was to him then that Jesus entrusted his Mother, and 'from that hour,' he tells us, 'he took her to his own home.'[7] As to where that was, and how long they lived together, there are two conflicting traditions.

One is that they remained together for a comparatively long time. When St John went to Ephesus, St Mary, it is said, went with him and kept house for him there. It is claimed that the site of their home there is known. The other tradition, however, is earlier and so the more probable. This is that they remained together in Jerusalem for three years before St Mary's earthly life came to its mysterious end there. In support of this tradition, it is surely significant that no mention of her is made in any of the Epistles.

Acts shows that St John from the earliest days of the Church acted as St Peter's chief lieutenant.[8] This relationship is confirmed by St Paul, who describes them, with James, the Lord's brother, as constituting a ruling triumvirate, those 'who were reputed to be pillars' of the Church in Jerusalem.[9] However, before long, as the Gospel spread into the more advanced and prosperous areas of the Empire, the centre of gravity in the Church moved away from provincial Jerusalem. The two greater Apostles then separated. St Peter went to Rome and St John to Ephesus, to become the leaders of the Christians in those major cities and their surrounding areas, where the Church was growing with such remarkable vigour despite its many enemies.

Tradition tells us that St John ministered in Ephesus and the Province of Asia for the rest of his long life. Jesus had nicknamed him and his brother 'Boanerges', sons of thunders,[10] and his fearless, combative personality had every opportunity to express itself in the course of his ministry there. Ephesus was the centre of the cult of the goddess Diana, which we can learn from Acts was bitterly hostile towards all rivals.[11] Among numerous fierce encounters between the Apostle and the High Priest of Diana, one is particularly remembered. To prove the power of Jesus to fulfil his promises to protect his followers,[12] St John drank a poisoned chalice, and to the awed consternation of his enemy took no harm. One of his mediaeval emblems, a cup with a viper in it, commemorates this extraordinary life-saving miracle. (The other emblems are an eagle and an open book.)

The pagan cults, however, were not St John's only enemies. Far more serious were those who came from Rome. In the earliest years of the Church, the imperial attitude towards Christians was ambivalent, as Acts shows. Judaism generally was treated with special tolerance, and while Christians were accepted as part of Judaism they remained comparatively safe. So we see St Paul appealing to Caesar, confident of receiving a fair trial.[13] This uncertain protection, however, did not last long, and in 64 Nero opened the flood-gates of persecution. St John, unlike Sts Peter and Paul and others of the Twelve, mercifully survived it, and so was able to enjoy the years of peace and progress for the Church that followed Nero's death. In 81, however, the full horror of persecution returned with the accession of Domitian. He decreed that all must reverence him as 'Lord and God', and although other religions were allowed, none might deny him either sovereignty or divinity. No true Christian, of course, nor Jew for that matter, could honour the Emperor as this law demanded, and in consequence many went to prison or to death. Among them we hear of another John, who in the past has been confused with the Apostle, who was sent to a prison camp in Patmos, and who subsequently wrote the Book of Revelation.[14]

Our St John did not escape this persecution. Refusing to worship the Emperor as the law required, he was sent as a prisoner of special importance to the Emperor himself to answer for his crime. What happened next is another, even more extraordinary, life-saving miracle! He was ordered to be thrown into a cauldron of boiling oil that was placed in public view before the gate of the city that led to Latinum. To the amazement of all who saw it, St John emerged unscathed, and Domitian was obliged to return him unharmed to Ephesus. This event is commemorated in St John's second Festival Day on May 6th, entitled St John ante Portam Latinam in our Calendar. In view of the dislike of the Reformers for all non-scriptural stories of the Saints, it is perhaps surprising that it is to be found there. It does show, however, that even they accepted its veracity.

Tradition has it that it was on his return to Ephesus after that miraculous escape from death that the now aged Apostle wrote his Gospel. In the famous way it ends there is a clear echo of Domitian's persecution. St Thomas in the Upper Room declares the faith of Christians in words that the Emperor had sought to expropriate to himself. 'And [Thomas] answered [Jesus], "My Lord and my God."'[15] It is considered most likely that the elderly Apostle would have used an amanuensis in writing his Gospel, as was common practice, and one used, we know, by St Paul.[16] It is suggested that he was another John, who is the true author of the 2nd and 3rd Johannine Epistles, where he describes himself as John the Elder. He was probably the amanuensis of the 1st Epistle, too, and also the one who later added the 21st chapter to the original version of the Gospel.

We hear several stories of St John from St Clement of Alexandria (c.200), who was devoted to his memory. The most moving is of how he was finally instrumental in converting 'the rich young man', who had come to Jesus seeking to be his disciple, but who had not then been able to bear the severity of his call to sell first all that he possessed.[17] St Clement also tells, lovingly, but with humour, how so fierce a personality in his younger days became something of a laughing-stock to the youth of Ephesus in his dotage. St John, he tells us, had two fixations, the need for all to love one another, and a horror of heresy. Both these convictions are, we notice, the two outstanding themes of his 1st Epistle, where heresies are called 'lies'. Consequently, the aged St John would urge everyone he met on every occasion, and repeatedly, to 'love one another', and then, on one memorable occasion, he rushed naked from the public baths rather than wash himself in the company of the arch-heretic, Cerinthus! Before he died, we might say, the fiery son of thunder had mellowed into the loveable 'fool for Christ'[18] , but to the end for St John the love of all did not mean the tolerance of everything.

This Collect was composed by Bishop Cosin in 1662, though based upon the shorter Collect by Cranmer in the 1549 Prayer Book, which was a loose translation of the Collect in the Sarum Missal. It is a distinct improvement on those earlier Collects, and without doubt a beautiful and devotional prayer.

Its theme is 'light'; a theme we especially associate with St John. In his 1st Epistle we find the words 'God is light', and they form part of the Epistle set for the day, the choice of which was another change made by Bishop Cosin. This truth about God, says St John, is central to the Gospel. 'This is the message that we have heard from him... that God is light, and in him is no darkness at all,' and if we want to be Christians, we must 'walk in the light'. If we walk in that light, then we will have fellowship with God and with one another.[19] That this may be true for us, and remain true for us, is the heart of this prayer.

In the Collect three lights are mentioned. There is, first, the divine light, 'thy light', that shines, and always has shone, both on and in our world. In Genesis this is seen as a creative light and the way that all began. For 'God said, "Let there be light", and there was light.'[20] As St John stresses in both the opening verses of his Gospel and his Epistle, this creative light, 'the true light that enlightens every man', shone forth in a special way in Jesus. In Jesus this light of God shines eternally and nothing 'overcomes it'.[21] So, too, Jesus says of himself, 'I am the light of the world',[22] and, he says, anyone who follows him, walking in the light that shines out from his life, will never live in the darkness; rather he will share in this 'light of everlasting life'.

Consequently this divine light is also a redemptive light. It shines for our benefit through the Gospel, 'the light of thy truth', and of this light, as the Collect reminds us, St John is an agent. This light is cast, we must also notice especially, 'upon thy Church'. When at Pentecost the Holy Spirit cast its light upon the early Christians 'with celestial fire', as Bishop Cosin described it in his famous translation of the Latin hymn *Veni, creator Spiritus*, it came as they were gathered together in the Upper Room.[23] This 'light' is what we must recognise as shining in the 'doctrines' of St John and the New Testament. This should not be too difficult for us, since this divine light 'casts bright beams'. So, having recognised this 'light of thy truth' in the New Testament, we are to set out to 'walk' in its light, 'for [this] word is a lantern unto [our] feet and a light unto [our] paths',[24] even brighter than the light that shone for the Psalmist out of the Old Testament Law.

Finally, we are encouraged in this Collect to look ahead by means of this 'light of thy truth' to 'the light of everlasting life', the heavenly goal to which we are being led. So the light of God in this Collect is shown to be also a sanctifying light, as well as a creative and redemptive light. It is the light of the Father and of the Son and of the Holy Spirit. More words from the Psalmist, therefore, come to mind, 'in thee is the well of life, and in thy light shall we see light'.[25] A sequence of spiritual activity and experience is consequently being depicted in this devotional Collect. The light of God shines upon us from the Father through Christ and his Church, which is indwelt by the Spirit in order to guide us through the darkness of this life to his heavenly home, so that there 'our joy may be complete'[26] in the ineffable 'light of everlasting life'.

The Church is especially mentioned in this Collect. We have noticed this, but it should be emphasised, for twice it is referred to in a way that may well be missed. 'It being enlightened...', 'that it may at length attain...', the 'it' here is the Church. Nowhere indeed in this Collect is the individual Christian precisely mentioned. So in our commentary so far we have taken, perhaps, a liberty in interpreting the Collect's petition as referring to us as individuals.

The light of God, Jesus teaches us, is like sunshine that shines on all alike, both the evil and the good.[27] God is 'our Father', and Jesus nowhere encourages us to pray to 'my Father'. The passage from 1 John, that is the set Epistle for this day and has obviously so influenced this Collect, stresses the idea of fellowship, both our fellowship with God and our fellowship with one another.[28] Even when we are praying alone we are not on our own. Even more obviously 'the everlasting life', that in this Collect is thought of as having its own special light, is a corporate life, characterised by mutual love for one another. By contrast, to live our lives 'in darkness', a possibility to which St John alludes in his Epistle, whether in our earthly or our eternal life, is to live essentially alone, for evil separates us both from God and from others.[29] Living together with others in loving fellowship, on the other hand, is the special characteristic of the life that is lived in the light, whether it be 'the light of thy truth' here, or 'the light of everlasting life' hereafter.

'Send out thy light and thy truth that they may lead me', says the Psalmist.[30] Although life lived in the light of God's truth is essentially a corporate life, each of us nonetheless has the responsibility to respond personally to its demands. The corporate emphasis in this Collect, therefore, does not prevent it being a prayer to challenge us as individuals. Indeed the call to live lovingly with others and for others, that is so central to the Gospel, is a major part of its personal challenge. This Collect surely highlights both this call and this challenge. The Apostle in his dotage, constantly urging all he met to 'love one another', also reflects the unrelenting insistence with which the Gospel calls and challenges us to love, because 'God is love'.[31]

'The light of everlasting life' ends the sequence of light depicted in this Collect. This light is what we usually call glory, whereas 'the light of thy truth', that guides us to it, is what we usually call grace. Grace is what we are especially able to find in the life of the Church on earth, the importance of which the Collect so clearly emphasises. Glory is what we may hope to experience in fellowship with Christ and his Saints in heaven. When Christ was transfigured on the mountain St John, we are told, 'saw his glory'.[32] He shone then with a light that was both very beautiful and very frightening. So it was also when that other St John was visited by the risen and ascended Christ on the island of Patmos.[33] And so it was too for St Paul when Christ revealed himself to him on the Damascus Road.[34] Our Christian hope is that we may share in 'this light of everlasting life', and presumably that means being able at last to bear, and indeed to enjoy, so much glory, something those three Saints, while here, were unable to do.

'What is man that thou art mindful of him?' says the Psalmist. 'Thou madest him lower than the angels to crown him with glory and worship.'[35] The idea of a 'life' of glory implies the perfecting of our nature to the extent that we can exist in the closer, glorious presence of God. Such a perfection was always true of Jesus, and it is 'in him' that this ultimate Gospel hope becomes even for us a reality. For him going into the glorious 'light of everlasting life' was, however, simply a returning to a life that he had left. In his great prayer in St John 17 we hear him saying, 'Father, glorify thou me in thine own presence with the glory which I had with thee before the world was made.' But then, amazingly, he says a little later, speaking, we may believe, of all who down the ages will become his disciples, and not just of the Apostles who heard him speak, 'The glory that thou has given me I have given to them...and I desire that they also may be with me to behold my glory.'[36] This Collect, therefore, points us to our extraordinary 'hope of glory', as well as to our 'means of grace'. It is for these twin blessings, along with 'the redemption of the world through our Lord Jesus Christ', that we should 'above all' thank God, according to our Prayer Book's General Thanksgiving. 'Beholding the divine glory' and 'attaining to the light of everlasting life' are but two ways of describing this ultimate hope of us human beings 'in' and 'through Jesus Christ our Lord'. It is this 'glory' and this 'light' that we believe St John and his fellow saints now enjoy, and would have us share.

THE INNOCENTS' DAY
December 28th

O Almighty God, who out of the mouths of babes and sucklings hast ordained strength, and madest infants to glorify thee by their deaths; Mortify and kill all vices in us, and so strengthen us by thy grace, that by the innocency of our lives and constancy of our faith even unto death, we may glorify thy holy Name, through Jesus Christ our Lord. Amen.

Although commonly called Holy Innocents' Day, as now it is officially in the A.S.B., the B.C.P. gives this Festival the title of The Innocents' Day. It was so called in the Sarum Missal, whose Collect was faithfully translated by Cranmer in 1549. In 1662, however, Bishop Cosin provided a new Collect, but by keeping the opening words of the petition, 'mortify and kill all vices in us', he retained a close connection between the old and the new Collect.

Bishop Cosin's new invocation, however, forces us to face up to the great problem that the events of this day create for us. Those pathetic, cruel deaths do mar the Christmas story dreadfully, and it is not at first easy to find any explanation that mitigates the horror of them. The invocation, however, boldly sets before us that necessary explanation. First, by quoting Psalm 8, which was the Introit for the Mass in the Sarum Missal, it declares that those deaths were foretold in God's Word long ago, and then, secondly, it declares that they served a glorious purpose. Indeed the Collect could hardly take a more exalted view of the matter; 'Almighty God', it declares, '..madest [these] infants to glorify [him] by their deaths'. Certainly the invocation does not evade the issue! But equally these words are not easy ones to pray.

The key to our understanding of this difficult opening lies in the scriptural understanding of glory. Essentially glory describes a quality that is unique to God, as the Glorias that we so frequently use in our worship properly emphasise. It is also the word that describes the life of heaven, where God lives in all the fullness of love and joy and peace, and where angels and Saints live too. And then, more mysteriously, it is especially used to describe Christ's Crucifixion. Christ's death was glorious because it was the redeeming act of divine love that saved from failure God's loving purpose for the human race, created in his own image. It thereby fulfilled God's will for his creation. It was 'the full perfect and sufficient sacrifice, oblation and satisfaction for the sins of the whole world'[1] that divine justice required, but since he made this sacrifice himself in his Son the glory of God's being, or Name, which is love, was revealed in all its perfection. It therefore glorified God.[2] And in so far as the way we live, or the way we die, are related to that glorious act of love, we may both share in its glory and reveal it. That this is possible is shown to us in the lives and deaths of the Saints, and St Paul goes as far as to say that the sufferings of Christians endured for Christ's sake actually add something of real importance to the glory of Christ's Passion, however 'full, perfect and sufficient' of glory his redeeming sacrifice on the Cross may be.[3] So in this Collect we are being guided to perceive how Christ, who saves us all by 'the blood of his Cross',[4] was himself saved from an untimely death by the blood of these infants and, therefore, his later glorious death throws a glorious light back upon their earlier ones.

This, then, is why the Church sees these infants as martyrs, and not simply as victims, and declares that their deaths glorify God, rather than mock him. The mediaeval Collect spoke of them 'confessing' their faith in Christ 'not by speaking, but by dying'. By quoting Psalm 8, in which 'babes and sucklings' are said to 'ordain strength', we may say that Bishop Cosin is making the same point. What is this 'strength' that they had a hand in 'ordaining', if it is not 'the redemption of the world by our Lord Jesus Christ'?[5] We may even say the Collect portrays these infants as prophets, as well as martyrs, for in what happened to them they foretold what must happen to Christ, and point to what he would achieve. Herod, in the grip of the Evil One, had every reason to fear the infant Christ. He failed, however, in his desire to kill him. The Roman governor who took his place, urged on by the Jewish authorities, succeeded, one may say, where Herod had failed. Jesus 'suffered under Pontius Pilate'; it was not Herod who killed him. But by then it was too late. The Saviour had grown into his role, and his death then was not simply the taking of his life by men of evil will. 'No ones takes it from me', said the adult Christ, 'but I lay it down of my own accord'.[6] So the glorious sacrifice was made and our redemption achieved. In it, however, the Holy Innocents played their part, and the Collect seems to imagine them now rejoicing in the fact that it was they, rather than the baby Jesus, who were put to death by Herod.

The vision of us glorifying God by our lives and, if need be, by our deaths is then taken up in the petition. What was true for the Holy Innocents we pray may be true for us. But how can such a wonderful thing become true for us? The petition tells us how. 'Mortify and kill all vices in us' is how it starts. One is reminded of several texts, but perhaps especially of St Paul's instructions to the Christians in Colossae. 'Put to death what is earthly in you',[7] he says, and then he gives us a list of the vices he has in mind. However, it is central to our faith that we can do nothing that is genuinely good without help from God, because within us there is a bias towards folly and evil, rather than towards what is wise and good. This is the reason why we need a Redeemer, and why we need to pray about everything we do. Neither as individuals, nor as a human race, can we redeem ourselves from this malign bias, which is why all merely human hopes are constantly frustrated. The Gospel, however, proclaims that our necessary Redeemer has come in Jesus Christ. Experience, however, and the Gospel, also show that he may all too easily remain for us a distant figure of history, for, unless and until his 'grace' enters our lives through our response of 'faith', as mentioned here, he is unable to 'save' us. Only then does he become our companion in life and so able to give us the power to overcome this bias towards folly and selfishness in all our relationships with others.[8]

But this is not all that we mean by our redemption. By 'the grace of our Lord Jesus Christ', a different bias, one that is towards all that is loving, wise and good, may be created in our hearts and minds, and this is what we recognise has happened in the lives of the Saints. Jesus has delivered them from what St Paul calls 'this body of death', and has given them instead his own 'spirit of sonship'.[9] This is what can be true of us too through the indwelling of grace, for which we must constantly pray. Through it alone do we have the power to 'mortify and kill all vices in us', and then go on to to live lives of genuine virtue. So, immediately, the Collect guides us to pray that we may be 'strengthened' by this all important 'grace'.

The word 'vice' here would seem to be used to cover all that St Paul calls 'improper conduct' and 'works of the flesh', and in most of his Epistles we find lists of them.[10] In ordinary language the word describes that which is seriously harmful to others; a vicious person or animal is one that is dangerous. This may lie behind the contrast in the Collect between 'all [our] vices' and the 'innocency of our lives', the innocent being seen as the opposite of the vicious, since they are no danger to anyone. Is this not the truth that makes the slaughter of the Holy Innocents so horrible, so vicious? And, consequently, does not what happened to those 'innocents' highlight the awful potential for evil that our 'vices' contain? Certainly we must at all costs 'mortify and kill' that which constitutes such a danger to others, and is not just a personal problem for ourselves. The contrast here is clearly supposed to add urgency to our prayer, and sincerity to our request to be 'strengthened' by God's 'grace'.

A virtuous sequence, therefore, is set before us in this Collect. First, we are reminded of the pressing need to face up to the reality of sin within us, in a spirit of repentance and mortification, all too conscious of its malign potential to harm others. Then we are straightaway reminded of our absolute need for the 'strengthened grace' of God, if this is to be done. Finally, going forward in a new spirit of love towards others and faith in God, both of which are to be so strong that we would rather die than compromise them, we may hope to live the kind of life, and, if need be, die the kind of death, that 'glorifies' God.

Since we are still within the Christmas octave, the Christmas Collect is always said with this Collect. There we pray that we may be 'regenerate', or born again, and made by 'adoption and grace' God's children. In 1 John we hear the Apostle addressing his faithful readers as 'little children'.[11] This Festival tells of little children, who in 'the innocency of their lives' and in their deaths 'glorified' God, and so one response to this Collect should be, therefore, to remind us that this is what we all are, our Father's little children, and recognise ourselves as being mere infants in the life of faith, however long now we may have been practising it.

This earthly life is like our spiritual infancy for, like little children, we live looking to a greater life that lies ahead of us. Just as children know that an adult life awaits them, so we know a greater life awaits us too. Just like them we view this truth with a mixture of fear and excitement. To grow up and leave the familiarity of the home is frightening for children, and yet there is also an impatience within them at the time it takes for this to happen. There is a natural reaching out in children to meet the future. So with us. We all know we must face up to the prospect of the eternal life that will take the place of this temporal one, and like children we are sure to look forward to it with a mixture of fear and excitement. We know that the life that awaits us is greater and more significant than this one. We know, too, that we are learning here, as children must, to take our place in that larger life to which we are all moving. Is there, therefore, anything more important for us than being well prepared for it when it comes? This is how St Paul speaks of this truth, as he looks to the hope of eternal life in heaven that he believes will be his by virtue of his 'faith in Christ'. It is 'not that I am already perfect; but I press on to make it my own, because Christ has made me his own. Brethren, I do not consider that I have made it my own; but one thing I do, forgetting what lies behind and straining forward to what lies ahead, I press on towards the goal for the prize of the upward call of God in Christ Jesus.'[12]

'Keep innocency and take heed unto the thing this is right, for that will bring a man peace at the last.'[13] 'Unless you turn and become like children, you will never enter the Kingdom of heaven. Whoever humbles himself like (a) child, he is the greatest in the Kingdom of heaven.'[14] 'Take my yoke upon you, and learn from me; for I am gentle and lowly in heart, and you will find rest for your souls.'[15] 'Like new born babes long for the pure milk, that by it you may grow up to salvation.'[16] Such texts remind us of this spiritual truth about ourselves. The 'pure food' that is suitable for us 'little children', as we prepare ourselves for the future, comes through the Church, its Word and Sacraments, on which we are to feed by faith with thanksgiving. Consequently, St Paul also writes about 'a maturity' that should characterise our childlike lives,[17] and he stresses that this is made evident by 'the constancy of our faith', which this Collect emphasises. There is no contradiction here. We are to be childlike but not childish. We must not allow ourselves to be 'tossed to and fro and carried about...by the cunning of men, by their deceitful wiles.'[18] Rather 'the constancy of our faith' is to uphold 'the innocency of our lives', and vice versa. The two virtues of constancy and innocence go together. Both are childlike, yet mature, virtues, leading us to the ultimate maturity of the heavenly life, in which, according to Jesus, the childlike are deemed to be the greatest.

THE CIRCUMCISION OF CHRIST

January 1st

Almighty God, who madest thy blessed Son to be circumcised, and obedient to the law for man; Grant us the true Circumcision of the Spirit; that, our hearts, and all our members being mortified from all worldly and carnal lusts, we may in all things obey thy blessed will; through the same thy Son Jesus Christ our Lord. Amen.

Added in 1928:

O Eternal Lord God, who hast brought thy servants to the beginning of another year; Pardon, we humbly beseech thee, our transgressions in the past, and graciously abide with us all the days of our life; through Jesus Christ our Lord. Amen.

This Festival became a major day in the Church's Calendar only very late. It was not recognised at all before the sixth century, before which time it was kept simply as the last day of the Christmas octave. The problem was lest the Church would be compromised by the pagan festivals of New Year, and that this fear persisted is shown by the later mediaeval Church authorizing a second Mass for the day, whose intention was to oppose all idolatrous and pagan practices. This Collect, however, is a new one, composed for the 1549 Book.

Jesus was circumcised according to the law on his eighth day, and there officially received his name, Jesus, according to St Luke's account of this event.[1] The other Gospels do not mention his circumcision, although St Matthew does mention his naming, without stressing the context.[2] 'The Naming of Jesus' is now the preferred title for this Festival in the A.S.B., with 'The Circumcision of Christ' being kept only as a secondary title. In both the mediaeval Calendar and in our B.C.P. Calendar, however, there is a separate Festival entitled 'The Name of Jesus' on August 7th, a Festival that has now been dropped in the A.S.B.

In the B.C.P. of 1662 no provision was made for a Proper for a second Sunday after Christmas. When there was such a Sunday the Proper for this Festival was used, as it was on other days until the Epiphany. In its 1928 revision, however, a Proper for Christmas II was provided, with the additional rubric that it should be used instead of that for the Circumcision on all other days before the Epiphany. This means that the Circumcision is now limited to its own day, like the other three Red-letter Saints' Days in the Christmas season.

No special mention is made in the Church's Calendar of New Year's Day, although in 1928 a second Collect for this Festival was provided, so taking notice of the fact that the Circumcision always coincides with the secular festival on that day. In Victorian times the custom of Watch-night Services began to develop, so that one's first act of the New Year could be to receive Communion, and it was probably this laudable custom that encouraged the composition of this extra Collect. In it mention is made of our being brought 'to the beginning of another year', but it has to be emphasised that the Church's year begins on Advent Sunday, not New Year's Day.

This major Festival of our Lord is a difficult one for us to keep with joy and enthusiasm. Not only is the physical rite of circumcision an indelicate one for us to dwell on, but also it is hard for us to see what relevance it can have for Christians. Has not circumcision as a ritual with spiritual significance been fully overtaken by the events of the Gospel? And does not St Paul go out of his way to make this plain? 'Was anyone at the time of his call uncircumcised? Let him not seek circumcision. For neither circumcision counts for anything, nor uncircumcision, but keeping the Commandments of God'.[3] Circumcision may have been part of the legal obligation of Jews under the Old Covenant, but it is not so for Christians. We know, however, from St Paul's Epistles and Acts that this understanding was only resolved after fierce controversy, the intensity of which is most evident in Galatians.[4] However, it soon became universally recognised in the Church that Christians were not required to keep that rite of initiation, which has been replaced by the sacrament of Baptism. It is faith in Christ that puts us right with God, and of this there is now the new 'seal of righteousness', our baptism 'into Christ'.[5] Why, then, do we still keep this Festival? In what way can it be important for us that Jesus was circumcised? Strangely, yet certainly, this Collect sees it as such. Christ's circumcision and 'obedience to the law' are declared to be things he was 'made' to do by God 'for man'. According to the divine purpose they are being portrayed here as definitely beneficial for us. How can we understand this?

It is in seeing Christ in his role as man's Representative, a scriptural role that is not an easy one for us to relate to, as, for instance, is his role as our Lord. It is, however, one that is nonetheless central to the truth of the Gospel. We especially associate this role with St Paul's teaching. It is he who speaks of Christ as 'the new Adam', who renews the whole human race for God. Through our relationship with 'the old Adam' we are all part of a fallen humanity, but now 'as one man's trespass led to condemnation for all men, so one man's act of righteousness leads to acquittal and life for all men'.[6] 'For as in Adam all die, so also in Christ shall all be made alive'.[7] 'For thus it is written, "The first man Adam became a living being", the last Adam became a life-giving spirit'.[8] 'Therefore, if any one is in Christ, he is a new creature; the old has passed away, and, behold, the new has come'.[9] This is the way St Paul puts this aspect of the 'truth as it is in Jesus'.[10] Christ has set in motion a new creation, and if we live 'in him' we step, as it were, out of the old fallen human race into the new redeemed humanity.

To enable this to be true for all, God had to become incarnate both as a man and as a Jew. For there was a second fall. Not only had all mankind, as symbolised in Adam, fallen, but also so had the chosen people, whose vocation was to be God's 'priests' to bring all mankind to him.[11] In this holy calling the Jews had failed both God and man, because, sadly, they understood 'neither the Scriptures nor the power of God'.[12] They failed to recognise that what mattered spiritually was faith in God rather than the keeping of the law. Circumcision had been meant to be 'a seal' of our faith in God, as it had been for Abraham. Instead, the Jews had made it the first step in a life dominated by law. The obligations of the law became a 'curse' rather than a blessing, for those who falsely put their faith in the law, rather than in the living God. They 'stumbled over the stumbling stone'.[13] Christ had to say to the godly, earnest Scribes and Pharisees, 'Woe to you, hypocrites, you traverse sea and land to make a single proselyte, and...[then] you make him twice as much a child of hell as yourselves'.[14] Strong words indeed, but they help us to understand the furious indignation that St Paul exhibits in his Epistle to the Galatians, for it shows how deeply he understood this problem, or should we describe it as this tragedy? He had himself passed through the saving fire of conversion, and his life now was totally dedicated to the proclaiming of the true Gospel and to fighting against the false one, peddled sometimes behind his back by false apostles.[15]

So we are to recognise how first God in Christ at his nativity became a man 'for man', placing himself alongside fallen humanity, in order to redeem all mankind, and then at his circumcision he became a Jew, making himself part of the failed chosen people in order to bring out of the old Israel the Church, the new Israel, that would carry the Gospel of our redemption to the whole world. As St Paul puts it, 'When the time had fully come God sent forth his Son, born of woman, born under the law' to redeem us all, so that all may enjoy 'the glorious liberty of the children of God'.[16] Cranmer in the Litany links these two closely connected Festivals of our Lord, and bids us pray, 'By thy holy Nativity and Circumcision...Good Lord deliver us'. This is why we can welcome this Festival with joy and enthusiasm. He became a man 'for us', and he also became a Jew 'for us'. In him we have been rescued not only from 'the curse of Adam', but also from what had become 'the curse of the law', and have received instead through Christ and his Church the freedom to live 'by the Spirit'[17] in newness of life.

Father Andrew S.D.C. said of the Circumcision of our Lord that it was the first shedding of his blood, and so pointed prophetically to the final redeeming sacrifice he was to make for us all in his blood upon the Cross. It is another central element of the Gospel that our Representative became there also our Substitute, 'according to the definite plan and foreknowledge of God'.[18] He was not only born and circumcised 'for us', he also suffered 'for us' 'once for all, the righteous for the unrighteous'.[19] However it was necessary that he was first 'circumcised and obedient to the law' 'for us', in order that his atoning sacrifice might be 'the blood of the covenant that God commanded'.[20] 'He appeared once for all at the end of the age (i.e. as the Old Covenant was brought to its end), to put away sin by the redeeming sacrifice of himself', for God 'sent his Son to be the expiation for our sins'.[21] Redemption has now been achieved 'for us', but we nonetheless must receive it by faith to make it our own. Christ has made atonement for us as our Representative and Substitute, but we still need by faith to accept him as our Saviour and our Lord. These great redeeming roles of Christ are brought together and seen to complement each other. All are vital for the Gospel. Jesus became 'obedient unto death', 'therefore...we [must] always obey', 'working out our own salvation with fear and trembling'.[22] Then we may receive power to escape those 'worldly and carnal lusts' that beset us, and do 'in all things' 'his blessed will', however hard it may be, according to the hope set before us in the Gospel, and in this prayer.

The Collect's petition is as dependent on the teaching of St Paul as its invocation. Its opening request, 'Grant us the true circumcision of the Spirit', is clearly based upon the closing verses of Romans Chapter 2: 'For he is not a real Jew, who is one outwardly, nor is true circumcision something external and physical. He is a Jew, who is one inwardly, and real circumcision is a matter of the heart, spiritual and literal. His praise is not from man, but from God'.[23] We might say that the 'real Jew' of this passage is one with the real Christian that this Collect is praying that we should all become. The Collect speaks of a 'true circumcision' which is to be 'of the Spirit', as opposed to a circumcision which is simply of the flesh.

Consequently this Collect talks about the need for mortification, as did the last Collect. We are being guided here, as in the last Collect, to face up to the uncomfortable truth that mortification must be a constant part of all our spiritual lives. Its elements, repentance, self-discipline and abstinence, are all unavoidable for all of us. No one can do without them, who is in earnest in his or her desire to be a true Christian, that is one who, according to this Collect, sincerely desires 'the true circumcision of the Spirit'. And it must be 'of the Spirit'. Unless God's Spirit controls what the Collects calls 'our worldly and carnal lusts', we will never live 'obeying his blessed will' for us.

St Paul aptly describes these as 'the deceitful lusts'.[24] The Devil is the great 'deceiver',[25] and he can all too easily make the essential areas of life his exclusive territory. And it does seem that in our time he has been noticeably successful in this. In sexual matters, particularly, an attitude that is clearly different from that taught in the Bible has become accepted wisdom among the opinion-forming elements in our society. The modesty and restraint in sexual behaviour, that is urged on us throughout the Bible and until quite recently was considered an essential part of civilised conduct, has been by so many otherwise civilised people unashamedly abandoned. The culture reflected by the media, the world of entertainment, and even by teachers and social workers, is openly hedonistic. This, therefore, is not a time when the call to 'mortify our carnal lusts' is likely to receive a ready welcome. This general change in attitude towards acceptable sexual behaviour is consequently creating great problems for all who want to live faithful Christian lives, and especially this is true for ardent young people who have grown up knowing no other spiritual climate. How to react to this sea-change in sexual *mores* is also creating undoubted difficulties for the Church. There are, as a result, 'great searchings of heart'.[26] Some in very high places have indeed openly parted company with the scriptural prohibitions on sex before and outside marriage and on homosexual sex. There is consequently undoubted confusion as to what is the Church's official teaching on sexual behaviour, and both confrontation and distress within its fellowship. It is fast becoming the main spiritual problem of our time.

In the Bible sex is portrayed as sacred. It is sacred because through its proper expression God continues to create those who are 'made in his image'.[27] This spiritual perception of sex lies behind the old wording in the B.C.P.'s Marriage Service, where the bridegroom says to the bride, as he gives her the ring, 'With my body I thee worship'. Sexual behaviour is constantly referred to in both the Old and the New Testament, showing us clearly that it is not something about which God is indifferent. It is mentioned in the Ten Commandments, and it is instructive to notice how the first casualty in the story of the Fall is sexual innocence.[28] While Adam and Eve lived wholly obedient to God their sexual desires were under perfect control. It was only when they were tempted to decide for themselves what was right and wrong behaviour that their 'carnal lusts' awakened to trouble their relationship. Jesus, the 'perfect man'[29] had, like us all, the sexual desires 'common to man',[30] but in him they were under perfect control. Is this not what we mean by the adjective 'pure', as used in the sixth Beatitude?[31] And does not that Beatitude reveal very particularly what was true about Jesus, and go far to explain his unique relationship with the Father? In his comments on the seventh Commandment Jesus makes it clear that it is not adequate for his disciples merely to refrain from adultery. They are required to be totally without such forbidden desires, truly 'mortified in [their] hearts and all [their] members'.[32] Such spiritual control of our 'carnal lusts' is asking much of us, but was he not speaking out of his own perfect humanity in this matter? Difficult as such control may be, however, no one who refuses to accept our Lord's teachings as being the truth in this matter can claim 'any inheritance in [his] Kingdom', according to St Paul.[33]

In this matter the Church clearly has a particularly difficult doctrinal and pastoral duty, for ours is a rebellious society. It stands, however, before the world in Christ's place, for it is his Body.[34] It must reflect his teaching and his pastoral love. The former, we know, is both clear and strict. Not only must we obey God's revealed will in this matter, but also no sacrifice is to be considered too great for us to make in order to do so. Pastorally it must relate truth to love. For our guidance we have that famous incident, in which a woman is brought before Jesus who had been 'taken in the act' of adultery.[35] In that meeting we notice three things. He protects her from her accusers, who are no better than her; he treats her with love, accepting her as a person in need of help; but he does not fail to stress that she has sinned and must change her ways. So the Church, too, must condemn any hypocrisy among those who judge others of sexual error and backsliding; it must be positive and loving, and not just negative and judgemental, in its pastoral handling of those who fail to keep God's Commandments; but it must be clear and definite in its upholding of scriptural moral values, and demand, at least of all its members, strict obedience to the scriptural norms of sexual behaviour. In a word, the Church must love the sinner, but hate the sin, and the compassion and concern it must have and show for Jesus's sake to all must not be allowed to blur to any 'the truth as it is in Jesus'.

In order to keep in touch with the 'world', however, this is all too likely to happen, and, as we have already had occasion to notice in this commentary, we can easily misunderstand the relationship between the law and the Spirit. The Spirit was not given to overthrow the law, but rather to enable us both to perceive its deep wisdom and give us the grace to obey it in spirit and in truth.[36] 'The written code' only 'kills' when it is made an idol to be worshipped. The Spirit, in contrast, makes us 'alive' by preventing this spiritual disaster, and enabling us to find, even as Jesus did, our fulfilment as God's children in 'fulfilling the law'. So through a 'true circumcision of the Spirit' that involves a constant wise 'mortification of all our worldly and carnal lusts', we can discover how true it is that 'the law is holy, just and good'[37] and so find both peace and joy, not merely frustration, in 'obeying [God's] blessed will' in this matter of sexual behaviour, as in all others. 'In the keeping of his commandments', said the Psalmist, 'there is great reward'.[38]

THE CONVERSION OF SAINT PAUL
January 25th

O God, who, through the preaching of the blessed Apostle St Paul, hast caused the light of the Gospel to shine throughout the world; Grant, we beseech thee, that we, having his wonderful conversion in remembrance, may show forth our thankfulness unto thee for the same, by following the holy doctrine which he taught; through Jesus Christ our Lord. Amen.

St Paul is by any reckoning one of the great men of history. His influence, certainly, on Christian thought and the Church's history cannot be overemphasised, and because his Epistles are part of Scripture his influence will never cease. Our admiration for him is not lessened when we consider how courageous and tough he was also. His brief autobiographical outburst in 2 Corinthians makes astonishing reading.[1] In order to preach the Gospel he was prepared to undergo any hardship or danger. Five times he was lashed by the Jews, three time beaten by the Romans, once he was stoned and left for dead. What he achieved and what he suffered is so remarkable that no superlatives to describe them seem an exaggeration.

Yet outwardly, at least at first sight, he was, we are told, an unattractive, even insignificant, looking man.[2] The apocryphal Acts of Paul and Thecla says he was small, bald and bandy-legged, with a long face, a long nose and bushy eye-brows. But he was also a man on fire with the Spirit of God, as well as a man with a great brain and a tough body. No doubt he would have had a kind of beauty as well as power, especially when he was telling of his beloved Master, for his spirit would have shone out then, even as it did in the face of St Stephen.[3] St Luke is eloquent in describing the affection in which he was held by his fellow Christians in Ephesus; 'They all wept and embraced Paul, and kissed him, sorrowing most of all because of the word he had spoken that they should see his face no more'.[4]

His most characteristic phrase is 'in Christ'. True life, he declares, is life lived 'in Christ'. In this regard St Paul was one who fully practised what he preached, as we can tell from another autobiographical passage, this time in Galatians. There we read, 'It is no longer I who live, but Christ who lives in me. The life I now live...I live by faith in the Son of God who loved me and gave himself for me'.[5] It is sublime; and we can fully believe that he was right when he said, without pride but in a spirit of blessed assurance, 'there is laid up for me the crown of righteousness which the Lord...will award me on that day'.[6] That day came for St Paul on 29 June 65. The head that was to wear that 'crown' was cut off by the Roman executioner at The Fontane in Rome, and his body was buried where the Basilica of St Paul now stands.

As already mentioned in the Introduction, it is the usual custom of the Church to observe the day of a Saint's death as his, or her, Festival day. In the mediaeval Offices it was called his *natalitia*, which may be fairly translated his 'birthday party', for it was reckoned that it was then that he entered his new life in glory, and when those already there joyously welcomed him into the life of heaven. This being so, it was fitting that the Church on earth should join in the heavenly celebrations, and annually rejoice for and with the Saint on that day. However, St Paul is not especially remembered by us now on the anniversary of his martyrdom. As we have said, that took place on June 29 in Rome. He was beheaded, while St Peter on the same day was crucified, St Paul's death being the more merciful because he was a Roman citizen. St Peter and St Paul consequently had traditionally enjoyed a shared memorial day, just as it was believed they would have enjoyed a shared *natalitia* in heaven.

The Reformers, however, rejected, sadly, such romantic notions. Moreover their new ruling was that no Saint, except for St Mary, should have more than one major Festival day. Consequently they restricted June 29 to remembering St Peter, and decreed that we remember St Paul only on this day, the Festival of his famous conversion. For emphasising his conversion rather than his death, however, it must be admitted that the Reformers had two sound reasons. First, it is so particularly emphasised in the New Testament, whereas St Paul's death is not recorded there. In Acts the account of it is given no less than three times,[7] and it is mentioned by St Paul twice in his Epistles.[8] Secondly, since his conversion so radically influenced the spread of the Gospel, its significance for the Church and for the world, it must be admitted, is infinitely greater than his final martyrdom.

The Collect is based on the Gregorian Collect in the Sarum Missal. However, first Cranmer developed it for the 1549 Book, and then in 1662 Bishop Cosin gave it a new invocation.

In the invocation the preaching of St Paul is stressed, and in the petition his teaching. The two go together, even though there is a distinction between them. In the early Church they had different names; the former was called the *kerygma* and the latter the *didache*. In some of his Epistles they follow each other in the most evident manner. This is particularly clear in his Epistles to the Ephesians and the Colossians. In Ephesians Chapter 1-3, and in Colossians 1-2:6 St Paul is clearly 'preaching' the Gospel, and in the remainder of these Epistles he is equally clearly 'teaching' what are the consequences for those who receive it.

It was St Paul's conviction that he had been specially called to preach the Gospel, and particularly to preach it to the Gentiles. 'Necessity is laid upon me', he says. 'Woe to me if I do not preach the Gospel'.[9] For this special ministry he had the right background, being the child of cosmopolitan Jews, who lived in Tarsus in Cilicia, and were Roman citizens. They were of the tribe of Benjamin and they gave their son the name of Saul, the Benjaminite King. Though a provincial he was, nonetheless, traditionally trained in Jerusalem in Gamaliel's famous school, and became a Pharisee.[10] The consequence was that he was able to hold his own in any company. The energy and determination, however, that he showed in his evangelistic journeys can only be explained by reference to the grace of God. He was chosen by God, he declares, 'as one untimely born' and clearly 'unfit to be called an Apostle, because I persecuted the Church of God'. Nevertheless, 'by the grace of God' he became the Church's greatest missionary, for, as he truly says, 'his grace toward me was not in vain'.[11] 'In Christ Jesus, then, I have reason to be proud of my work for God', he wrote to the Romans. 'By word and deed, by the power of signs and wonders, by the power of the Holy Spirit' working through him, St Paul 'fully preached the Gospel of Christ' throughout much of what is now Turkey and most of Greece.[12] His ambition, which was thwarted by his martyrdom, was to preach the Gospel also in Spain,[13] for, having reached Rome, he did not leave it. However, although imprisoned there, he continued his apostolic ministry by means of his Epistles to the converts that he had left behind in Turkey and Greece. In view of all this intensive and fruitful activity, conducted by every means and regardless of every danger, it was surely right that Bishop Cosin introduced 'the preaching of the Gospel' in his new invocation and stressed it as the outstanding feature of St Paul's life.

However, here let us stress the truth that his preaching of the Gospel has not ceased! The thousands, who heard him proclaim the Gospel in his lifetime, are but a fraction of the millions that have heard the Gospel from him since then by reading and studying his Epistles. We know that this was particularly true for the Reformers in our country, and throughout Europe, in the 16th and 17th centuries. In a special way St Paul was the

Father of the Reformation. Luther especially tells us of the enormous impact the reading of Romans had on him, and Calvin was a Pauline theologian in the same basic way that St Augustine had been centuries earlier. It was St Paul who inspired them to fight so bravely to preserve the Gospel from corruption in their time, even as he had fought to preserve the Gospel from corruption in his.

His unique influence has continued down the years to our own time. Here, perhaps, a personal witness may be allowed. The pioneering work of Canon Dr J. B. Phillips in translating St Paul's Epistles, and the other Epistles, into simple language had a most profound effect on many in the immediate post-war period, not least myself. If we ask, "What is the secret of their unfading influence?" perhaps it lies in the fact that these letters, which are the earliest parts of the New Testament, have within them so much of that Pentecost power, about which we read with wonder in Acts. After St Peter had preached his first great sermon, we are told, 'When they heard this they were cut to the heart'.[14] A good modern translation can unlock this power so that the modern reader is suddenly similarly affected, and then St Paul has made another disciple for Jesus Christ.

So it is that 'the light of the Gospel' goes on 'shining through the world', as this Collect expresses it, and the voice of its greatest preacher continues to be heard. Perhaps this thought, arising from this Collect, may move us, even now, to read, or re-read, these remarkable letters, using, maybe, a good modern translation. To do so is to hear one who went through the fire of a 'wonderful conversion', brought about by a personal encounter with the risen Christ. To hear him speak of Christ, what he did for him and meant to him, is possible for us all now. The Collect speaks of us being especially 'thankful' for St Paul's 'wonderful conversion'. We should also be 'thankful' for this modern availability of these letters, in virtually all the languages of the world, the reading of which has been a life-changing experience for so many, and the means under God of so many other 'wonderful conversions'.

The Collect's invocation stresses St Paul's vocation as a preacher; in the petition it stresses his role as a teacher.

St Paul was not a systematic theologian, but an active Apostle, moving from place to place and writing to his Churches to meet the needs of the moment. However, both his teaching and his preaching have one special characteristic; they are totally Christ-centred. Two truths were dominant for St Paul; Jesus was both the Messiah of the Jews and the Saviour of all mankind. As the eternal Son of God Jesus had come from God to repair the damage done in both the fall of man and in the failure of Israel. This he had achieved on the Cross and in his Resurrection, and now 'in him' a new redeemed Spirit-filled humanity was emerging which manifested the truth that the last phase of God's eternal purpose for his creation had begun.

This for St Paul is the thrilling core of the Gospel. Through it God 'has made known to us...the mystery of his will...(which is) in Christ...to unite all things in him, things in heaven and things on earth'.[15] To the Corinthians he puts the same truth, but this time stressing the part we are called upon by God to play in this divine redemption of his universe. 'God was in Christ reconciling the world (the Greek is *kosmon*, so the translation should be 'universe', no less) to himself not counting their trespasses against them, and entrusting to us the message of reconciliation. So we are ambassadors for Christ, God making his appeal through us.'[16]

What above all matters, therefore, is that we should become through Christ reconciled to God. This is achieved by faith in Christ and in what he came to do. This is the vital first response, to be followed by repentance for past folly and sin, and loving obedience to his Spirit and Word in the future. In this way we enter into the new humanity started by Christ, when God became a man in him. So to St Paul Christ was a 'second Adam,'[17] the originator of a new race of human beings, those who live according to the dictates of God's Spirit, freed from the slavery of living by the dictates of sin, experiencing through Christ the joys of divine sonship, able to cry out from the heart to God, 'Abba, Father.'[18] 'If anyone is in Christ,' he cried, 'he is a new creation, [for that person] behold the old has passed away, the new has come.'[19] The effect of this spiritual transformation is revealed in the way that for those so changed all their old racial divisions and social attitudes are also changed. For them, as he puts it, in the context of society then, there was suddenly 'no longer Greek and Jew, circumcised and uncircumcised, barbarian, Scythian, slave and freeman, but Christ is all and in all.'[20] It is not difficult to transpose such a text into modern terms. To experience this is to discover a joyous liberation of the spirit and the ability to 'walk in a newness of life.'[21]

This is the essential heart of his 'holy doctrine'. There are, however, no half measures possible for those who believe in this truth, 'the truth as it is in Jesus,'[22] and would seek to 'follow' it. It must be for us, spiritually speaking, a life and death experience, in which our all must be offered so that God's all may be received. If, therefore, there is a single text that can possibly sum up St Paul's 'holy doctrine', that we pray here we may be given grace to 'follow', it is, perhaps, Romans 6 v.11. 'You must consider yourselves dead to sin, and alive to God in Christ Jesus our Lord.'

It expresses, after all, exactly what happened to him. Paul was not his original name. When he became a Christian he 'died' to the life of Saul, the Pharisee, and came 'alive' to God in a new way altogether. Paul the Christian was born, as 'a man in Christ'.[23] He had found God, not in the law, but 'in Christ Jesus', who was now his loving and ever-present 'Lord'. What he experienced, we believe, is the essence of true Christianity, and the reason why he spoke and wrote with such power and authority was because he did so out of own experience. He too could say, '[I] speak of what [I] know and bear witness to what [I] have seen'.[24] That this life-changing and life-giving Gospel spread so quickly throughout the people of the Roman Empire, and is still wonderfully converting people today, is due under God to the life and letters of St Paul more, perhaps, than any other single human factor. How much we have cause to be 'thankful', not only for his 'wonderful conversion', but also for his total contribution to the presentation and passing on of the Gospel, is beyond calculation. It was our Lord who said to Ananias, 'He is a chosen instrument of mine'.[25] Perhaps that might be better translated 'the chosen instrument'. It would seem then less of an understatement.

The Collect speaks of us 'following the holy doctrine which he taught', as an act of thanksgiving for the Gospel he presented. Since his teaching is so Christ-centred, it is appropriately phrased. We are to 'follow' one 'who loves [us] and gave himself for [us]',[26] and who 'has made [us] his own'.[27] St Paul may seem to us to have known for himself the truth of such 'doctrine' and 'followed' it himself, possibly better than any, 'with far greater labours, far more imprisonments, with countless beatings and often near death.'[28] Yet he also says of himself that he has not 'already obtained' all that is involved in 'following' this 'holy doctrine'. As it was for him, so it is for us, the ultimate goal always lies ahead of us, and as 'followers' we are to live as those who are ever 'straining forward to what lies ahead'. This he describes as 'the prize of the upward call of God in Christ Jesus.'[29]

Consequently, although St Paul never mentions the Gospels, because, of course, they were not written when he was writing his Epistles, his teaching points us to them in the most insistent manner. We cannot stay with the teaching of St Paul. We need a knowledge of the life and teaching of Jesus too, as he so vehemently emphasises to us. 'Was Paul crucified for you? Or were you baptised in the name of Paul?' he asks with irony and passion.[30] Of course not! For him one thing only is of supreme importance, such as makes all else superfluous, and that is 'the surpassing worth of knowing Christ Jesus my Lord'.[31] To the Philippians he put the meaning of this truth for him with sublime simplicity in six words of one syllable, 'For me to live is Christ'.[32] This is 'the holy doctrine' which this Collect urges us to accept, and 'follow'.

THE PRESENTATION OF CHRIST IN THE TEMPLE
commonly called
THE PURIFICATION OF SAINT MARY THE VIRGIN
February 2nd

Almighty and everliving God, we humbly beseech thy Majesty, that, as thy only-begotten Son was this day presented in the temple in substance of our flesh, so we may be presented unto thee with pure and clean hearts, by the same thy Son Jesus Christ our Lord.

The Collect refers only to the Presentation, although the title of the Festival makes it clear that there are two events being commemorated. The Collect is Gregorian, and therefore comes out of the Church of the late sixth century. It reflects the attitude of the Church then to this Festival, which was seen primarily as a Festival of our Lord. During the later mediaeval period, however, this Festival in the West became increasingly celebrated as a Festival of St Mary rather than of Jesus, in spite of its Collect in which she is not mentioned. Cranmer, inheriting this later mediaeval emphasis, called the Festival in the 1549 Book simply, 'The Purification of St Mary the Virgin'. Bishop Cosin in 1662 made three minor changes to the wording of the Collect, but also one major change to the Festival itself by giving it its present title. By making it also, if not primarily, a Festival of Jesus, however, he was in fact returning to the earliest traditions of the Church, and it is a mistake, therefore, to see this change of name in 1662 as a Protestant inspired alteration. It is noteworthy, nevertheless, that the Marian title is always set in larger type in our prayer books.

In the East, however, the tradition that this is essentially a Festival of

Jesus rather than one of his Mother was never lost. There the Festival is called 'The Meeting' rather than 'The Presentation', and the central event commemorated is the meeting of Simeon with the infant Christ, and the old man's recognition of this baby boy as 'the light of the world'.[1]   In his song of joy Simeon called Jesus 'a light to lighten the Gentiles',[2] as well as one that would bring glory upon the Jews, and this gave to this Festival its popular title, Candlemas. This title, that started in the East, soon spread to the West and with it, as the most popular part of the celebrations, the blessing and lighting of candles while the Nunc Dimittis was being sung. The fact that this Festival always comes within the Epiphany season, which traditionally has a missionary character, has meant that its message has blended perfectly with the Church's wider concerns. Coming on the fortieth day after Christmas, the Festival also points us back to whence 'the true light that enlightens every man'[3] comes, as well as forward to the time when this blessed truth will become known to everyone.

Behind the two events that we are remembering in this Festival lies the law set out in Leviticus Chapter 12. What was happening was special for the reason that Jesus was both the first-born and a boy, and for such there was a particular ceremony. The oldest tradition in the Old Covenant was that God meant his priesthood to be recruited from all first-born male children.[4] Later came the development that the priesthood should be confined to one tribe, the Levites,[5] and then it was further restricted to one family, the Aaronites.[6] All first-born male children, nonetheless, continued to be ceremonially redeemed from this original divinely ordained obligation to become priests, and this is what Joseph and Mary were doing when they 'presented' Jesus in the Temple. They were 'presenting' him to God as a priest, and 'redeeming' him from that obligation by means of the required sacrifice.[7]

The mystical significance of what they were doing was hidden from them, though it was revealed, at least in part, to the two holy people, Simeon and Anna, who welcomed the little boy Jesus with such strange words and with such unexpected joy. It is not, however, hidden from us, who know that he is indeed a Priest, our great High Priest, but of the New Covenant, not of the Old.[8] Subsequent Priests in this Covenant do not have to come from one race, one tribe or one family, but they are those whom God calls 'from every nation, from all tribes and peoples and tongues'.[9] The Epistle to the Hebrews is especially concerned to develop this important truth, but since it is not precisely part of the substance of this Collect, perhaps we may leave it there.

As well as to 'present' and to 'redeem' Jesus, St Mary came also to be 'purified', according to the same law. The sacrifice she offered for her purification was the minimum, which may seem to imply that she and Joseph were poor. Joseph, however, as a carpenter in Nazareth would have been considered well off, but here, away from home, we may well imagine that he was temporarily hard up. How long this situation lasted we cannot tell, for the accounts of Jesus's earliest years are quite different in St Matthew's and St Luke's Gospels. Nor are they easily blended. If we wish to do so, then we must surmise that soon after this event came the visit of the Magi, and then the flight into Egypt. St Luke, however, apparently knew nothing of such things, and tells us simply that the holy family next returned home 'to their own city Nazareth'.[10] However this matter also, in spite of its interest, need not detain us, as it, too, is not central to the substance of this Collect.

The substance of the Collect concerns the important Biblical concepts of 'presentation' and 'purification' as they apply to us.

First, we should notice that in this Collect God is addressed as 'thy

Majesty', and this is a title that emphasises from the perspective of Scripture God's role as Judge as much as it does that of King, for it was the duty and prerogative of Kings to judge. The events we are commemorating in this Festival took place in the Temple at Jerusalem, the place of God's 'earthly throne'. It was there that the prophet Isaiah saw 'the King, the Lord of Hosts' 'sitting upon his throne and his train filled the Temple'. Immediately, he tells us, he recognised his sinfulness and God's inevitable judgement against him, and was filled with fear and foreboding. What happened next, however, reveals how God's forgiveness can alter totally the situation for us, who are equally 'of unclean lips, and dwell in the midst of a people of unclean lips'. An angel came to Isaiah with God's fiery sign of forgiveness and acceptance. The impure, he was being shown, can be made clean. We need not be 'lost' as Isaiah thought he must be, but we may be safe even in the intimate presence of the All-holy Judge.[11] In the same vein, in Hebrews we are assured that we may 'with confidence draw near to the throne of grace',[12] and St Paul's final verdict is that 'there is no condemnation for those who are in Christ Jesus'.[13] We must not therefore fear, because we are the kind of people we know ourselves to be, to 'present' ourselves to God, because his forgiveness is offered us through Christ. Rather, to do so is our 'spiritual worship', and 'acceptable' to him.[14]

This 'presentation' of ourselves before God, moreover, must be a constant part of our spiritual lives, just as our 'purification' must be too. They are indeed inextricably connected. In Baptism we are sacramentally both 'presented' and 'purified'. In Communion we come regularly to 'present' ourselves before God, and to be 'purified' by him. Whenever we turn to him in prayer the same is true. So we may in faith and hope and love look forward with awe, but without fear, to our final 'presentation' on the Day of Judgement. By prayers of repentance and by genuine efforts to purify our lives, we prepare ourselves for that Day; with awe at the thought, certainly, but without fear. We have received 'the Spirit of sonship'; we need not 'fall back into fear'; we may indeed hope that in our final 'presentation' we may recognise him whom we see upon 'his throne', and to him 'cry, Abba! Father!'[15] That is the hopeful picture that St Paul's famous words depict for our comfort.

The wording of the main part of the invocation reminds us of the Nicene Creed; indeed it seems deliberately to echo it. 'The only-begotten Son'..'in substance of our flesh', these are phrases of the greatest theological significance. In the Nicene Creed Jesus is described as 'the only-begotten Son of God...begotten, not made'. The sense of the Greek word *monogenes* (only-begotten) is not just that Jesus has an unique relationship with God, but also that he is morally and spiritually perfect because of it. He is not essentially a mere creature of God, as we are. He is 'begotten, not made', fully divine, 'very God of very God', and 'of one substance with the Father'. Yet, although he was 'begotten not made', he became, nonetheless, 'incarnate...and (thereby) was made man', and this is the significance of the phrase in our Collect 'in substance of our flesh'. He, who was 'of one substance with the Father' became, through his birth 'by the Holy Ghost of the Virgin Mary', also of one substance with you and me. This is the mystery of our Lord's being, and of his relationship both with the Father and with us. This is the truth that the Nicene Creed establishes against all other beliefs and ideas about Jesus. Just as there were many false beliefs and ideas being taught in the Church, when the wording of the Nicene Creed was being worked out, so there are today. Since this Collect stresses and emphasises the historic doctrine of the Church about Jesus, it would seem to be particularly a Collect for our time.

In the Collect this final 'presentation' of ourselves before God is seen as something Jesus will do for us. There are, however, two other ideas of our final 'presentation' in the New Testament. The first is that it will be made to Christ, rather than to the Father, who has committed our final judgement to him.[16]   Then the agents of our presentation are seen in St Matthew's Gospel as angels,[17] although St Paul in his mind's eye seems to see himself as being allowed to present to Christ at least those who are his own converts.[18] Secondly, there is the idea that we are finally 'presented' to the Father 'in the Son', rather than by the Son, although in this case by whom is not mentioned.   This concept is also part of that constant emphasis, so characteristic of St Paul's Epistles, that what matters is that we 'live in Christ' so that at the end we are 'found in him'.[19] Christ is the one that redeems all mankind and reconciles all things to God. If we are to be presented to God 'holy and blameless and irreproachable' this can only happen if we are 'in him'. Then we are to believe the 'day' will come when even the Son is finally 'presented' to the Father, and 'God will be everything to everyone'.[20]

It is a curiosity of this Collect that its ending is unique among all the Prayer Book Collects. In 1662 one of the changes Bishop Cosin made was to alter the usual 'through' to 'by'. Scripture, as we have just seen, does not require it, so why was it made?   The Rev. W.E. Buckley, a Victorian scholar, suggested that the change was made to prohibit the idea that St Mary is our final presenter! Since she had presented Christ in the Temple, the belief had grown in the Church that in the end she would present us to God too. By the late mediaeval period this Festival, as we have seen, had become dominated by St Mary, and she rather than Jesus had become its central figure. So this might well have seemed to Bishop Cosin a wise change to make to overcome this undoubtedly unscriptural, though nonetheless delightful and devotional supposition.

There was also one other change made in the translation of this Collect, in this case by Cranmer in 1549. He rendered purificatis mentibus (with purified minds) in the Sarum Collect by the phrase 'with pure and clean hearts'. The word pure, however, is surely a difficult one for us ever to use of ourselves! It can be used of the sinless Christ, of course, and many would say it can be used of St Mary, 'the immaculate'. But hardly of us. Clean, however, may be considered acceptable since it implies, even when appropriate, that we were previously dirty. So 'purified', the literal translation, would seem to be a much better word to have used here than 'pure', that is if we alone are being referred to in this Collect. However, in view of the scriptural notion that when we are finally 'presented' to the Father we shall be united with Christ (in him), perhaps devotionally we can make this final phrase in the Collect stretch to include him as well as ourselves. He then is the 'pure' one, and we are those who have been made 'clean', 'cleansed from all unrighteousness' in him.[21]

SAINT MATTHIAS'S DAY

February 24th

O Almighty God, who into the place of the traitor Judas didst choose thy faithful servant Matthias to be of the number of the twelve Apostles; Grant that thy Church, being always preserved from false Apostles, may be ordered and guided by faithful and true pastors; through Jesus Christ our Lord. Amen.

This Collect is by Cranmer, composed for the 1549 Book. The Collect in the Sarum Missal prayed that St Matthias's intercessions might help us to recognise God's hand in all that befalls us, and so was objectionable to Cranmer. The Sarum Collect mentioned St Matthias becoming one of the Twelve, as does Cranmer's, but it did not mention Judas, as the new one does. St Matthias, God's 'faithful servant', is here contrasted favourably with the traitor Judas, but, somehow, the centre of interest fails to remain on 'the faithful and true pastor', as one feels it should, and seems to rest instead on 'the false Apostle'! Consequently, as we think about the meaning of this Collect for ourselves we cannot possibly concentrate only on the one and forget the other. Indeed, the probability is that we will learn more from the fate of Judas than from the story of St Matthias.

All that we know for certain about St Matthias is told us in Acts. There, however, we are reminded that he was one of the quite large number of both men and women that followed Jesus throughout his ministry. In the Gospels we hear so much of the Twelve that we tend to overlook the part that others played. Just as some of the Twelve were first disciples of St John the Baptist before becoming disciples of Jesus, so were others. St Matthias and his rival for a place among the Twelve, Joseph Barsabbas, were among them, according to what St Peter said in his introductory speech before the casting of lots.[1] We may presume, too, that both of them would have been among the Seventy that Jesus sent on an evangelistic mission.[2] They would both have been part of the excited crowd of disciples that welcomed Jesus into Jerusalem.[3] They would have been also among those devastated disciples who 'stood at a distance and saw' Jesus crucified,[4] and, crucially for their qualifications for becoming Apostles, they would have been among those who were gathered in the Upper Room when the risen Christ so suddenly appeared in their midst.[5]

Nothing else is known for certain of St Matthias. An apocryphal book, however, called The Acts of Andrew and Matthias, was apparently very popular in the early Church, and was translated into several languages. It tells of him visiting cannibal tribes with success, and that his preaching exploits took him into as widely separated areas as the shores of the Caspian Sea and Ethiopia. He was finally martyred; but all is uncertain. From the evidence of pictures there seems to have been also some confusion between him and St Matthew. So we have to accept that the real St Matthias has receded out of sight into those mists that surround so much of early Church history. That he was indeed 'a faithful servant' of Jesus we may be sure, and that, having been elected to join the Twelve he would have fulfilled his apostolic ministry as 'a faithful and true pastor', as this Collect suggests. That, however, is all we can say of him for certain; yet that surely is honourable enough.

———————————

If St Matthias's memory remains a remote and uncertain one, that of 'the traitor Judas' continues to fascinate us with a perverse intensity. Why did he do what he did? It is a compelling question. And it is probably followed by the thought, "Could I have behaved like that? Could I even now behave like that?" In 1 John there is a passage that seems to echo that great betrayal, and, perhaps, one that we should ponder. Some Christians had renounced their faith in Christ and left the Church, and St John says, 'They went out from us, but they were not of us'.[6] Was he remembering Judas? Now Judas, we know, was the only Judaean in the Twelve. He came from Kerioth in southern Palestine (Iscariot means 'of Kerioth'), whereas the rest were Galileans. How much, one wonders, does that explain? Did he feel, and was he made to feel, an outsider? However, does a realisation of this lie behind the special consideration with which Jesus appears to have treated Judas, at least at the Last Supper? He was given there the place of honour beside Jesus and he received from him first 'the morsel', a special sign of intimacy and friendship.[7] By this gesture Jesus clearly was appealing to Judas, knowing full well what was fomenting in his mind. But the black resolve of Judas is dramatically emphasised by St John's closing comment to that scene: 'Immediately he went out; and it was night'.

Strangely, however, the Gospels do not attempt to explain why Judas betrayed Jesus. St John comments that Judas was a thief; he was the treasurer for the Twelve and misused the funds as treasurers sometimes have, and still may do.[8] Could anxiety about a debt, however, or the fear of being found out as a thief, have caused Judas to do such a deed? 'The love of money is the root of all evils', says St Paul, or 'evils of all kinds',[9] and we are told particularly of Judas's furious indignation at the waste, as it seemed to him, of Mary of Bethany anointing Jesus with precious nard.[10] Moreover in St Matthew's and St Mark's accounts of this story we are told that it was immediately after it that Judas went to the Chief Priests, and St Matthew tells us also how he bargained with them for money and of the sum that was agreed.[11] But, even so, the evidence of the Gospels does not really point to avarice as the reason why Judas betrayed Jesus, but rather to something much deeper. The sum he received was, after all, so paltry, and, much more revealing, when Judas repented of his betrayal, as we know he did, he returned the money with the anguished cry, 'I have sinned in betraying innocent blood'.[12]   That does not sound like a man simply regretting his avarice. What it does sound like is a man who has come to believe that the one he has just betrayed was after all innocent of that (how strange this sounds!) of which he believed he had been guilty. (We are rejecting St Luke's rival version of what happened both to the money and to Judas as being manifestly less likely, in spite of his assurances.)[13]

Bizarre, to the point of being grotesque, as it may be, it does appear that Judas believed Jesus to be guilty of some evil that at the time fully justified his betrayal of him to the Chief Priests. But what could that possibly have been? St John, we may notice, says simply that 'Satan entered into him',[14] and leaves the matter there. But can we not go further? This we do know. More than eyebrows had been raised at the way Jesus befriended and treated 'tax-collectors and sinners'. Moreover, in St Luke's Gospel there is a story that reads as a duplicate to the story of Mary's anointing of Jesus, which we know so infuriated Judas, and since he omits the story of Mary's anointing, it is likely that St Luke meant it to be seen as a such.[15] Now, in the Lucan story, the woman who showed her love and gratitude to Jesus in that particular way was a prostitute, and this fact was noticed critically at the time.

We know nothing of Judas's background. Perhaps he had been Pharisee-trained and still admired their strictness according to the law. The title 'Pharisee' had the meaning of one who had 'separated' himself from all dealings with the worldly and godless, among whom prostitutes would most emphatically have been included. The power of the Evil One to build much on little is surely known to us all. Jesus warns us against the 'unsound eye' that can fill us with darkness. And then he adds, 'If the light that is in you be darkness, how great is that darkness?'[16] Do not such words almost read like a prophecy of Judas's betrayal? Prejudice and self-righteousness are desperately dangerous states of mind, but equally commonplace. At all events, it seems clear that somehow Judas had become persuaded that Jesus was guilty of that which made his claims to be the Messiah utterly false, and therefore for his presumption was deserving of death. Judas, we may take it, knew exactly what he was doing. He knew what the consequence of his action would be for Jesus. If, then, what really lay behind the betrayal of Jesus was prejudice and self-righteousness, and the 'unsound eye' that sees evil in good and good in evil, then what Judas did is certainly not an act of depravity to which none of us could ever stoop. Rather it is all too typical a deed.

Our eyes, too, if the truth be told, are all too likely to be 'unsound'. All of us are prone to look at others and to assess situations in a prejudiced manner. Consequently all of us are capable of appalling errors of judgement. In the Collect for Purity, with which we start the Holy Communion Service, we pray for the 'cleansing of the thoughts of our hearts by the inspiration of the Holy Spirit'. How necessary such an inner cleaning is for us all! And are there any who have not in hindsight recognised that they 'have sinned' condemning the 'innocent' in their minds at least? Judas, we must not forget, was chosen by Jesus, and therefore potentially as great a Saint as all those we are honouring in these Collects. How fine is the line, then, between moral disaster and blessedness! If in the end we are left in Scripture with the verdict that to have done what he did Judas must have been overcome by Satan, let us not forget that we are also told there that 'our adversary the Devil prowls around like a roaring lion seeking someone to devour'.[17] Nearness to Jesus did not save Judas. So something even more than that is clearly required for our salvation. It is the verdict of Scripture that it is only when we live 'in Christ' that we are completely safe.[18]

––––––––––––––

The petition in this Collect is for our Bishops. It speaks of 'Apostles', but those being referred to are not the Twelve, but the apostolic men that succeeded, and down the centuries have successively succeeded, to their original leadership of the Church. It is such men who have kept for the benefit of the Church that special 'ministry and apostleship' from which Judas 'turned aside'.[19] Later they were given the title of Bishops, and supporting them, but subordinate to them, there arose the inferior orders of Priests and Deacons. This three-fold ministry was clearly emerging in New Testament times. The Apostles, St Paul, St James and St Peter, we know had 'Elders' under them,[20] and we hear, also, of the order of Deacons, which may have included women.[21] 'It is evident unto all men diligently reading Holy Scripture and ancient Authors, that from the Apostles' time there have been these Orders of Ministers in Christ's Church, Bishops, Priests and Deacons' is how the B.C.P. describes the matter.[22]

The Collect, however, speaks also of 'false apostles'. Even in New Testament times there was considerable internal conflict within the Church, and St Paul in Galatians tells us of how he had to fight tooth and nail to withstand 'false apostles' who were preaching 'a different Gospel'.[23] In 3 John we hear of John the Elder's bitter struggle with Diotrephes, who sought to usurp his authority. We hear, too, of 'false apostles' in the Church in Corinth and Ephesus. These were either Judaisers or Gnostics. The former sought to keep Christianity within Judaism. They accepted Jesus as the Jewish Messiah, but not as 'the Saviour of the world', and if they had succeeded there would have been no Gospel for all mankind. The latter sought to mould Christianity into the prevailing religious philosophy of the time, known by the composite term Gnosticism. Its basic belief was that matter was inherently evil, and that only the intellect and the spirit had any real value. Therefore, although Gnosticism took many forms, all Gnostics would have agreed that a divine Incarnation was totally impossible. Because of its pervading influence at that time, all educated Gentiles entering the Church would inevitably have been influenced by Gnosticism, and if it had succeeded in moulding Christianity to fit its preconceptions, as, humanly speaking, it could so easily have done, there would have been no Gospel at all. The later books of the New Testament all show how fierce the contest was with these 'false apostles'.[24]

Mutatis mutandis, however, we cannot fail to see how the Church today is similarly threatened. As then, there are those who actively seek to graft the core teaching of other religions onto Christianity, and in so doing to eradicate its distinctive doctrines. As then, there are others who, out of sympathy towards the prevailing liberal hedonism of these days, are seeking to realign the Church's distinctive moral teaching and religious language to fit these modern preconceptions. The Church, however, is 'not of the world'.[25] All the time, because we live in it, hard decisions will always have to be taken and brave leadership given, if its life is to be 'ordered and guided' aright. The onus for this decision-making and leadership rests upon our Bishops, however much they may properly seek to share it through Synods with those they lead. They are today's apostolic men, the main ministers of Word and Sacrament, and consequently essential for the Church's ministry and fellowship. At their Consecrations their duty to keep 'our most holy faith' free from error and in line with Scripture is three times pressed upon them. Therefore a Bishop who is guilty of heresy, or who encourages unworthy compromise with 'the world', because of his office has the power to harm the Church far beyond that of anyone else. This Collect clearly recognises this danger, as it bids us pray that it may be preserved from any such, and may always be 'ordered and guided' only by those that are 'faithful and true'.

St Paul said that a Bishop's office is a 'noble task',[26] but surely it is much more. Before God to be so called is also an awesome responsibility. Our Lord warned St Peter and the other Apostles how 'Satan demanded to have (them)'.[27] Then, however, it would appear that he only succeeded in 'having' one, but what a judgement was passed by Jesus on that false Apostle![28] It is, consequently, an excellent and proper change that nowadays we always pray for our Diocesan Bishop by name. He is our responsibility no less than we are his! It is under his 'ordering and guiding', we acknowledge, that 'we are to grow up in every way into him who is the head, into Christ, from whom the whole body, joined and knit together..makes bodily growth, and upholds itself in love.'[29] He, therefore, needs our prayers, that we may receive from him the 'faithful and true' spiritual leadership, for which this Collect bids us pray, and without which the Church cannot flourish.

THE ANNUNCIATION OF THE BLESSED VIRGIN MARY

March 25th

We beseech thee, O Lord, pour thy grace into our hearts; that as we have known the incarnation of thy Son Jesus Christ by the message of an angel, so by his cross and passion we may be brought unto the glory of his resurrection; through the same Jesus Christ our Lord. Amen.

In the Church of both East and West, St Mary has been honoured above all the Saints with a veneration to which a special name is given, *hyperdulia*. From the beginning she has been recognised as *theotokos*, the Bearer, and so, the Mother of God. Traditionally she is honoured on six Festival Days, her Conception, her Nativity, her Assumption, the Annunciation, the Visitation and the Purification. In a sense the chief of these is her Assumption (August 15), the day of her final entry into the joys of heaven, her *natalatia*. This Festival is her Coronation day, when she was welcomed as Queen in Heaven. In the B.C.P., however, it was the only one of the six Marian Festivals to have been dropped, although in some parts of the Anglican Communion it is still retained under the Festival's eastern title of 'The Falling Asleep of the Blessed Virgin Mary'. It is a very early tradition that, like Enoch, '[she] was taken up so that [she] should not see death, and [she] was not found, because God had taken [her]'.[1] There is importantly no record of her tomb or of stories about her relics, as is the case of the Apostles and other Saints. The teaching of the eastern Fathers is that St Mary lived with St John in Jerusalem for three years before the end of her physical life occurred. Another less credible version, however, that later became established in the West, declares that she kept house for St

John in Ephesus, and that her assumption to heaven at some unspecified time took place from there.

In the later mediaeval period the Feast of her Conception (December 8) came increasingly into prominence. Now in the Roman Catholic Church it is called the Feast of the Immaculate Conception and, with the Assumption, is one of the two major Marian Festivals in the Roman Calendar. In our Church, however, the Annunciation has traditionally been and remains the great Marian Festival, and even after the Reformation it continued to be known by its popular mediaeval title, Lady Day. However, like the Purification, the Annunciation is a Festival in which the honours are inevitably and properly shared with our Lord; in the one we remember how Jesus was conceived in his mother's womb of the Holy Spirit, in the other how he was presented by her in the Temple. Perhaps because of this in the A.S.B. St Mary is given a Red-letter Day on her birthday (Sept 8), a day that is, like The Visitation (July 2) and her Conception, only a Black-letter Day in the B.C.P Calendar.

In the B.C.P., as we have just said, the Annunciation is celebrated as St Mary's greatest day. We are remembering how 'the angel brought tidings to Mary, and she conceived of the Holy Ghost.'[2] How important was that moment for all mankind and so for us! As we read of that event, so beautifully told by St Luke,[3] we should surely notice with gratitude how simply and trustingly she accepts her amazing vocation that means so much for us, and not only for her. We should recognise that her simple words, 'Behold, I am the hand-maid of the Lord; let it be to me according to your word' are a vital element in our salvation. By humbly, yet willingly, accepting her role as the mother of the Messiah she allows the Incarnation to take place, with all its blessed consequences for us, and for the world. So our generation, too, as she foretold, calls her 'blessed',[4] and in the B.C.P. she is usually given the honoured and devotional title, 'The Blessed Virgin Mary'.

Her great and proper prominence in the Church's devotions, however, is in marked contrast to the place that she takes in the Gospel narrative. In his active ministry she did not go with Jesus. She certainly figures prominently in the story of the wedding in Cana of Galilee;[5] she is mentioned also in the Synoptics for being over-anxious for Jesus, as he gave himself to the sick and suffering in the early days of his Galilean ministry;[6] and she arrives on the scene dramatically when Jesus is on the Cross.[7] But that is all. She is, however, mentioned as being with the disciples who gathered in Jerusalem after Christ's ascension to await the coming of the Holy Spirit, and was no doubt also with them again on Pentecost Day when he came,[8] but even then she remains in the background.

Very little is known for certain about St Mary's early life. She was living in Nazareth when the angel Gabriel came to her, but the Book of James tells that she lived in Jerusalem as a child. Her parents were called Joachim and Anne, and until she was twelve she was especially associated in her education with the activities of the Temple. Do we hear echoes of this time in the phrase she uses to describe herself, 'the hand-maid of the Lord'?[9] At twelve she was betrothed to Joseph, and we must presume that she left Jerusalem then to live in Nazareth with Joseph or his relations. Betrothal was an integral part of marriage, a solemn commitment being made then to proceed to marriage when the time was right, so when she conceived Jesus we are told that Joseph is called her 'husband', and he thought of 'divorcing' her, even though it is clearly stressed that he was then only 'betrothed' to her, and it was 'before they came together'.[10]

We are told that she was related to Elizabeth, the mother of John the Baptist, which means he and Jesus were cousins.[11] We are told, too, of a sister who accompanied St Mary to the Cross; Hegesippus identified her as

Salome, the wife of Zebedee and so the mother of Sts James and John,[12] but this important relationship is not confirmed by Scripture. Scripture does, however, tell of Jesus's brothers and sisters, the four boys being James, Joseph, Judas and Simon, according to St Mark.[13] Were they, however, children of whom Joseph was the father? Although there is nothing in Scripture to suggest this, from the 4th century it became the official doctrine in the West for St Mary to be considered 'ever-virgin'. These 'brothers and sisters' were deemed to be the children of Joseph by an earlier marriage, of which, one must also add, nothing is known. This supposition would presumably make Joseph much older than St Mary, and certainly Joseph disappears from the Gospel narrative after Jesus's early years. St Mary also does have the appearance of being a widow on the few occasions when we hear of her there. The Reformers, however, rejected this unscriptural doctrine, although fully accepting that St Mary was a virgin when Jesus was conceived in her womb on this day; and this remains the general Anglican position on this matter. However, whatever the truth may be of St Mary being physically the mother of other children than Jesus, Scripture certainly encourages the devotional concept that spiritually she is the Mother of all who believe that Jesus is their Brother, for did he himself not claim us all as his brothers and sisters?[14] And also did he not say to St John, our Christian brother, 'Behold your Mother,', and to St Mary of him, 'Behold your son'?[15] So may we not all look to her also as our Mother too? We certainly may, is the witness of the Saints, as well as the traditional teaching of the Church.

———————————

This Collect comes from the Gregorian Sacramentary, but it is the Post-Communion prayer that was said before the Blessing, not the set Collect in the Proper. The set Collect stressed the intercessory prayers of St Mary, and so was not acceptable to Cranmer. Both the old and the new Collects, however, emphasise that the Incarnation began at the Annunciation, and not as so many wrongly suppose at Christmas. This truth is confirmed in the Creeds, where we declare that 'our Lord...was conceived by the Holy Ghost, born of the Virgin Mary'. The redeeming life of Christ began, as all human life begins, in the womb, when the miracle of conception takes place. It was there in St Mary's womb that God was 'made man...for our salvation'.

There is, of course, a special relevance today about this essential Christian truth. Abortion in consequence of this doctrine must be seen, at least for Christians, as a taking of life. The divine gift that we call life does not begin at birth, nor at some agreed time before birth. It begins at conception, and God, the Creator of life, is at work in every womb whenever that mysterious moment comes upon a woman.[16] In the case of St Mary she was a 'pure virgin'[17] when that moment came upon her. We believe that Christ's conception was a unique miracle, but that is not to say that there is not a genuine element of the miraculous about every conception. It may be that the eyes of a scientist may not see this. Looking into the womb of a woman, as he now can, he may see only that which looks like jelly in those first days of her pregnancy. So he may believe it is merely what he sees, but in that case his eyes are 'not sound',[18] for in truth God has acted, and what he is seeing is in fact a child of God.

It is for every mother as it was for St Mary. In those first days of her pregnancy St Mary went to her cousin, Elizabeth. She, 'filled with the Holy Spirit, exclaimed with a loud cry, "Blessed are you among women, and blessed is the fruit of your womb! And why is this granted me that the mother of my Lord should come to me".'[19] That beautiful scene of the meeting between those two expectant mothers is the centre-piece of the next Marian Festival, the Visitation, but we may stress it here, both because it is so relevant to the issue we are now considering, and also because, since it is not a Red-Letter Day in the B.C.P., we shall not be covering that attractive Festival in this book.

The traditional teaching of the Church is that abortion is always a great evil, which may only be contemplated if the mother's life cannot be saved in any other way. Life is of God and is his gift to us, and it cannot be accepted merely as the consequence of sexual intercourse. Men and women are procreators, not creators, of life. To spurn this divine gift, therefore, is a sign of unbelief. Nothing indeed illustrates the official rejection of traditional Christianity more vividly than the way in which abortions are permitted now simply in order to convenience the life of adults who have become parents by mistake; or even, in some places, to reduce the population. The subject is indeed a form of religious litmus paper for Christians. The joy of St Mary and Elizabeth may, sadly, be contrasted with the dismay felt by so many women today, either young teenagers, like St Mary, or middle-aged women, like Elizabeth, who 'find that [they are] with child'. But, however conceived, that which lives within them is also 'of the Holy Spirit', and not just of a man. This joyous Festival, therefore, seems to throw the light of judgement upon this very dark and distressing fact of modern life, and to demand of us our prayers for all involved in the so regrettable, but now increasing, use of abortion.

We hear in the invocation of the need for 'grace' to enter our 'hearts'. It is this grace that inspires our faith, and enables us to see God at work in all manner of ways in the world. Especially it is grace that enables us to recognise 'God in Christ reconciling the world to himself, not counting [our] trespasses against [us]'.[20] The faith that saves us, that puts us in a right relationship with God, and opens our eyes to 'the truth as it is in Jesus',[21] comes to us through grace. Yet this grace of God is not simply 'something' he gives us,[22] and then that is the end of the matter. It is 'something' that we must 'receive' and then live out in obedience and, possibly, suffering. So St Paul urges his converts in Antioch 'to continue in the grace of God',[23] in spite of the difficulties they are certain to meet if they do so. In this Collect this truth about the activity of Christ's grace in us is being stressed, as we pray for its saving activity in our lives. First, through grace, we pray that we may believe in the 'Incarnation', that 'God in Christ' has indeed come into the world as a man. Then, through grace, that may understand why he came, and the reason for 'his Cross and Passion', and how 'it was for us all and for our salvation' that 'he hung and suffered there'.[24] Finally, that we may through grace take up our cross and so reach out in faith and hope to share in 'the glory of his Resurrection'.

It is a marvellously inclusive prayer, with the whole Gospel encapsulated within it. And is this not appropriate for a prayer that has St Mary especially in mind? Yet, although this is our Church's prayer on her great day, she is not mentioned in it! The prayer is wholly Christ centred. But that is, surely, we may believe, just as she would wish it to be. Indeed, how typical it is of her role in Christ's ministry. However, at the start of that ministry, on the occasion of his first miracle, we do hear one clear word from her, and, humble as she may have been in his presence, to us it is a firm word of command; 'Do whatever he tells you.'[25] It is sublime in its simplicity, its straightforwardness and its trust. 'Pour thy grace into our hearts', we pray here. For what purpose? To believe as we should in all the articles of our Faith, certainly, but also that we may do whatever Christ requires of us. God's Word, which in the womb of Mary took flesh, must always be obeyed by us whatever the cost. 'Do whatever he tells you' is St Mary's command because like a good Mother she wants only the best for her children. This Collect, then, leads us to contemplate the life, death and resurrection of Jesus, to apply their meaning to our lives and to do so constantly, in a spirit of eager obedience. Consequently it is a prayer that is suitable to be used on virtually any occasion.

This Collect points us, as St Mary always does, to Christ and to the need for 'grace' to appreciate and respond to all that he has done for us. The traditional teaching of the Church, based on a devotional reading of the Gospels, declares, however, that St Mary is not someone who should be left behind, as it were, in her simplicity and obedience in the pages of Scripture. Nor even that she is one to whom we should simply look up, rejoicing in her glory in heaven. Rather she is one who should play a constant part in our spiritual lives. She is, through our Lord's own sanction, not only his Mother but also the Mother of his disciples, and so two related considerations have been believed of her. The first is her certain love of us, for Christ's sake, and, consequently and secondly, her loving intercession to God for us in all our needs, whatsoever. As she is both the Mother of God and our Mother in God, she is someone to whom we may always go, assured of love and acceptance, and one who can intercede to God for us with unique wisdom and power. It is these two very simple considerations that have made, and still make, the ancient prayer, the Hail Mary, as firmly part of the regular prayers of millions of Christians as the Lord's Prayer itself.

It is notable that Marian devotions down the years have developed rather than diminished. They have also tended to return from whence they were once excluded at the Reformation, and this is especially true of our own Church and the Anglican Communion generally. Historically, the most crucial figure in the development of Marian devotions is probably St Dominic (1170-1221). He initiated the Rosary devotion that has played, and still plays, so great a role in deepening the spiritual lives of ordinary Christians. Another simple devotion initiated in the mediaeval period that still holds its place as a powerful aid for ordinary Christians is the Angelus. In both these popular devotions we are, as it were, by the repeated use of the Hail Mary prayer, being instructed by her into the meaning and importance of all that her Son has done for us.

St Mary's role in the devotional life of the Church has also been, and still continues to be, greatly strengthened through the activities of the several Marian shrines that are found around the world. The best known of these, to which millions of ordinary Christians continue to go, are perhaps Lourdes (France), Fatima (Portugal), Guadalope (Mexico), Czestochowa (Poland), and our own Walsingham. At all these places, St Mary's loving presence and mystical power are still as evident as ever to the faithful who visit them, and they continue to be places where life-changing miracles occur. Now to these older shrines there has suddenly been added a new one which, although so recently established, is attracting pilgrims in their millions. Its story is exciting and extraordinary. On June 25 1981, St Mary appeared to six local children on a hill near the Bosnian village of Medjugorje, and since then on the 25th of the month she has sent out messages through these six children, who have now grown into young adults. Though including various instructions and admonitions that often reflect a knowledge of what is currently happening, these messages have a consistent pattern and a recurring theme. All start by addressing us as her 'Dear children,' and in them St Mary regularly claims our attention by virtue of her role as our Mother in God. Then she repeatedly emphasises her desire that we should be faithful in our prayers, through a persistent turning to God (conversion is her word for this) and never to doubt their importance for ourselves and the world. Then, further, in our daily living she constantly demands of us total obedience to God's will, after the example of Jesus; that, she says, must be the most obvious characteristic of 'her children'. Finally she invariably ends these messages with the gracious phrase, 'Thank you for your response to my call.'

Although we hear all too little of St Mary in the Gospels, we can nonetheless easily visualise, from what we are told, what kind of person she was. 'Be it unto me according to your will,'[26] 'My soul magnifies the Lord and my spirit rejoices in God my Saviour.'[27] 'Your father and I have sought you anxiously.'[28] 'And Mary pondered all these things in her heart.'[29]   [She] said to him, "They have no wine."[30] 'Whatever he says to you, do it,'[31] 'Standing by the Cross of Jesus [was] his Mother.'[32]   From these sayings and teachings, we recognise her total obedience to God's will, her constant concern for the happiness and well-being of others and the depth of her spirituality.

If one can define the purpose of our spiritual lives as the maintenance of a personal loving relationship with God through Jesus Christ, then having a devotional relationship with St Mary as our spiritual Mother is, simply, an immense help to us in it. A Madonna and Child icon, or picture, may be for us something much deeper than a devotionally nice thing. It may be a family picture. The point is this. The truth we may experience through it is both that St Mary is being given us by Jesus as our Mother and, more importantly, that St Mary is giving us Jesus as our Brother. In this way we discover a new depth in our relationship with him as 'our great Redeemer, Friend and Brother.'[33] Jesus gave us the Eucharist as a special 'means of grace' whereby our relationship with him may be cemented. We are handicapped in that relationship if we spurn this Sacrament or remain uninstructed in how to partake of it. He gave us also his Mother for a similar purpose, and we are similarly handicapped in our relationship with him if we are prejudiced against her, or do not know how to develop a loving relationship with her. It is, consequently, the experience of those who visit the Marian shrines as expectant pilgrims to discover a great strengthening of their commitment to Christ. It is also the whole purpose of the Marian devotions to unite us more obediently to Christ, just as it is St Mary's only concern, we know, that we 'do whatever he tells us.'

The Angelus ends with the recitation of this wholly Christ-centred Collect, but before we recite it we pray the versicle and response:

> Holy Mary, Mother of God, pray for us,
> That we may be made worthy of the promises of Christ.

These promises St Mary long ago rejoiced in, recognising them as blessings that God had from earliest times 'promised to our forefathers, Abraham and his seed, for ever.'[34] These promises have been fulfilled in Jesus or, as St Paul quaintly puts it, 'all the promises of God find their "Yes" in him'.[35] The essence of this prayer is that we obtain them, being 'brought unto the glory of [Christ's] Resurrection' 'by his Cross and Passion.' To this blessed end, God does indeed 'pour his grace into our hearts', yet for this blessing to be received by us, our own prayer is vital, and the prayers of others for us are of great importance too. 'God will deliver us,' said St Paul, 'and on him we set our hope..[but] you also must help us by prayer.'[36] Now, the great ones of prayer are the Saints and the greatest of these is St Mary. As we pray this prayer, we may look up and know that she is wholeheartedly sharing with us in it. And so she is whenever we pray.

SAINT MARK'S DAY
April 25th

O Almighty God, who hast instructed thy holy Church with the heavenly doctrine of thy Evangelist Saint Mark; Give us grace that, being not like children carried away with every blast of vain doctrine, we may be established in the truth of thy holy Gospel; through Jesus Christ our Lord. Amen.

St Mark is one of the most interesting as well as important of the Saints. Important, naturally, because he wrote the first Gospel, and this is fully emphasised in this Collect. He is most interesting, too, because of what the New Testament tells us of him, which we will come to shortly.

This is a new Collect by Cranmer. Since the Sarum Collect stressed the value of St Mark's prayers, as well as the importance of his Gospel, he could not use it, at least in its entirety. The importance of his Gospel, however, remains the crucial theme of Cranmer's new Collect, a theme very much after his own heart. He describes it as 'heavenly', and it is an appropriate adjective. Let us stress an important point here. What St Mark was doing was a truly extraordinary thing, and, what is more, he knew what he was doing. He was not writing a mere account of a man's life and death, a biography, but rather a book that he believed was a Word of God to the world, no less. He believed that he was proclaiming, in his account of Jesus, in his life and especially in his death, good news from God that was destined to affect the history of the world and the lives of all mankind. Consequently he describes his book as 'The Gospel of Jesus Christ, the Son of God.'[1]

This strange English word, Gospel, translates the equally strange Greek word *euaggelion*. Both Gospel and *euaggelion* are words coined to describe something unique and wonderful that God has done for the world in and through Jesus Christ; and that something is to redeem it from sin, and so from the finality of death, sin's consequence, thus bringing to us his promised 'gift of eternal life'.[2] They refer to nothing else, and have no meaning in any other context. St John describes his Gospel like this: 'It is written that you may believe that Jesus is the Christ, the Son of God, and that believing you may have life in his name.'[3] It excellently describes the purpose of all the Gospels. Now St Mark was the first to write such a uniquely important kind of book, and therefore the significance of what he did is incalculable. The actual opening words of his Gospel are, 'The beginning of the Gospel of Jesus Christ, the Son of God.' Yes, and what a 'beginning' is contained within his short book of so few pages! The reading of it, certainly, has 'begun' the Christian lives of millions.

The Collect stresses the enormous value and importance of St Mark's Gospel. It is consequently extraordinary to realise that the Church very nearly lost it altogether! St Mark's Gospel as we have it is unfinished, for its original ending has been lost. Its final chapter is only eight verses long, and ends, we can see, in mid-sentence, since in Greek the last words, *ephobounto gar*, (for they were afraid), cannot properly stand alone.[4] So what happened? The implication is that when the Church came to decide upon the Canon of the New Testament in the 2nd Century, all that could be found of St Mark's Gospel was a mutilated copy! To understand how this could all too easily have been the case one must recognise how the Gospels were then all hand-written books. The obvious similarities between the first three Gospels were quickly recognised, hence the description 'synoptic' given to them by scholars. Between St Mark and St Matthew, moreover, the similarities are particularly great, with St Matthew reproducing nearly everything St Mark mentions in his shorter Gospel, often word for word. Therefore, when it came to choosing which Gospel to transcribe, St Matthew's was the usual choice. Contrariwise, St Mark's became the neglected Gospel, and so in the end was nearly lost.

False endings, however, have been added to it, but because of its lost ending we do not, sadly, hear from St Mark himself of the effect of the Resurrection on his disciples. The event is declared but, regrettably, not reported fully. So much that we would have liked to know from St Mark, who would have been himself an eyewitness, we shall therefore never know. We must simply rejoice, as the Collect bids us, that the vast majority of this precious book, that should by right be printed as the first of the Gospels, has been preserved. In the Collect Cranmer makes us pray that we be 'established [by it] in the truth of thy holy Gospel.' That, we may say, is what in fact St Mark's book did. It established this unique form of sacred literature, and others then built upon his pioneering achievement.

St Mark's Gospel is notable for two characteristics in particular. The first is the innumerable realistic touches that add such interest and conviction to his narrative. These reveal that behind his story must have been an eyewitness of the events about which St Mark writes. And who might he be? Papias, an early Christian writer, tells us. It is none other than St Peter, and the internal evidence of the Gospel confirms this in a fascinating way. Not only is St Peter constantly at the centre of the action, but also we notice that quite often the part he plays is portrayed in a thoroughly discreditable light![5] Considering what a revered figure St Peter would have been in the early Church it is inconceivable that such unflattering stories would have been so vividly remembered and so faithfully recorded by anyone else than St Peter himself! Then to add to this internal evidence, there is the external evidence of St Peter's first Epistle. There his very special relationship with St Mark is made clear as he speaks of him affectionately as 'my son'.[6] So it has been said that St Mark's Gospel may be taken as St Peter's Gospel too, and this, naturally, gives enormous extra authority to it.

In addition, however, to this special 'filial' relationship that he had with St Peter, we can also say that St Mark was himself very well qualified to write a Gospel. His home in Jerusalem, we know, was the meeting place of the early Church. We learn this from Acts. When St Peter so miraculously escaped from prison he went immediately to 'the house of Mary, the mother of John, whose other name was Mark'.[7] On that occasion many had 'gathered together' there, and 'were praying'. It is consequently likely that the home of St Mark was also where that famous Upper Room was, where Jesus and the Twelve had their Last Supper, where also he came so suddenly to be with his gathered disciples on the first Easter evening, and where the Holy Spirit came upon those same disciples at Pentecost. All these tremendous events, then, would have been shared by St Mark, even the Last Supper, perhaps by him then acting as a servant. St Mark, revealingly, tells us of a 'young man' who followed Jesus and the eleven Apostles after that supper into the garden of Gethsemane, and who was very nearly arrested there by the soldiers. This young man was surely St Mark himself! Who else would have known that he was only dressed in 'a linen cloth' and when grabbed by the soldiers was able to shed himself of it and to 'run away [from them] naked'?[8] From his youth, therefore, St Mark would have been part of that inner circle of Jesus's closest disciples, even if because of his age he would only have hovered on the fringe of it. Nevertheless to realise this also adds weight and authority to all he tells us.

———————————

The second characteristic of St Mark's Gospel is the great emphasis it places on the Passion. One third is concerned with the last week of Christ's life, and in the other two thirds regular and repeated reference is made to it.[9] This emphasis may be explained by the fact that St Mark was writing during, or just after, the terrifying Neroic persecution (64-65) that claimed the lives of so many Christians, including St Peter and St Paul. As in the garden of Gethsemane, however, St Mark, now a mature man, was once again fortunate to escape. This was the first wide-spread time of Passion for the early Church, fulfilling all Jesus's warnings, but also, through its horror, linking it more closely than ever with its crucified Lord.

St Mark's Gospel, consequently, stresses that vital aspect of the Gospel, that suffering and sacrifice are central to it. In his Gospel it is the role of Satan, not so much to cause Jesus suffering, as to tempt him to evade it! So in one of those incidents, in which St Peter is the villain rather than the hero, Jesus is telling the Apostles of the need and inevitability of his Passion, and St Peter presumes to contradict him. Jesus turns on him, saying, 'Get behind me Satan! You are not on the side of God, but of men'.[10] The Passion of God's Son is God's way of redeeming sinners, and if we want to follow Christ into the Kingdom it must be for us our way too.[11] It is a special feature of St Mark's Gospel that the moment of the world's salvation is depicted as a moment of total darkness, both physical and spiritual. 'There was darkness over the whole land', he says, as Jesus hung on the Cross, and as he died he 'cried out with a loud voice, "My God, my God, why hast thou forsaken me?"'[12] Because of its lost ending St Mark's Gospel does not, as we have said, tell us either the details of Christ's Resurrection or its effect upon his disciples. What we are left with is his Crucifixion, and in particular its effect upon the Centurion who supervised it. 'Truly this man was the Son of God',[13] said that soldier, and those words do seem to make a remarkably appropriate as well as most powerful ending to his Gospel, which, as we have recalled, started with the same assertion. In those words, perhaps we can say, we have what Cranmer meant by 'the heavenly doctrine of St Mark', and they remind us of St Paul's words to the

Corinthians about how the Gospel cannot be taught 'with eloquent [worldly] wisdom, lest the Cross of Christ be emptied of its power'.[14] For all its interesting and homely realism, this is a Gospel that must be approached with awe as well as faith. It will not read as 'good news' to the simply curious or half-hearted. It is such a devotionally challenging book. Only to those who 'repent and believe' and are ready to 'follow', 'taking up their cross' after Christ's insistence, will it be 'the Gospel'.[15]

Such thoughts prepare us well to consider the Collect's petition, but before we do so, let us complete the story of St Mark. He was the cousin of St Barnabas, and we hear of him accompanying St Barnabas and St Paul back to Antioch after that historic meeting with St Peter and James, the Lord's brother, in Jerusalem, when it was decided how Gentiles might become Church members.[16] He then went with them on their first missionary enterprise, but clearly failed to fulfil the role of assistant, or perhaps secretary, that had been expected of him. For reasons we are not given, but would much like to know, he turned back when they were poised to go into the hinterland of Turkey. This so annoyed St Paul, however, that he refused to take him on his subsequent return journey. It also created so serious a rift between him and St Barnabas that they parted company and do not seem to have worked together again. St Barnabas, however, took his cousin with him on his own independent return missionary journey to Cyprus.[17]

It is very good to know that the story of St Mark does not end there. His reconciliation with St Paul took place when he was a prisoner in Rome, where St Mark was no doubt also working closely with St Peter. On three occasions in his Epistles St Paul makes honourable mention of St Mark.[18] Though St Peter was St Mark's main source, the fact that he was intimate with St Paul as well could not have failed to have greatly influenced him.

After leaving Rome, Eusebius tells us St Mark went later to Alexandria, where be became that city's first Bishop, and where he was martyred in 74. Later tradition has it that his relics were moved to Venice, whose patron Saint he became. His emblem is the lion, the second of the four faces of the living creatures in Ezekiel[19] that are interpreted as foretelling the four Gospels, and this emblem is much in evidence in Venice, and also in later portraits of the Evangelist.

In the petition of this prayer, a comparison is made between 'vain doctrine' and 'the heavenly doctrine' with which St Mark in his Gospel has 'instructed the Church'. It is not an improper comparison, because 'vanity' in the Scriptures means 'worldliness', and so is rightly to be compared with godliness, not modesty. The force of the famous complaint of the Preacher in Ecclesiastes, therefore, is that 'everywhere there is worldliness'.[20] So things have not changed very much! The Collect, however, urges us to recognise the danger this poses for us all, and for the Church in particular. We must at all costs not become 'like children', who are attracted only by what is pleasurable and new. How easily this can happen! St Paul reminded the Christians in Galatia that before Christ came to rescue them they were 'like children', slaves to the 'elemental spirits of the universe'.[21] And it seemed to him that they were reverting to that sad state. The spirits of the world, the flesh and the Devil will retain their insidious powers while time lasts, for to live according to these 'elemental spirits' always appears so natural. To be up-to-date, to move with the times, to be relevant to modern society and responsive to all new thinking seems surely only sensible. The desire to be popular, moreover, is inevitably particularly strong for those who know themselves called to influence people and society as a whole. So the Church may be led into temptation, and allow the world to dictate its agenda. There can all too easily take place a watering down of 'the truth of [God's] holy Gospel', an evading of its stricter demands, and the making of compromises with 'vain doctrine' for pity's sake. The Collect, however, reminds us that the Gospel is God's, not ours. It shows that any such tampering with its truth can turn 'heavenly doctrine' into 'vain doctrine'. And according to St Paul the difference between obeying one rather than the other can be likened to the difference between freedom and slavery, such is the seriousness of the matter.[22]

There can be little doubt that the temptation to depart from the demands and the truths of the Gospel are very strong indeed today. The prohibitions in the Ten Commandments, which Jesus so uncompromisingly confirmed,[23] his teaching on divorce and remarriage,[24] and his condemnation of all sexual activity outside marriage,[25] are perhaps the most obvious matters that are creating tension for and within the Church these days, because they are so widely rejected outside it. In his parable of the Wedding Feast,[26] however, although Jesus stressed that all without exception are welcome into God's Kingdom with all its joys and privileges, he also warned that no one is exempt from wearing the required 'garment' of faith and repentance, love and obedience. All are equal within the Kingdom, since all are equally the objects of God's love, but that means that none can claim dispensation from its obligations, neither the advantaged nor the disadvantaged, neither the comfortably off nor those gathered in from 'the streets and lanes of the city'. The truths of the Gospel are to govern the lives of all without exception. To suggest anything less is to teach 'vain doctrine', and to advocate a false Gospel.

As individual Christians and the Church face up to the tensions and temptations of our times, St Mark's Gospel points us uncompromisingly to the truth that alone can prevent 'heavenly doctrine' from being turned into 'vain doctrine'. There, so very clearly, the Cross and Passion of Jesus is shown to be the essential lynch-pin of all Christian doctrine. If there is one text that characterises 'the heavenly doctrine' of St Mark's Gospel it is probably this; Jesus 'called to him the multitude with his disciples, and said to them, "If any man would come after me, let him deny himself and take up his cross and follow me, for whoever would save his life will lose it, and whoever loses his life for my sake and the Gospel's will save it."'27 We notice that all are included in this call, 'the multitude' no less than 'his disciples'. Herein lies the only way to life and glory for us all without exception. Without sacrifice and self-denial there is no Gospel. That is the essential heart of St Mark's 'heavenly doctrine'. As it was for the Centurion, so it is for us all; we have to see Jesus on the Cross before we can truly recognise in him 'the Son of God', and so become able to make in a spirit of faith and repentance the required response both to him and to 'the truth of his holy Gospel'.

SAINT PHILIP AND SAINT JAMES'S DAY
May 1st

O Almighty God, whom truly to know is everlasting life; Grant us perfectly to know thy Son Jesus Christ to be the way, the truth and the life; that, following the steps of thy holy Apostles, Saint Philip and Saint James, we may steadfastly walk in the way that leadeth to eternal life; through the same thy Son Jesus Christ our Lord. Amen.

This is the first of the two Red-letter Saints' Days that are shared Festivals. Originally this Festival was for St Philip alone, and St James was only added some time in the 5th century, that is after the Martyrology of St Jerome, where St Philip is on his own, and the Sacramentary of St Leo where he is joined by St James. Even though St Philip has always been thought of as the senior partner in this Festival, Cranmer's 1549 Collect made curious reading. He omitted naming St James altogether! The Sarum Collect had mentioned St James as well as St Philip, and in it the Church 'rejoiced in their merits' and sought to be 'instructed by their examples'. Cranmer, however, seeking to give the Collect a scriptural flavour, as was his wont, took the famous words 'the way, the truth and the life'[1] from the Festival's Gospel and made them the centre-piece of his new Collect. In it, we prayed, that all might know Jesus to be 'the way, the truth, and the life' as he had 'taught St Philip and the other Apostles'. It was, therefore, a most curiously worded Collect for this Festival, since not only was St James lost amid 'the other Apostles', but also that particular teaching, as the Gospel makes plain, was addressed to St Thomas, not St Philip! Bishop Cosin came, however, to the Archbishop's rescue in 1662. In his redrafting of the 1549 Collect he managed to keep the wording of

Cranmer's scriptural invocation, and make it the first element of the petition in which St James as well as St Philip is mentioned in the second.

Why, however, St Philip and St James were ever combined and made to share a Festival remains a liturgical mystery. In the various lists of the Twelve in the Gospels,[2] and in all that we know about them, they are not shown in any way to be close. As far as St Philip is concerned, there would be a good case for joining him with either St Andrew or St Bartholomew. We have already stressed his closeness to St Andrew, but his link with St Bartholomew is equally close. In St John's Gospel we hear how St Philip is instrumental in bringing him to Jesus,[3] (the Nathanael of St John's Gospel is the Bartholomew of the Synoptics—see his commentary) and in all the lists of the Twelve, St Bartholomew follows St Philip. Now in St Matthew's Gospel the Twelve are named in six pairs, and the setting for this list is the start of an evangelist mission. We are told that on such missions, of which we can gather there were several affecting not only the Twelve but others too, Jesus sent his disciples out 'two by two'.[4] It seems, therefore, most probable that the way the names of the Twelve are set out in St Matthew's Gospel shows us who paired up with whom on these enterprises, so that one of the pairs was St Philip and St Bartholomew. By the same token, on these occasions St James was paired with St Jude, (who like St Bartholomew is given other names, Thaddaeus and Lebbaeus), yet St Jude is paired liturgically, as we know, with St Simon (October 28). There is a reason for the latter pairing (see relevant commentary), but there is no obvious reason why St Philip and St James should have been for so long paired liturgically.

All we know for certain about these two Apostles is confined to the Gospels. St Philip was from Bethsaida in Galilee,[5] and so would, we may presume, have known St Peter and St Andrew and the two sons of Zebedee. He was certainly Greek-speaking, as indeed his name suggests, for the Greeks in Jerusalem, who wanted to meet Jesus, went first to him as one, presumably, who would understand their wishes.[6] From the other two times in which St Philip is mentioned we may gather he was both a practical, sensible man, and also among the more articulate of the Twelve. When Jesus was faced with the problem of feeding the crowds who had come to him in the Galilean hills, St John tells us that he turned first to St Philip.[7] Perhaps he was the quartermaster of the apostolic band. Then, in that famous last discussion between Jesus and the Twelve in the Upper Room, we hear of St Philip, who was clearly confused by what Jesus was saying to them, being willing to speak up and question him.[8] That he was gently rebuked by Jesus for his spiritual blindness does not, however, imply that he was particularly so. St John honestly indicates that he had spoken for them all, for even then, it seems, they had not fully understood who Jesus is.

St Philip's subsequent career, like that of most of the Twelve, is shrouded in legend. There are stories concerning his daughters that suggest that he may have been confused with Philip the Deacon, who had, we are told in Acts, four notable daughters who possessed prophetic powers.[9] It is likely that he preached the Gospel in Phrygia, in modern Turkey, and met his death in Hierapolis, perhaps by crucifixion and perhaps on a specially tall cross. In pictures St Philip is either portrayed holding loaves and fishes, or carrying what seems to be a very long cross. However, since another tradition tells of him killing a dragon in a pagan temple in Hierapolis, this long cross may be a large sword! Such legends, however, so typical of those that surrounded other great Saints, add nothing to the fine, straightforward character that shines out so clearly from St John's Gospel, in which he plays a notably prominent part.

If there are several Philips in the New Testament there are even more Jameses. There were two among the Apostles, and these are usually distinguished by the titles James the Great and James the Less, or James the son of Zebedee and James the son of Alphaeus.[10] It is, of course, the latter James that we are honouring in this Festival. One has to concede that almost nothing more than the name of his father is revealed for certain in Scripture about this St James. It is, however, likely that one of the many Marys mentioned in the Gospels is his mother. St Mark tells of a Mary who is 'the mother of James the younger (or perhaps, 'the less', *mikros* being the Greek word used) and Joses'.[11] She was the companion of St Mary Magdalen and Salome, or Joanna, who bought spices to anoint Christ's body. (St Matthew leaves out Salome in the matter of the anointing, and St Luke substitutes Joanna for Salome).[12] Consequently, we may know the names of both St James's parents.

The Epistle for this day is taken from the opening verses of the Epistle of St James. Was the author our St James? Certainly for centuries this was thought to be the case. However, today this is widely rejected, and the James that was Jesus's brother is considered a more likely author. There is, also, an apocryphal book called The Book of James that tells several stories about our Lord's infancy and childhood, and also gives us the names of St Mary's parents. This book, too, in earlier centuries was attributed to our St James, but again James, the Lord's brother, is now considered a more likely author. However, it is quite likely, even probable, that the author of these two books are two more Jameses that must be added to all those others that we read of in the New Testament.

Tradition declares that St James died in a fierce persecution of Christians in Jerusalem in 62. His emblem is a fuller's club, with which he is said to have been finally beaten to death, after having been stoned. If this is true he was the last of the Twelve to die, as his Master had died, in Jerusalem, just as his greater name-sake was the first. It must be said, however, that in his death he may again be being confused with James, the Lord's brother, who, according to Hegesippus, was also martyred in this persecution.

In this devotional Collect the word 'know' is used twice, and the word 'life' three times. These words, linked to Jesus, constitute the heart of this prayer. In it we are asking God for the kind of knowledge that will enable us really to live, or perhaps we should say, really to come alive. 'God is the giver of life',[13] but there are different qualities of life, such as God has willed for the different kinds of creatures that he has made. For human beings, however, God wills that we 'know' 'life', not just of one kind, but of two. We are to 'know' both the temporal life of the plant and animal, but also the eternal life of himself and angels. This is well described in the Burial Service. 'Man that is born of a woman hath but a short time to live...He cometh up and is cut down, like a flower; he fleeth as it were a shadow and never continueth in one stay.' In death our bodies are consequently committed to the ground or to the fire, 'earth to earth, ashes to ashes, dust to dust', sharing the material fate of all merely temporal creatures. But then the fuller truth about us in pronounced. Unlike them, for us this is done 'in sure and certain hope of the resurrection to eternal life through our Lord Jesus Christ'. This eternal life, revealed by Jesus in his Resurrection, God wills us to experience also, and it is this supernatural, eternal life through Christ that we are praying here 'truly to know'.

The word 'know' in Scripture usually has a spiritual and moral element to it that is not ordinarily the case today, since now science and technology dominate its use and meaning. There it has to do with our perception of good and evil rather than our understanding of facts and figures. In Scripture, therefore, 'to reject the evil and choose the good'[14] is true knowledge. And best of all is 'truly to know' God himself, as Moses did, 'whom the Lord knew face to face'.[15]

For the generality of people in the Old Testament, however, to 'know life' meant simply to obey God's Law. 'Obeying his voice...means life to you.'[16] Obedience to the law for both the nation and the individual was 'life and good', disobedience 'death and evil'.[17] 'Man does not live by bread alone, but by [obedience] to everything that proceeds out of the mouth of God'.[18] So God raised up spiritual leaders to reveal it and expound it, and monarchs to see it was obeyed. Nevertheless despite this insistence on obeying the law the prophets and poets of Israel foresaw an altogether 'truer knowledge' of 'life', which would one day become available to all 'from the least...to the greatest'.[19]   Then the Law would no longer have to be taught to reluctant people 'precept upon precept, line upon line'[20], for then God would communicate himself directly. Then all would 'truly know life'.[21]

This prophecy was fulfilled through the coming of Jesus and the Holy Spirit. Through them this 'truer knowledge' of 'life' may now permanently infuse our temporal lives with the eternal.[22]   Faith in Christ is the essential conduit of this newness of 'life'. As he sought to explain his own experience of this new 'life' in himself, St Paul said, 'It is [now] no longer I who live but Christ lives in me; and the life I now live in the flesh I live by faith in the Son of God.'[23] Through a similar faith in Christ our lives may be similarly changed. Although outwardly we remain creatures of time and space, inwardly we 'know' that a transformation has taken place, that Christ's Spirit has entered our spirit and that we have begun to live the 'life' of eternity. It is the whole purpose of the Church's greater Sacraments of Baptism and Holy Communion to enable us to receive and retain this new gift of 'eternal life' that God has granted to us now through Jesus and the Holy Spirit.

Nevertheless this 'eternal life' of God, though it may be genuinely 'known' by us here through our faith in Christ and our fellowship in his Church, is yet to be further 'known' by us in eternity. Even though we experience it here as a reality in which we may rejoice, it still remains a hope that is set before us; but it is one to which we may look with blessed assurance. 'May the God of hope fill you with all joy and peace in believing, so that by the power of the Holy Spirit you may abound in hope',[24] said St Paul to the Romans. When writing to the Ephesians he used an interesting word to explain it. It is a*rrabon*, which in secular usage is a first instalment on a debt or promise, and the sign that full and final payment will be made. 'In Christ', he said, 'you who have believed were sealed with the Holy Spirit, which is the *arrabon* of your inheritance until you acquire possession of it'.[25] The fullest reality, therefore, of what it means 'truly to know everlasting life' awaits us in the hereafter, and all the spiritual experiences of our Christian lives here are God's guarantee, his *arrabon*, to assure us that our hopes of a final fulfilment to them hereafter are 'sure and certain'.

Nonetheless, being people of all too little faith, we will always need the support of our fellow believers in the Church, which includes our fellowship with the Saints in heaven. Indeed this Collect stresses this fellowship as being vitally helpful to us in this matter. And is not this just as we would expect? It is by 'following in their steps' that our limited temporal 'knowledge of eternal life' may surely grow and deepen hereafter into the full experience of it that they in heaven now 'know perfectly'.

―――――――――――

This Collect, then, reminds us how Christ said, 'I am the way and the truth' as well as 'the life'. As we have just stressed, through our relationship with him here, made constant and personal by the indwelling of the Holy Spirit, we may begin now to 'know' by faith and hope, as the Saints have before us, 'the life' that is 'eternal'. However to experience this 'life' here, which Christ claimed as his own, we must, naturally, follow his 'way' and accept his 'truth'. Does that not seem reasonable? Yet when the Apostles first heard these words and Christ's explanation of them, they were all strangely baffled. 'How can we know [this] way?' they said. 'What does he mean...? We do not know what he means.'26 So we should suspect there is a mystery hidden within these simple words. There is, for they relate both to his own Crucifixion, and to the crucified life that he demands of us. 'For this you have been called because Christ suffered for you, leaving you an example that you should follow in his steps.'27

It is inevitable that we should be reluctant to accept the full implications of what Christ means by this famous saying. It is only the Saints who, having understood its meaning for themselves, have embraced it gladly and willingly. That is why they have 'such honour'. But there is, as one would expect, a loving purpose behind this sharp requirement. The truth is this, that only the crucified life is the kind of life that can be a certain instrument of God's will in our sinful world. Naturally not all see this, or care about such considerations. As St Paul observed, 'the word of the Cross is foolishness to those [who are without faith],28 and even the Apostles needed to experience Christ's Resurrection and the coming of the Holy Spirit before they could understand 'the power and wisdom' of the Crucifixion. Therefore in a sense we are more fortunate than they, since we experience the fellowship of the Holy Spirit in the Church. We have been baptised into this 'truth', and were there dedicated to follow this 'way', God being our helper. 'We were buried with Christ by baptism into death, so that we may walk in newness of life'.29   We have also God's Word in Scripture constantly at hand to guide and inspire us, and we have the example and fellowship of the Saints to encourage us. Yet, as we all know, for all these advantages the same essential difficulty in 'truly knowing' 'the way and the truth' of 'the [Christian] life' remains for us today.

'Show me thy ways, O Lord, and teach me thy paths. Lead me forth in thy truth and learn me, for thou art the God of my salvation, and in thee hath been my hope all the day long.'30   The ancient prayer of the Psalmist remains as relevant as ever, therefore, even though Jesus in his life and his death has shown us perfectly 'the way' of 'life', and has taught us all that we need to know about 'the truth' of it. The call for us to live the crucified life, to deny ourselves, to cross out self, will always be our problem. Why we must, and what exactly this demand means for us will always be as hard for us to understand as it will be difficult for us to put into practice. But his teaching is as clear as his example. We cannot possibly avoid either and claim in any sincerity to be Christ's followers. 'If any would come after me let them deny themselves, and take up their cross, and follow me. For whoever would save their life will lose it, and whoever loses their life for my sake will find it.' [31] Indeed, this teaching creates for us a new law of life, the law of self-denying, self-sacrificing love, that transcends and supersedes all the earlier commandments of God, and one that must be even more fully obeyed. Here, more than ever, it is true that 'obedience [to God's law] is life to us.'

Jesus said to St Philip and St James and the other Apostles as they were together in the garden of Gethsemane, 'A new commandment I give to you, that you love one another as I have loved you.'[32] That is the difficulty; we must love as he loved. And, of course, we can only do that if he indwells us. That is the essential requirement for the keeping of this life-giving commandment. For us sinners it is otherwise impossible for us to obey it as we should. But if by his grace we do keep it, there is 'great reward'. 'If you keep my commandments,' Jesus said a bit later, 'you will abide in my love...for these things I have spoken to you that my joy may be in you and that your joy may be full.'[33]

How hard Christ's teaching is for us, but how wonderful too! Once the vision of life in Christ has been perceived, how can we be satisfied with the prospect of life without him? Here it may help us to recall the little conversation between St Philip and Jesus recorded for us in this Festival's Gospel. St Philip said, 'Show us the Father and we shall be satisfied,' to which Jesus replied, 'He that has seen me has seen the Father.'[34] The truth is that the only 'satisfactory' God is the God that allowed himself to be crucified for us, and the only 'satisfactory' life for us to live is that which unites us to him. To be thus 'satisfied' is to follow in the steps of St Philip and St James and all the Saints, and to walk with them 'in the way that leadeth to eternal life.'

SAINT BARNABAS THE APOSTLE
June 11th

O Lord God Almighty, who didst endue thy holy Apostle Barnabas with singular gifts of the Holy Ghost; Leave us not, we beseech thee, destitute of thy manifold gifts, nor yet of grace to use them always to thy honour and glory; through Jesus Christ our Lord.

This Collect was composed by Cramner for the 1549 Prayer Book. The discarded Collect in the Sarum Missal extolled St Barnabas as an intercessor for the Church and as one that had 'enlightened' it by 'his doctrine and his passion'. The new Collect is therefore more obviously based on Scripture, and also in its attractive wording more obviously appropriate for one that was such an attractive person.

St Barnabas was not one of the Twelve, but he was one who very quickly became a leading figure in the Church. The affection in which he was held by the Apostles is particularly shown by the fact that he was given a nickname by them, and thereafter was always known by it. Barnabas is a nickname, for his real name was Joseph.[1] St Luke interprets it by the Greek phrase *huios parakleseos*, which is variously translated as 'son of consolation' (A.V.), 'son of exhortation' (R.V., N.E.B.), and 'son of encouragement' (R.S.V.). This explanatory phrase is all the more interesting because of the relationship between the word *paraklesis*, used here, and *parakletos*, the special word St John uses to describe the Holy Spirit in his Gospel, and the fact that St Luke makes the comment, when describing St Barnabas, that he was 'a good man, full of the Holy Spirit'.[2] Linked with the account of his receiving this name is the story of St Barnabas giving the proceeds of the sale of a field to help the general funds.[3] No doubt such generosity was a great encouragement to the Apostles, and may have had something to do with their choice of it for him, but other references make it clear that St Barnabas was valued by all in the early Church much more highly than simply as a financial benefactor.

The early Church did not have only external enemies to deal with. It also had its own internal problems, and these were very considerable. Within Judaism, for instance, there were deep-seated rivalries and prejudices that soon emerged to disturb the common life of the Church in Jerusalem. The Greek-speaking Jews were not being given their fair share of food by the Aramaic-speaking Jews, who were in the majority; and the Church, we know, solved that problem by establishing the order of Deacons.[4] That, however, was a minor matter compared with the furore that arose when Gentiles started to join the Church. None at first had imagined that this would happen. Certainly all believed that Jesus was the Messiah of the Jews, but clearly they had not all perceived that this meant that he was also 'the Saviour of the world'.[5] The Roman centurion, Cornelius, was the first to ask to join, and from the story of St Peter receiving him it is clear that even he had not earlier perceived this truth.[6] Soon, however, others in Antioch, having heard the Gospel preached, sought to join also. Into this situation, which was one of the greatest possible importance, as well as of delicacy and potential divisiveness, the Apostles in Jerusalem sent St Barnabas. In their eyes, therefore, we may take it that he appeared qualified to deal with it wisely. Maybe the name 'Barnabas' should be also translated 'son of wise counsel', for clearly it was especially for this quality that the Apostles and the Church trusted him at this critical moment in its history.[7]

The remarkable influence he had is again illustrated by the way in which he helped to reconcile the Apostles and other members of the Church to the conversion of St Paul. Very understandably all in Jerusalem were extremely suspicious of St Paul, when he fled back there from those who had wanted to kill him in Damascus. 'But', says St Luke, 'Barnabas took him and brought him to the Apostles, and told them all that had happened'. His sponsorship was all, it seems, that St Paul needed; and it was also one, as we know, that was later to have special significance for the spread of the Gospel.[8]

Another story of him does seem to confirm that St Barnabas really was a very 'good man', for he was apparently as generous in his treatment of others as he was with his money. When he and St Paul set out on their first historic evangelistic mission to Cyprus and Turkey they took with them his cousin, St Mark. Sadly, however, the young man did not last the course. When later the two Apostles began to plan a second follow-up mission St Paul refused to consider taking St Mark, whereas St Barnabas was equally insistent that his young relative deserved a second chance. In the event they parted company, St Barnabas returning with St Mark to Cyprus, and St Paul going straight to Turkey taking with him St Silas this time as his companion.[9] 'Son of consolation', perhaps, was the rendering of Barnabas that St Mark would have particularly favoured.

St Barnabas, we may presume, was a man of large physique and handsome appearance. We are told in the heathen town of Lystra the healing of a cripple so excited the people there that they believed the two Apostles were Olympian gods come to visit them. St Barnabas was taken to be Zeus, no less, and St Paul, his messenger Hermes. In the case of St Paul this was because he was the main speaker, but by implication St Barnabas by his manner and commanding presence would have appeared to be the leader of the party and a person of greater authority.[10]   That St Barnabas, however, was also a speaker of power and eloquence is shown by the effect he had on the Church in Antioch, when he visited them on that vital occasion already mentioned. Then we are told that 'he exhorted them all to remain faithful to the Lord with steadfast purpose ... and a large company was added to the Lord'. It was, interestingly, at that time, when Gentiles were beginning to join the Church, that its members first called themselves Christians.[11]   Perhaps St Barnabas had a hand in inventing this famous title. At all events the occasion shows that Barnabas can very properly be interpreted 'son of exhortation'.

Scripture, therefore, makes it plain that St Barnabas was indeed an exceptional person. He had great charm and courage; he was wise, kind and generous. He was the ideal kind of man to be a leader in the Church. This Collect, surely, justly describes him as a man of 'singular gifts of the Holy Ghost'. The earlier Sarum Collect, however, as we have noticed, spoke also of both 'his doctrine and his passion', as well as his gifts, 'enlightening' the Church. This points to the belief, now rejected, that St Barnabas was the author of the influential book entitled the Epistle of Barnabas. This book nearly became part of the Scripture, and indeed since it is part of the Codex Sinaiticus, the important manuscript of the Bible found in the monastery on Mount Sinai in 1844, it must have been thought in some areas to have been so. However, in the final analysis, it was omitted from the Canon of Scripture. It emphasises the difference between Christianity and Judaism, and has much in common with related passages in Romans, Galatians, Thessalonians and, very particularly, Hebrews, so much so that St Barnabas has been thought by some, particularly Tertullian, to be the author of Hebrews. However, this too is now generally rejected.

His 'passion', mentioned in the Sarum Collect, took place in his beloved Cyprus in Salamis in 61. He had, however, a much wider ministry than just to the island of Cyprus. He is mentioned by St Paul in Galatians and 1 Corinthians in such a way as to suggest that he would have been well known to both those Churches[12], and in Colossians 4:10 it is just possible that it is St Barnabas, not St Mark, that is due to visit the Church there. Tradition also declares that St Barnabas evangelised in north Italy, and that he founded the Church of Milan, where there is still an order of monks bearing his name and accepting him as their Patron.

———————————

Behind this Collect is the teaching in 1 Corinthians 12 on 'spiritual gifts'. The Collect extols St Barnabas as one whom God 'endued' with 'singular', meaning special, spiritual gifts. As one should expect, God does not treat us all alike in the area of the spiritual life any more than he does in any other, yet Scripture teaches that there is a basic equality in our treatment by him there. 'There are varieties of gifts, but the same Spirit'.[13] The Collect, we notice, contrasts 'singular' gifts with 'manifold' gifts, that is those for 'the few' and those for 'the many'. But since all are 'of the same Spirit', there is an underlying unity of purpose behind all these various gifts of God that gives an essential equality of value to them all, and taken together they enable the Church to fulfil all its mission. All are important and necessary. No one can think, let alone say, 'I have no need of you'. Then beside the need to acknowledge the common value of all spiritual gifts, be they higher or lower, goes the need to recognise their suitability, and to accept gladly that they are gifts given to us, rather than chosen by us. We are given individually what God decides; we do not take what we think we should have. So there is to be 'no discord in the Body'. The great truth that enables 'all (to) rejoice together' is that we are all 'individually members' 'of the Body of Christ'. Yet, none the less, perhaps strangely, St Paul ends that Chapter by encouraging us to 'earnestly desire the higher gifts'.[14]

Is there, we may ask, a danger here? Even a leading into temptation? The Zebedee brothers were not praised, we know, for seeking the highest places in the Kingdom, and did not Jesus teach us that we must not attempt to exalt ourselves?[15] There is, however, a truth that, if acted upon, dissolves this danger. Yes, all gifts are wholly of God, but once given they then become wholly ours. In their use our full co-operation is required. In this way, therefore, through his gifts, God enables us also to be givers. This is very much what he wants us to become. Thereby we are drawn more closely to him and share in his loving activities, even to becoming 'ambassadors for Christ, God making his appeal through us'.[16] 'All things come of you', said David, 'and of your own do we give you?'[17] So the more we receive of God, the more we can give to God, and to others for his sake. If this should be at the heart of our desire, there can be no danger in 'desiring the higher gifts'.

Nonetheless, the higher gifts do bring with them special temptations, even the temptation of pride, the worst of sins. Was it his recognition of this that inspired St Paul to conclude his teaching on spiritual gifts with his great chapter on the primacy of love?[18] Indeed, perhaps he had himself in mind as he did so! Love is 'the more excellent way' that must control and inspire all the life of the Church and the lives of all who are members of it. To be given 'the higher gifts' does not, unfortunately, mean that we are sure to use them properly. Consequently the Collect ends with the prayer that we may have 'grace' to use all God's gifts, be they higher or lower, 'always to his honour and glory', which means in the spirit of love.

It is love, *agape* in Greek, that is the supreme gift of God to man, being nothing less than his own innermost Spirit. Scripture talks of higher and lower gifts, and the Collect contrasts 'singular' with 'manifold' gifts. All, however, are to be subject to this greatest gift. St Paul said, 'Rekindle the gift of God that is within you'.[19] Perhaps we can take those words out of context and use them to speak to us in this one. We must always keep this vital truth in mind, that unless all is done in love nothing will be done well, certainly not to God's 'honour and glory'.

The list of 'the gifts of the Spirit' in 1 Corinthians 12, that lie behind this Collect, are not actually easily understood.[20] They need scholarly analysis and, for study, a commentary. They refer to 'singular gifts' rather than 'manifold gifts'. For us who may be likened, (as it were) to hands and feet, or even fingers and toes, in the Body of Christ, other lists are much more likely to help us devotionally. There is the list of 'the fruits of the Spirit' in Galatians: love, joy, peace, patience, kindness, goodness, faithfulness and self-control.[21] There is an inspiring little list in 1 Thessalonians, 'Rejoice always, pray constantly, give thanks in all circumstances, for this is the will of God in Christ Jesus for you all'.[22] Then in St Paul's final exhortation to his friends in Corinth we read, 'Be watchful, stand firm in your faith, be courageous, be strong, and let all that you do be done in love'.[23] There is also that famous list of positive thoughts in Philippians that, if indulged in, bring into our lives 'the peace of God'. 'Whatever is true, whatever is honourable, whatever is just, whatever is pure, whatever is lovely, whatever is gracious, if there is any excellence, if there is anything worthy of praise, think about these things'.[24] It is advice worthy of the stirring language in which it is given. Best of all, however, is the analysis of love in 1 Corinthians 13: 'Love is patient and kind; love is not jealous or boastful; it does not insist on its own way; it is not irritable or resentful; it does not rejoice in wrong, but rejoices in the right. Love bears all things, believes all things, hopes all things [and] endures all things.' It is a passage to which we should surely return repeatedly as we seek to 'rekindle the gift of God that is within [us]'.

All such holy and virtuous things seem to be characteristic of St Barnabas. He was one, certainly, who received 'singular gifts of the Holy Ghost', but it was not the receiving of these higher gifts that made him a Saint. It was that he 'used them' according to the 'more excellent way' of love, and so in all that he did he gave 'honour and glory' to God. That is what made him one. Yet, we must not forget that we have all received gifts 'by the same Spirit'. The Saints may have lived in an exceptional manner, but in all ordinary respects they were unexceptional people. The 'grace' we pray for here is no less available to us than it was to them, and so the life that gives 'honour and glory' to God is equally possible for us all. Some prayers of the

Church, especially those honouring the Saints, may appear to apply only to the few and not to the many, and therefore not to us. However, we must not allow such thoughts. We have all been 'baptised into Christ',[25] and so been given 'grace' to make, fully and lovingly, whatever is our proper contribution to the Church's life, after the example of St Barnabas. We have all been called to be Saints,[26] and therefore, God helping us, can become saints.

SAINT JOHN BAPTIST'S DAY

June 24th

Almighty God, by whose providence thy servant John Baptist was wonderfully born, and sent to prepare the way of thy Son our Saviour, by preaching of repentance; Make us so to follow his doctrine and holy life, that we may truly repent according to his preaching; and after his example constantly speak the truth, boldly rebuke vice, and patiently suffer for the truth's sake; through Jesus Christ our Lord. Amen.

This is another Collect by Cranmer. The Sarum Collect, which it replaced, was in this case particularly bland and impersonal, rather than theologically objectionable, and what we have now is far worthier of so important and remarkable a man. In his revision of Cranmer's Collect, however, Bishop Cosin made one small, but interesting change. He changed the word 'penance' to 'repentance' in the invocation. There was a pleasing alliteration in the phrase 'preaching of penance', but to reformed ears in 1662 it was apparently not acceptable. However, it is interesting to perceive that the word 'penance' had not acquired in 1549 the objectionable overtones that it had a hundred years later. The only place in the B.C.P. outside the Articles of Religion in which the word 'penance' is still found is the service of Commination. This service was introduced in 1549 as a special service for Ash Wednesday only. Although the practice of 'auricular and secret confession to a Priest' is encouraged in the homily that is part of the Holy Communion Service, 'for those who think it needful and convenient for the quietness of their own consciences', Cranmer in 1549 did not provide an independent order for that sacrament. Instead he gave it a place within 'the Order for the Visitation of the Sick', and this arrangement remains in our 1662 B.C.P. There, however, Cranmer's special Ash Wednesday service was given the title, 'A Commination', meaning a solemn warning, and is described as a service to be used at any time as 'the Ordinary shall appoint'.

Cranmer's reason for providing this service was to prevent any misunderstanding among the faithful occasioned by the Reformers' insistence that auricular confession should be practised only voluntarily. Previously this sacrament had been obligatory, and its regular use had formed part of their ordinary religious duties. In addition they had been taught that if they were conscious of serious sin, 'mortal sin', they should not receive Communion before 'making their confession'. Shrove Tuesday (Confession Tuesday) and Ash Wednesday, moreover, had been the two days especially appointed for the regular use of this sacrament. By quite suddenly changing this custom that had so stressed the seriousness of sin, and especially of 'mortal sin', the Reformers were not only upsetting the established rhythm of the spiritual lives of ordinary churchgoing people, but also were possibly encouraging the idea that evil-doing was not really as wrong in God's eyes as they had previously been taught. Now this most definitely was not what the Reformers desired. In this matter at least they wanted all to recognise that the Reformation had changed nothing. The Pope's writ no longer ran, certainly, but God's Word most certainly did. Although no one now had to prove their penitence by confessing to a Priest, it was definitely still considered true that 'if any of you be a blasphemer of God, an hinderer or slanderer of his Word, an adulterer, or be in malice, or envy, or in any grievous crime' such had still to 'truly repent' before receiving Communion, 'lest the Devil enter into you, as he entered into Judas, and fill you full of all iniquities, and bring you to destruction both of body and soul', as the homily in the Holy Communion Service teaches. This special service, with its solemn warnings against evil-doing and evil-doers, which the faithful were all expected to attend, was devised to press home these truths, and to create a regular corporate occasion for self-examination and repentance to be used at any time, but especially at the time that hitherto had been associated with the saying of their confessions.

Now, it must be said, this service of Commination has been quite forgotten, and one wonders when it was last used anywhere in our country. But then it must also be said that in our land, and even in our Church, a liberal, even dismissive, attitude towards those who wilfully set aside God's Command-ments has steadily gathered pace, and it is no coincidence that there is no equivalent to this service in the A.S.B. Bishop Cosin may have been uneasy about using the word 'penance', but he and his predecessors and associates were not uncertain about their attitude towards all forms of evil-doing, or uneasy about demanding repentance of sinners. Indeed they desired passionately that our Prayer Book would be a permanent bulwark against evil in our land, and the very last thing that they desired was to take away from the faithful a proper fear of evil's consequences, which the Commination Service so earnestly stresses.

St John the Baptist, called, somewhat strangely, 'thy servant John Baptist' in this Collect, was also one that equally definitely stressed the need for repentance and the confession of sin.[1] His baptism was a 'baptism of repentance',[2] and he is here described as a preacher of repentance. Further we pray especially in the Collect that 'we may truly repent according to his preaching'. However he may be misunderstood. In his own day he certainly was. His appearance was strange and his life style austere.[3] 'He came eating no bread and drinking no wine', and to the worldly Scribes and Pharisees he seemed a harsh fanatic.[4] We too may be tempted today to feel alienated from him for similar reasons. So let us notice that Scripture declares that 'he preached good news to the people',[5] and his understand-

ing of repentance is of a life-changing experience that brings great blessings to others as well as to ourselves. How positive and attractive, for
instance, were his answers to those who sought his guidance! Repentance,
he taught, should be shown in generosity towards those in need, honesty
in doing our job, gentleness in exercising authority, and sympathy towards
the weak.[6] The Greek for repentance is *metanoia*, and it means a change
of mind or attitude. 'To truly repent', therefore, is not just to reject what
is wrong and evil, but also to embrace what is right and good. This, then,
is the positive concept of repentance for which we are praying here, and
which was 'according to his preaching'.

However, impressive as this advice is, both Scripture and this Collect make
it clear that St John's teaching on this subject is deeper still. The greater
purpose of repentance, he taught, is that we may be emptied of self, that
seed-bed of all our sins, in readiness to being filled by God.[7] So this Collect
rightly calls us, not just to remember his 'doctrine', but also to emulate his
'holy life'. His holiness was fully perceived by the common people of his
time, indeed so much so that even the Chief Priests, who in their jealousy
and ignorance despised him, dared not criticise him openly,[8] and it is even
more clearly revealed in his joyous acceptance of Jesus as the one who
would both fulfil his preaching and supplant his influence.[9] He may have
been more of an Old Testament Saint than a New Testament one, being
likened by Jesus to Elijah[10]; but then Elijah's holiness was considered
equal to that of Moses himself, Elijah being the fount of Prophecy, even as
Moses was the fount of Law; and let us notice how he was the recipient of
our Lord's unstinted praise.[11]

This Collect twice mentions 'truth', and Scripture portrays St John the
Baptist pre-eminently as a man of truth. It was his refusal to compromise
scriptural truth that led to his death in Herod's prison.[12] Jesus repeatedly
emphasises the supreme merit of truth. It is 'truth [that] will make [us]
free'[13], and those 'who are of the truth hear his voice'.[14] The Collect

stresses the need for us to 'constantly speak the truth', but just as vital, or indeed perhaps more vital, is our ability to hear the truth, and to listen prayerfully to it. Only then will we be able always to speak it, and live according to its demands. These, as the Collect and the fate of St John warn us, may be hard and difficult, and even dangerous. It was for Jesus, who told Pilate that he stood before him for 'bearing witness to the truth'.[15] For us to 'truly repent' is to seek the real truth about ourselves and acknowledge whatever that may be. That truth about ourselves will be revealed to us only as we are willing to perceive it as it is in God's Word, and, very particularly, 'as it is in Jesus'.[16]

Some element of 'patient suffering for the truth's sake' cannot be avoided by any who will 'truly repent', and then seek 'boldly' to live out the implications of 'all the truth' revealed to us by the Holy Spirit and by Scripture.[17] We must, therefore, interpret the prayer that we may 'constantly speak the truth', and 'boldly rebuke vice', as widely as 'the doctrine and holy life' of St John demands. Mercifully none of us in this land will be risking our lives if we do so, even though some hardship incurring genuine sacrifice and some unpopularity, even approaching persecution, may conceivably be asked of us by God 'for the truth's sake', yet the whole Gospel, and not just the example of St John, assures us that to accept such 'patiently' will be infinitely worthwhile, no matter how unpleasant or protracted it may be. For those 'who are persecuted for righteousness sake', and so presumably for the truth's sake, 'great rewards' are promised.[18]

––––––––––––––––

Our consideration of St John's special theme of repentance has led us to consider the petition in this Collect before the invocation. So let us return to the Collect's beginning where we recall how, according to God's 'providence, thy servant John Baptist was wonderfully born'. We are told that he 'did no miracle'[19], but his birth was certainly miraculous, and an event that God revealed to be 'providential' by the sending of his angel.[20] By keeping this day as a major Festival, the Church recognises it as playing a vital part of 'his redemption of the world by our Lord Jesus Christ',[21] no less. No doubt every one of us is 'wonderfully born', but our births are not accompanied by signs and wonders, and the visitation of angels, nor were our parents old and barren when we were conceived.[22] Scripture certainly assures us all that God is our Creator and our Father. Moreover, it tells us that we each have a Guardian Angel.[23] Yet, however special we may properly consider our own birth to have been, not only to our earthly parents but also to our heavenly Father, that happy event was not significant for the 'redemption of the world', and so, surely, less 'wonderful' than that of 'John Baptist'.

For the Saints, as we have said, the day of their death rather than the day of their birth is considered by the Church to be their most 'wonderful' day. It was then that they entered into the life of heaven. Here, however, we are commemorating St John the Baptist's earthly birthday, not his heavenly one. That day is kept on August 29, but for reasons already considered (see Introduction) our Church has chosen to make St John's nativity rather than his martyrdom his major Festival. For us, we must say, if not for him, his birth is certainly of far greater significance, and the invocation stresses why. St John was born to 'prepare the way of [the] Son our Saviour'. Even before he was born Scripture tells us that mysteriously he was aware of his vocation. His mother, Elizabeth, cried out to St Mary, who had come to see her, 'Behold, when the voice of your greeting came to my ears, the babe in my womb leaped for joy'.[24]

St John's main message may have been that sinners must prepare for Christ's coming into their lives by repentance, but he also stressed that, when that happens, he comes to bless, 'to baptise us with the Holy Spirit and with fire'.[25] These words remind us not only of Pentecost, when this prophecy was so exactly fulfilled,[26] but also of 'the fruits of the Spirit', such as 'love, joy and peace', and all other such 'blessings of goodness' that the Holy Spirit brings into our lives.[27] Even though persecution and sacrifice come with the Gospel's blessings, its main consequence, for those who hear it and accept it, is that they shall 'rejoice greatly' after the example of St John.[28] In prison, as his end drew near, we read how he knew then the joy of renewed faith in the fact that 'thy Son, our Saviour' had indeed come, that his preordained work of redemption was under way, and that St John's own part in that divine activity, which he had been providentially 'sent' by God to do, had been faithfully accomplished.[29]

This devotional Collect, then, does not only tell of truths that relate to St John the Baptist. Yes, though less so, we are all 'wonderfully born',[30] and like St John we all live under God's 'providence' and are 'sent' to fulfil his purposes. The Incarnation guarantees that this is true for every one of us, for it throws the reflection of God's glory over every human being.[31] Since God became a man, every human being has become God's brother or sister as well as his child. So we are quite sure that 'there is joy in heaven [as well as on earth] when a child is born into the world',[32] and that 'the Lord is loving unto every man'.[33] And with his love for us go his purposes for our existence. 'Thy hands have made me and fashioned me; O give me understanding that I may learn thy commandments', says the Psalmist.[34] We must learn for what purpose he made us, and then walk in that way. What can be more important for us than that? But how can we know this truth about ourselves? And then how can we fulfil it in our lives? Jesus said, 'When the Spirit of truth comes, he will guide you into all the truth'.[35] We have been 'baptised with the Holy Spirit', as St John the Baptist said we would be. He has come to 'guide us into all the truth' about ourselves, according to God's providential will for us. We are, therefore, to go forward, 'constantly', 'boldly' and 'patiently' in faith and hope as did St John the Baptist, seeking the Spirit's guidance and trusting his ability to help us follow it. 'He who calls you is faithful, and he will do it.'[36]

SAINT PETER'S DAY
June 29th

O Almighty God, who by thy Son Jesus Christ didst give to thy Apostle St Peter many excellent gifts, and commandest him earnestly to feed thy flock; Make, we beseech thee, all Bishops and Pastors diligently to preach thy holy Word, and the people obediently to follow the same, that they may receive the crown of everlasting glory; through Jesus Christ our Lord. Amen.

Until the Reformation this day was kept in our Churches in honour of both St Peter and St Paul. Tradition has it that they were martyred on the same day, although Dionysius, a second century Bishop of Corinth, who is the earliest known person to comment on this matter, says only that they were martyred about the same time. For them to have been brought together, however, to share a Festival Day was to endorse the New Testament's perception that they were the two outstanding personalities of the early Church. St Luke called his book on how it all began, 'The Acts of the Apostles', although most of them are hardly mentioned. It could, perhaps more accurately, have been entitled, 'The Acts of the Apostles Peter and Paul'. They are presented there as the two main human instruments used by the Holy Spirit in both founding the Church and spreading the Gospel.

Although the pairings of St Philip with St James and St Simon with St Jude were kept, Cranmer altered this double Festival to give each of these supremely important Saints their own Red-Letter Day. This day, June 29, was given to St Peter and, as we have already noticed, January 25 to St Paul. This change, however, naturally necessitated a fresh Collect. The Sarum Collect for the double Festival was very simple. It prayed that, since the Church 'took its rise' from these two Saints, it might 'in all things' follow the precepts which they gave. This simple theme may be said to have been kept in a general sense by Cranmer, but it has been overshadowed now by two important, but also controversial, new elements, the first being the emphasis on St Peters special 'gifts' and pastoral responsibilities in the invocation, and the second being the mention of 'all Bishops and Pastors' and their preaching ministry in the petition. The consideration of these two new elements will, inevitably, constitute the main part of our commentary.

In the Roman Catholic Calendar St Peter has a second Festival Day called St Peter's Chains (St Peter ad Vincula), that is not included in ours. It falls on August 1st, which means that it coincides with the ancient agricultural Festival of Lammas, which is a Black-Letter Festival in our Calendar. In our Prayer Book, however, the main event commemorated by the Feast of St Peter's Chains, his miraculous escape from prison, is not forgotten, for it is the reading set for the Epistle on this day. In the Scottish Book of Common Prayer Lammas Day is given special consideration, since it is one of that country's Quarter Days, which fall on different days from those in England, the others being All Saints' Day, Candlemas and the Feast of St Philip and St James. The Proper, however, set for Lammas Day in the Scottish B.C.P. is, perhaps surprisingly, the traditional Proper for St Peter's Chains, and so the day is kept liturgically as a Petrine Festival rather than an agricultural one, without that fact being recognised in its title.

St Peter's real name was Simon, and Peter (or Cephas) was Jesus's nickname for him.[1] Why Jesus gave him this name is a matter both of importance and controversy, which we must consider in due course. St

Peter's home was Bethsaida,[2] where he and his brother ran a fishing business in partnership with the Zebedee family.[3] We know he was married and his wife accompanied him on his travels, and we hear in the Gospels of his mother-in-law, whom Jesus healed.[4] In the apocryphal book, The Acts of St Peter, there is also an attractive story of him healing a daughter who was paralysed.

None of the Evangelists, sadly, gives us any personal descriptions of the Apostles, but in the mediaeval paintings of St Peter a certain similarity between them has been noticed. It may be, therefore, that they give a reliable indication of his appearance. Certainly what they show is wholly believable. He is portrayed there as a sturdily built man of late middle age, with a wide forehead, thick hair, a curly beard and strong chin. From the Gospels we may reasonably suppose he was the oldest of the Apostles, but nonetheless he is shown there to have been a very active man. He was fit enough to run with St John from Jerusalem to the tomb of Jesus that lay outside the city; he was able to swim ashore to Jesus, when he came to those Apostles who had gone fishing after his Resurrection; and he was up to attacking the High Priest's servant with a sword with notable success.[5]

St Peter's attractive, yet forceful, personality comes through very clearly in the many stories of him in both the Gospels and Acts. Many inevitably concern his special relationship with Jesus, and from them we can perhaps generalise about him. They show us a man who was trusting to the point of rashness, devoted to the point of folly, and loyal to the point of violence.[6] His great love for Jesus was, we know, cruelly tested in the High Priest's courtyard, but his failure then, we may believe, did much to develop him spiritually.[7] His first Epistle is a beautiful book, full of his faith in and love for Jesus, but also notable for its personal humility, its compassion for the tempted and frightened, and its encouragement to the suffering and oppressed.[8]

In the end St Peter followed his Lord to a martyr's death, as Jesus had foretold he would,[9] but in his case he was crucified upside down. Tradition has it that this was at his own request, since he did not believe himself worthy to die exactly as his Master had. In the apocryphal Acts of St Peter we hear the famous story of how St Peter was urged by his fellow Christians to flee from Nero's soldiers who were seeking him, and how, as he was hurrying along the Appian Way to safety, he met Jesus going the other way. *'Domine, quo vadis?'* he asked (Lord, where are you going?). 'I am going to Rome', Jesus said, 'to be crucified again'. At this St Peter turned back to go with him; and then Jesus disappeared. So Jesus's prophecy and his own eager declaration were both fulfilled.

St Peter's first Epistle opens with a remarkable passage, which has been seen as unintentionally autobiographical. If we may take it in that sense, he is declaring that he is one 'chosen and destined by God the Father, and sanctified by the Spirit for obedience to Jesus Christ and for sprinkling with his blood.'[10] Even if he really had his Christian readers in mind when he wrote them, could any words describe St Peter better? Indeed since these words are part of God's 'holy Word', that is so stressed in this Collect, we may perhaps accept them, not only as describing what St Peter may conceivably have believed was the truth about himself, but also as descriptive of what God declares to us to be the truth about St Peter.

Behind the wording of this reformation Collect lies that crucial reformation issue, the claims of the Papacy. Since these claims, and the Reformers' rejection of them, govern its wording, and are essential to its meaning, we must consider both in some detail.

The invocation obliquely refers to two very special passages, both of which were, and still are, used as proof-texts for the Papal claims. We should keep them in mind. The first is St Matthew 16 vv 18-19. This passage is part of the Gospel for the day, and in it we hear of 'the keys of the Kingdom' that Jesus 'will give' to St Peter. These 'keys', we may presume, are the main items referred to in the phrase 'many excellent gifts' in the Collect's invocation. The second passage is St John 21 vv 15-20, in which the risen Christ urges St Peter to fulfil his pastoral responsibilities in the coming Church with special faithfulness before he is taken away by martyrdom. The phrase in the invocation, 'earnestly to feed thy flock', clearly refers to our Lord's admonitions to St Peter on that occasion. Now, the most crucial element of the Papal claims is that St Peter was set apart by Jesus from all the other Apostles to fulfil a unique ministry, and for the fulfilling of it Jesus gave him supreme spiritual and pastoral authority in the Church, and, as we have said, it was to these two passages that the Papacy particularly appealed. Before we go on to consider them from, as it were, both sides, it is perhaps worth noticing that, since Cranmer goes out of his way to draw attention to both of them, he is showing himself unafraid of their force in this dispute.

Although the Collect alludes to both of these passages, it is the Matthean passage that is unquestionably the more significant. There are two outstanding elements in it. The first, which is implied in the invocation, and to which we have just referred, is Jesus's promise of 'the keys of the Kingdom'; 'I will give you', he said to St Peter, 'the keys of the Kingdom'. These 'keys' have messianic overtones, no less. They remind us both of Isaiah's prophecy of a Davidic Messiah, who will possess 'the keys to the house of David',[11] and also of the risen Christ in Revelation, who now controls 'the keys of Death and Hades'.[12] Cranmer describes these 'keys' as simply 'excellent gifts', but 'awesome' would surely be a more appropriate adjective to use. After all, control of who enters, and who is refused entry, into God's Kingdom is involved, as Jesus's mention of 'binding and loosing' ('whatever you bind on earth will be bound in heaven and whatever you loose on earth will be loosed in heaven') to explain their use makes plain.

These 'keys of the Kingdom' are not mentioned directly elsewhere in the Gospels. There are, however, passages with which, clearly, they may be linked, especially in regard to the important concept of 'binding and loosing' that Jesus used to explain their use. One such is the saying of Jesus, spoken, we notice, to all the Apostles and not just to St Peter, about the mysterious power of his 'parables of the Kingdom'. Their use was to have a similar effect to that of 'the keys', for they would control who would understand the truth about God's Kingdom (or its 'secrets'), and who would not.[13] Another related passage is the great occasion in the Upper Room on Easter Day, as described by St John. Then Jesus gave to the faithful disciples gathered there, who included more than the Apostles, the gift of the Holy Spirit, that was to endow them with similar powers of 'forgiving or retaining sins'.[14] Then later in St Matthew's Gospel there is a second mention of 'binding and loosing'. This time, however, this awesome power is not given just to St Peter, nor even to all the Apostles, but generally and directly to 'the disciples', and within the unexceptional context of some teaching by Jesus about pastoral practices and common behaviour in the coming Church.[15] In these three related passages Jesus is seen giving special powers and responsibilities either to the Apostles as a body, or to the Church generally, and in none of them, we notice, is St Peter singled out, nor is any sign given in them that Jesus willed for St Peter a special or controlling ministry in this crucial matter of 'binding and loosing'. It is reasonable to suggest, however, that if Jesus had willed such a ministry, as the Papal claims assert, these related passages would have indicated it, if not emphasised it.

———————————

The second crucial issue in this Matthean passage, not referred to in this Collect, is the matter of St Peter's name. 'You are Peter', said Jesus, 'and upon this rock I will build my Church', and the promise of 'the keys' immediately follows this saying. (We have here a play on words. In Greek Peter is *petros* and rock is *petra*.) The change of St Peter's name, however, is not dependent on this passage, for, according to St John, Jesus gave it to him when they first met.[16] The other Evangelists also refer to this change of name in their lists of the Twelve, which suggests that, at least in origin, its purpose was to establish St Peter as their leader.[17] St Matthew and St Luke also allude to it in their respective stories of his call, but in both cases without emphasis.[18]

A person's name in Judaism was a matter of great significance. It was supposed to reveal the truth that really mattered about that person, his or her character as well as position and family connections. So Joseph was told by the angel what Jesus was to be called, and why. 'You shall call his name Jesus, for he shall save [God's] people from their sins',[19] (Jesus being the same name as Joshua and meaning 'God saves'). To change a person's name, therefore, was to indicate that a vitally important change had taken place in that person's life that all should recognise. So it was that Saul the Pharisee became Paul the Christian. Even though the Gospels indicate that Jesus still called St Peter 'Simon', as in the Johannine passage that lies behind this Collect,[20] the evidence of both Acts and the Epistles is that he was always Peter (or Cephas, the Aramaic for rock) to the early Church. To this generalisation there are only two exceptions; James, the Lord's brother, called him Simon at the Council of Jerusalem, and in his second Epistle St Peter does so himself, if one accepts the Petrine authorship of that Epistle.[21] The point at issue here, however, may be put in the form of two queries: "What did Jesus mean by changing Simon's name to Peter? And what did the early Church understand by that change of name?"

The Matthean passage is very powerful. Having stressed his change of name, Jesus goes on to say, 'On this rock I will build my Church'. Clearly Jesus did mean something of great importance, and it is central to the

Papal claims that these words must be accepted as prophetic, that is as having meaning for the whole future of the Church. Although initially they referred to St Peter personally and to his leadership within the early Church, being prophetic, so it is claimed, they refer to the future also. Their meaning, it is claimed, did not die with St Peter, and so all who have succeeded him as Bishops of Rome have inherited all that was envisaged in that utterance of Jesus. Since it is a word of God, having gone forth it must be fulfilled, and men and women assist its fulfilment as they accept the Popes as men who have been granted supreme authority in the Church by Jesus. Such is the understanding of this passage by the Roman Catholic Church. The pastoral responsibilities that are involved in the Johannine passage, although of secondary importance, would seem, certainly, to augment the more far-reaching implications of the Matthean passage. This doctrine of the Popes' unique ministry, gives them, it is claimed, infallible wisdom in defining the truth in matters concerning faith and morals. Although undoubtedly claimed in Cranmer's day, this was not, however, confirmed as Catholic dogma until the promulgation of the doctrine of Papal Infallibility in 1870.

The Reformers, however, interpreted this crucial Matthean passage very differently. From the evidence of the New Testament, they argued, nothing could be clearer than that the foundation on which the Church was built was Christ himself, and none other. This truth is stressed by both St Peter and St Paul, who both significantly describe him as 'the Rock'. In 1 Corinthians 3:11, we read, 'No other foundation [for the Church] can anyone lay than that which is [already] laid, which is Jesus Christ'; and then in Romans 9, reminding his readers of Isaiah's prophecy of 'the Rock' that God would 'set up', and on which he would rebuild his chosen people, he says, quoting Isaiah, 'They [the Jewish authorities] have stumbled over the stumbling stone', 'the Rock' that would both 'make men fall', but also would enable all 'who believed in him not to be put to shame'.[22] In 1 Corinthians 10:4, also, we have the emphatic words, 'the Rock was Christ'. In that chapter St. Paul is urging the new Christians in Corinth to beware of the spiritual danger of acknowledging any other authority than that of Christ. He likens them to the Israelites of old, who like them were journeying to a promised land. They were all the time being tempted, he said, just as the old Israelites had been, to be faithless and disobedient. Then, to stress the essential unity of the old and the new Israel, St Paul said that what, or who, sustained the old Israelites was exactly what, or who, sustains them, the new Israelites. 'They drank [even as you do] from the supernatural Rock that followed them, and that Rock was Christ.'[23]

In 1 Peter we also read of the same Isaianic figure of the 'messianic' Rock that St Paul refers to in Romans. Again there can be no doubt that St Peter sees this 'messianic' figure as Jesus. In the context of this reformation Collect, 1 Peter 4 vv 4-10 is a passage of particular significance. It appears to give St Peter's own interpretation of this dispute, that was so central to the Reformation, but which the New Testament clearly shows had its roots in the earliest years of the Church, for in the Corinthian Church we read that some said, 'I belong to Cephas' (*et al.*) and others said, 'I belong to Christ'.[24] St Peter, we notice, in his Epistle lays special emphasis on the fact that the true foundation-stone of the Church is Jesus, 'the stone...in God's sight chosen and precious'. His readers consequently were to be as 'living stones' used to build 'a spiritual house' on this foundation 'to offer spiritual sacrifices acceptable to God through Jesus Christ'. The passage reads as if St Peter is concerned that no one should be in any doubt that Jesus, and no one else, is 'the Rock' on which the Church is built.

Nevertheless the words of Jesus, 'You are Peter and upon this rock I will build my Church and the power of death shall not prevail against it', are part of Scripture. The Reformers did not seek to deny them, but only to reinterpret them. They must be taken in their context, and this, they claimed, the Papacy wholly failed to do. The context, which is so crucial to its proper interpretation, is the questioning of the Apostles by Jesus. First he asked them what others were saying about him, and then what they themselves believed. It was to this second question that Peter made his famous answer, clearly speaking as their spokesman, 'You are the Christ, the Son of the living God'. To this statement of spiritual recognition Jesus cried out, 'Blessed are you Simon Barjonah! For flesh and blood has not revealed this to you, but my Father in heaven'. What, the Reformers claimed, so excited Jesus was not so much the Apostles' faith expressed by St Peter, as his recognition of the Father's influence and inspiration behind St Peter's words. It was that, rather than St Peter's or any man's faith, on which he could completely rely, and which made him then so certain that the Church, that would emerge out of his earthly ministry, would survive all 'the powers of death', including his own. What is translated in the R.S.V. 'the powers of death', however, is literally 'the gates of Hades', and so might be better translated 'the powers of evil'. The Church throughout its history would have to contend, he knew, against 'the rulers of the darkness of this world, and against the forces of spiritual wickedness in the heavenly realm'.[25] Without the protection of the Father, Jesus knew that it would be no match for these evil powers, but since the truth St Peter articulated had come direct from the Father, and the Apostle's faith in Jesus had been inspired by him, Jesus knew for certain that nothing could eliminate it. This saving truth had at last been spoken. It was at last believed. The sure foundation of the Church had consequently at last been laid. This was the light that would for ever shine in the darkness, and the darkness would never prevail over it.[26] The future was, therefore, now assured. Yes, St Peter's contribution to this was, of course, important, but it is the message rather than the man that was of supreme importance. After all, the Reformers could point out, immediately after this saying St Peter was rebuked by Jesus for serious foolishness, and even called 'Satan'![27]

The New Testament undoubtedly shows that St Peter was the leader both of the Twelve and later of the early Church, even though James, the Lord's brother, from the evidence of Acts 15 may have been deemed while he lived his nominal superior. St Peter's leadership, however, as shown there, was never more than that of a *primus inter pares*. In the life of the early Church he did not take the place of Jesus. That place was taken by the Holy Spirit, as St Peter himself frequently made clear.[28] His leadership, therefore, had no 'messianic' overtones. His relationship with St Paul, as described in Galatians 2, is particularly relevant to this truth. Clearly to St Paul (and should he not have known?), St Peter inherited from Jesus none of his 'supreme' authority. The Reformers' contention, therefore, that from the evidence of the New Testament he cannot, as claimed by the Papacy, be separated in his ministry from the other Apostles, beyond his undoubted role as *primus inter pares*, does appear to be soundly based.

We continue, however, to have to face this divisive situation. The Papal claims have not been mitigated since Cranmer's time, and they remain the major barrier between ourselves and others and the Roman Catholic Church. It can be said, however, that there are not a few within our Communion and outside it who are willing, even eager, to acknowledge the primacy among bishops of the Bishop of Rome, believing that this is scripturally supported and ecumenically required, but who believe that describing his nature as one of infallibility, and so in effect likening him to Jesus rather than to St Peter, is both unfounded according to a proper understanding of Scripture, and also disastrous for the greater good and unity of the Church. (See further St Simon and St Jude.)

This Collect, then, while acknowledging the special place of St. Peter in the early Church, by the way it continues subtly confirms our Church's rejection of the later Papal claims for him. Having specially mentioned St Peter's ministry in its invocation, it proceeds by conscious contrast in the petition to pray generally for 'all Bishops and Pastors'. These are seen primarily as preachers of the Gospel. Although the Reformers rejected any 'messianic' claims for St. Peter and, therefore, his successors, they nonetheless believed strongly that the Church, as the Body of Christ, did possess 'messianic' status. From the Church God's 'holy Word' does go forth down the ages to all mankind, the preaching of which does have the power to bring judgement, either leading to salvation or condemnation, on all who hear it. Because the Church is ordained of God to preach and teach his 'holy Word', being itself the incarnate Word's new Body, it does hold those awesome 'keys' of which Jesus spoke, for it is through the response of men and women to that Word of the Gospel that there is a binding on earth that binds in heaven and a loosing on earth that looses in heaven. As Jesus taught, amid life's 'floods' and 'winds', only those who have built their lives upon that 'rock' will be safe in their day of judgement.[29] The absolutely vital thing for the Church and its leaders to do, therefore, was, and is, to preach that 'holy Word', which wonderfully does have power to open the way that leads to the place of 'everlasting glory'.

'But how are they to believe in him of whom they have never heard? And how are they to hear without a preacher?'[30] This Collect, therefore, prays not only for those who will hear God's holy Word, and hearing will 'obediently follow the same', but also for the preachers of that Word. As is only logical, they are mentioned first. We pray specifically that they may be 'diligent' in their preaching, but, bearing in mind the special importance the Reformers attached to this ministry, the adjective Cranmer chose here sounds strangely inadequate. Perhaps we should interpret it in terms of the more impressive biblical word 'trustworthy'.[31] Even in the earliest years of the Church there were 'preachers of a different Gospel', who were apparently very 'diligent' in the mischief they caused,[32] and it was indeed the battle cry of the Reformers that this was exactly what was happening again in their time.

This overwhelming concern of the Reformers for the purity of the Gospel, echoing the concern of St Paul, ignited and fuelled the Reformation. It also alerts us to the truth that a perversion of the Gospel is an ever-present danger for the Church. Certainly we believe that 'the powers of death' will never 'prevail over' the Church, but surely we must also recognise that these 'powers' will never cease attempting to do so, and their main line of attack will be to cause a perversion of the Gospel. It is, therefore, right that we should constantly be asking, "Are they succeeding in our time?"

As we have had occasion to remind ourselves, we are concluding a Decade of Evangelism, a time when the preaching of God's 'holy Word' has been officially emphasised. (Is that why the last ten years have been such fraught ones?) We have already recognised the undoubted difficulties facing the Church today as regards evangelism (see St Stephen's Day). They are real and not easily overcome and, though most relevant to our thoughts here, it would be tautologous to repeat them. Nonetheless, since it is St Peter's Collect that we are considering, we cannot but remind ourselves that it was he who led the Apostles 'every day in the Temple and at home to teach and preach Jesus as the Christ'.[33] Moreover, it was St. Peter who said, clearly establishing his own priorities in this ministry, 'There is no other name under heaven among men by which we must be saved'.[34] As we are praying here for all preachers, other relevant words of Scripture also come to mind: 'I charge you in the presence of God and of Christ Jesus...preach the Word, be urgent in season and out of season, convince, rebuke and exhort, be unfailing in patience and in teaching. The time is coming when people will not endure sound teaching but...as for you, always be steady, endure suffering, do the work of an evangelist, fulfil your ministry.'[35]

'If [however] the bugle gives an uncertain sound, who will get ready for battle?'[36] After praying for the preachers, we pray that, as a result of their preaching, 'the people will obediently follow' to where God's holy Word alone can lead them, a sharing in God's 'everlasting glory'. However, it may be that the wording of this petition does not sound as relevant today as it would have done 500 years ago. 'Obediently following God's holy word', 'receiving a crown of everlasting glory', are these 'the sounds of the bugle' that are certain to get 'the people' of today 'ready for battle'? The fact is that the spiritual life nowadays is seldom seen in terms of 'obedience' to 'God's holy word', be it preached or written. That understanding of it is likely to be described derogatively as fundamentalist. Nor is its ultimate aim usually perceived as seeking to obtain some glorious heavenly reward. That is likely to be seen as misguided, selfish and irresponsible. How then are we to pray this prayer? Is it one we can still pray with sincerity and conviction?

Let us remind ourselves of the most basic of scriptural truths. God's 'holy Word' for us is not limited to the spoken or written word: it has become incarnate in Jesus. The phrase 'obediently follow' much better describes a relationship with a Master than a devotion to a script. Nonetheless God's 'holy Word', through being incarnate in Jesus, is, as he is, 'the same yesterday, today and for ever.'[37] The living Master, therefore, can never be separated from the sacred script. Although Jesus is now risen and ascended, he remains the historical Jesus of the written Gospels. There is a correlation here. On the one hand the discipleship of a living Lord frees us from a blind obedience to the written words of Scripture from the error of fundamentalism. The Old Testament Law, we know, became a 'curse' to the many who most 'obediently followed' it, because their obedience to it tragically prevented them from recognising in Jesus the fulfilment of all they held most dear,[38] and a similar tragic perversion can spill over into the spiritual lives of 'the people' of the Church. They, too, can have a spirituality wholly dominated by 'the letter' of Scripture, and so be unable to be led by its 'Spirit'.[39] However, on the other hand, we must never imagine that Jesus in glory can be separated from the earthly Jesus of the written Gospels. There can never be a 'modern' Jesus, who has 'outgrown', as it were, the man who walked the lanes of Galilee and died on a Cross outside Jerusalem 2000 years ago. Through his indwelling Spirit Jesus may indeed be our contemporary, but he has not changed from the man who was the contemporary of St Peter, and demanded of him unqualified obedience. It is always the scriptural Jesus who must be our Master too, for there is no other. If we should imagine otherwise, we are deceiving ourselves and 'the truth is not in us.'[40]

We may ask, perhaps, why anyone would ever want to make this basic mistake. The answer is, of course, because the scriptural Jesus is above all else the Jesus of Golgotha. It was in fact St Peter who was the first of so many to take exception to this truth about Jesus,[41] and then who later, when put under pressure by the company he found himself in, was the first of others to deny that he knew that Jesus.[42] He had to learn, as we all must, the meaning of Jesus's insistence that following him involves 'taking up our cross.'[43] This is the 'stumbling block' (or scandalous requirement; in Greek the word translated 'stumbling block' is *skandalon*) that so put off the Greeks in Corinth that had at first shown interest in the Gospel that St Paul was proclaiming.[44] So it is now as it was in the beginning. If we ask why Christ makes the demand that we live the crucified life of obedience to him, his answer is as uncompromising as it is uncomfortable. 'Truly, truly I say to you, everyone...is a slave to sin,'[45] and unless we allow him to redeem us from sin's bondage, the slaves of sin we will remain. Towards him, and the Word of God that he has fulfilled, there has to be a wholehearted obedience, born out of our sense of need and our consequential trust in him. Only then, said St Peter, teaching us, we may presume, out of his own bitter experience, can Christ live in us as 'the Shepherd and Guardian of our souls.'[46]

But what of the ultimate aim of our spiritual lives suggested by the last phrase of this Collect? The truth is that it is only those who have accepted gladly and willingly the restrictions on their own wills and judgement, that is implied by the call to take up our cross, who are able to live wisely, unselfishly and responsibly. 'I can will what is right, but I cannot do it,'[47] said St Paul; such is the power of sin. So it is only those who have been truly 'baptised into Christ', 'into his death', that are 'free', 'no longer enslaved to sin.'[48] It is, in a word, the Saints who are the great contributors to the real needs of the world; indeed, as St Paul says, 'the whole creation groans' and 'waits' for their arrival.[49]

They 'receive the crown of everlasting glory', but it is the reward of sacrificial service. Christ wore 'the crown of everlasting glory' on the Cross,[50] and those who live the crucified life will receive one too. St Peter, again: 'When the Chief Shepherd is manifested you [also] will obtain the unfading crown of glory.'[51] This Collect's wording, therefore, as is always the case with our Prayer Book Collects, points us to the truth that really matters, 'the truth as it is in Jesus'.[52] This is the truth all 'people' no doubt really desire to know, but too often fail to look for where it may be found. How sad this is! 'When Jesus saw the people he had compassion on them because they were harassed and helpless like sheep without a shepherd.'[53] How important, therefore, that 'all Bishops and Pastors' really are 'diligent' in preaching God's 'holy Word' to inspire 'the people obediently to follow the same', according to this prayer. Its message is not therefore one that has lost, or ever will lose, its relevance. Rather, without it it is we are lost.

Let us end, however, with thanksgiving. Many 'Bishops and Pastors' do most faithfully and 'diligently' fulfill this ministry, and also many 'people' live lives of wonderful 'obedience' to Jesus and all God's 'holy Word'. They are the spiritual heirs of those to whom St Peter wrote so encouragingly; 'Without having seen him you love him; though you do not now see him you believe in him, and rejoice with unutterable and exalted joy. As the outcome of your faith you obtain the salvation of your souls.'[54] What more, then, can we say? Maybe only this. In view of the history lying behind this Collect, it is perhaps ironic that of 'all the Bishops and Pastors' called to this vital ministry of preaching God's 'holy Word', none today have been more obviously 'diligent' in it than the Bishop of Rome.

SAINT MARY MAGDALEN
July 22nd

O Almighty God. whose blessed Son did call and sanctify Mary Magdalen to be a witness to his Resurrection; Mercifully grant that by thy grace we may be healed of all our infirmities, and always serve thee in the power of his endless life, who with thee and the Holy Ghost liveth and reigneth, one God, world without end. Amen.

St Mary Magdalen was throughout the Middle Ages identified with 'the woman of the city, who was a sinner',[1] who so lovingly washed and anointed Jesus. This error became officially established by the Gregorian Proper for her Festival. The Collect portrayed St Mary Magdalen as the supreme example of a truly repentant sinner, and the Gospel was this Lucan story. Cranmer clearly accepted this mistaken identification, for his Collect in 1549 was based on the Gregorian Collect and the Day's Gospel remained the same. The Festival then, in spite of this error, was given very properly Red-letter status. This reflected not only St Mary Magdalen's great importance in the Gospel narrative, but also her particular popularity in mediaeval England. Two of the most famous mediaeval Colleges in Oxford and Cambridge are dedicated to her, and 187 of our mediaeval Churches own her as their Patron Saint. In 1552, however, her Festival Day was relegated to Black-letter status for unrecorded reasons that can now only be surmised. One may have been the demands of agriculture. Her Festival is so close to St James's Day, and, as mentioned in the Introduction, major Festivals meant holidays for working people, and were not welcomed during the harvest. Another, however, may have been the growing strength then of Puritanism in our Church. Such honour being heaped on a prostitute, however repentant she may have been, and however faithful she may have become, may well have been frowned upon. Be that as it may; it was one of the more excellent changes made in 1928 that both this important and popular Festival was given back its Red-Letter status, and also that a new Proper was provided, which correctly identifies St Mary Magdalen with the Mary whom Jesus 'healed of seven demons', and who was the first 'witness to his Resurrection'.[2] Very properly now her earlier mistaken identification with 'the woman...who was a sinner' has been officially laid to rest.

St Mary Magdalen has also been mistakenly identified with Mary, the sister of Lazarus and Martha. Certainly the two Marys were equally devoted to Jesus, but they are clearly distinguished from each other by reference to the places that were their homes, the one being Mary of Bethany, the other Mary of Magdala, which is the meaning of Magdalen. This mistaken identification is also due, however, to the similarities between the story, already referred to, of the prostitute, who anointed Jesus at a supper in the house of Simon the Pharisee, and that of Mary of Bethany, who anointed Jesus also at a supper but in the house of another Simon, this one called Simon the Leper.[3]

Yet even now the real St Mary Magdalen remains largely unrecognised! Although we rightly remember her, as the new Collect stresses, as someone that Jesus healed and as the person who was the first to meet him after he rose from the dead, it is not, nonetheless, generally appreciated that during the years of Jesus's ministry she was particularly valued as a leader and organiser. The real St Mary Magdalen was a very capable woman, who was pre-eminent among that important group of women who sustained Jesus and his disciples in their evangelistic activities. These women are given all too little credit, though it is clear that they played a major part in his ministry.[4] It is only in passing, we notice, that St Luke, the interested doctor, mentions St Mary's healing. In the relevant passage, clearly, his main concern is to tell of Jesus's evangelistic work, and in doing so he gives us the names of some of his female supporters, stressing the great importance of their contribution. No doubt there were many others, for we hear of 'the women who followed him from Galilee (that) stood at a distance' when Jesus was on the Cross.[5] All the Evangelists mention the names of some, but only St Mary Magdalen is mentioned by all of them. Consequently such evidence as the Gospels give suggests that she was their accepted leader. It would have been, so it would seem, just as all would have expected that it was St Mary Magdalen who organised the preparation of spices to anoint the dead body of Jesus, and who led that valiant party of women to render those last services to their Lord 'while it was yet dark'[6]

The healing of St Mary is naturally of peculiar interest, and what she was healed of has understandably been the subject of much speculation. St Luke's mention of 'seven demons' suggests a complex state of both mental and spiritual disorder, with physical complications too. Elsewhere in his Gospel St Luke mentions a man who was possessed by a 'legion of demons'.[7] Demon possession was clearly then accepted as a valid medical description of conditions to which, no doubt, the medical profession today can give precise names. All we can say, then, for certain about St Mary Magdalen when she was healed by Jesus is that she was in a dark and terrible state, and that her subsequent total devotion to him arose out of her intense gratitude to him for her healing. It is for the quality of this devotion that she is so specially remembered, the intensity of which is so poignantly emphasised by her lonely vigil by the Cross. That the risen Jesus should have come to her first of all seems, therefore, so very fitting. And her special relationship with him is again vividly shown by her rapturous greeting of him in the garden. The word she used then was *Rabboni*, which St John translates simply as 'Teacher', but 'dearest Master' would give its meaning so much better.[8]

Because of her two mistaken identifications the mediaeval Church made St Mary Magdalen both the Patron Saint of repentant sinners, and also of those who embraced the contemplative life. Although no doubt she does not mind being so honoured, one has to say that neither patronage is really appropriate. She would, we may presume, have been associated by the Church with the healing of the sick, the obvious area to choose for her patronage, if those unfortunate mistakes about her had not been made. It certainly does seem strange that she has two famous Colleges of academic study named after her, but no great Hospitals dedicated to her memory! At all events the new Collect in the 1928 book, which we are considering, cannot easily be faulted. Her particular connection with the healing of the sick, her total commitment to serving Jesus, and her honour in being the first to 'witness to his Resurrection' are all given proper emphasis in it.

The 1928 Collect brings together healing and service within the context of our risen life in Christ. This three-fold bond, however, is not, unfortunately, one that is generally recognised.

It is natural enough for Christians to be concerned about health, and about the healing of the sick, and also to believe that God is too. It is easy to believe that when God's Kingdom comes on earth as it is in heaven, according to our constantly repeated prayer, the needs of the sick and suffering will be fully met. Did not Jesus say, 'The Kingdom of heaven is at hand. Heal the sick, raise the dead, cleanse the lepers, cast out demons.'?[9] We surely could insert words like 'therefore' or 'consequently' before that string of commands, because we know that meeting of the needs of the sick and suffering are among the main signs that God's Kingdom is indeed even now being established here.[10] In a perfect world none would be crushed by sickness or cut off by untimely death.[11] We readily understand that healing of body, mind and spirit expresses God's loving will for us, and that all who are involved in bringing it to us, whatever their personal religious views may be, are doing God's will.[12] Yet, for all that, we do not so readily recognise what health is for, that is, what we are meant to do with it when we have it.

This Collect stresses the truth that health is for service. Our desire for health should be part of our desire to serve God and man. Health, like wealth, is for using. To desire health simply to maintain our own comfort or to fulfil personal ambitions, avoiding at all costs anything that might threaten it, is to turn an obvious blessing into a potential curse. We can turn it into an idol, 'a thing to be grasped'.[13] Rather, our health, such as it may be, must be put to its proper use, that is, be used in service according to God's will, after the pattern of God's Son, who came among us 'taking the form of a servant.'[14]

Consequently in this as in all other areas of our lives, we must be ready for the unexpected, if we are genuinely seeking to do God's will. 'His ways are not our ways,' Scripture warns us.[15] Jesus is, the Athanasian Creed assures us, 'perfect man', and so, like the prophesied servant of God in Isaiah who foreshadowed him, he gave himself totally in service to God. Yet this did not mean for him a long life of health and happiness. In spite of that being God's general will for mankind, his will for the 'perfect man' involved much physical suffering and an untimely death. So, as St Paul pondered the sacrifice of Jesus in the prime years of his vigorous life, he warned his converts in Philippi (and through them us), that since they were called to live by Christ's Spirit, they may well be called to share his physical fate. What seems both commonsensical and good may yet not be God's will for us. St Paul, we know, had to learn this mysterious truth for himself, and it is the measure of his sanctity that he did so. He was handicapped by some serious condition, perhaps affecting his eyes, from which he prayed repeatedly to be healed. He prayed this, moreover, only for the worthy reason of being made more able to fulfil his vocation in God's service. Yet God revealed to him that he was mistaken in this request. His disability, he was taught, was in fact for him creative of much good. In God's Kingdom, he was shown, the weak are often better instruments than the strong.[16] So St Paul accepted his disability gladly and willingly, and thereby became an even more useful servant of God.[17]

Even though in God's Kingdom men and women are always being inspired to go out to heal the sick, that does not mean it is necessarily a Kingdom of fit people. Indeed many of its most effective advocates are to be found among 'the poor and maimed and blind and lame' that are made so welcome there.[18] Yet it is nonetheless the usual way for God first to heal, and then to empower for service, as was true of St Mary Magdalen. Healing for her was a life-changing experience, something glorious, not just something convenient, and this can be just as true for us, when it is the work of doctors and surgeons, as it was for St Mary, whose healing came directly from the hand of Jesus. For us, too, it can be the start of us living our lives in a totally new spirit of service. When that happens, our healing has not just made us better, it has enabled us really to come alive and to understand what our health is for.

From St Mary Magdalen Jesus 'cast out seven demons'. As I think of her, I am reminded of another woman who experienced an even more amazing healing, being actually raised from the dead. Dorothy Kerin, who founded the Home of Healing at Burrswood in Sussex, and who surely will be soon included in our official list of Saints, having died after a prolonged period of acute and progressive illness, was made in a moment, as she says, 'every whit whole'. In her case, she was told by Jesus what she was to do with her miraculous gift of new health. This he described to her as 'giving faith to the faithless, comfort to the comfortless and healing to the sick,' and this she wonderfully fulfilled in the fifty extra years of life here that were granted her.[19] Although St Mary Magdalen is accredited with no special gifts of healing, as Dorothy Kerin was, both women were given grace not only to be 'healed of all their infirmities', but also to 'always serve Jesus in the power of his endless life'.

Even though the experiences of the Saints are so exceptional and ours so unexceptional, their example can still inspire us to live much better lives, 'doing our duty in that state of life unto which it shall please God to call us'.[20] Whatever health we may enjoy must be used, as they used theirs, in service, and our healings, too, must become 'life-changing', in the way of making us better able, or perhaps able for the first time, to do whatever is God's will for us. Such thoughts suggest that there is a great difference between being healed, and simply being made physically fit once more. The latter is not the same as being 'healed of all our infirmities'. Doctors may be able to make us better again, but it is for a deeper and fuller healing than that that we are really praying here. To the woman who touched 'the fringe of his garment' Jesus said, 'Your faith has made you well'.[21]   What happened to her by that touch, however, we may be sure, was that she was 'healed of all her infirmities', and so released from 'her bonds' to serve others.   This is the healing that remains Christ's special gift, which requires our faith, as well as very probably medical assistance too, to be both given to us and received by us. This Collect guides us to seek the 'grace' that inspires in us this healing faith and hope.

This Collect links health not only with service, but also to our risen life in Christ. It emphasises the scriptural truth, that governs all references to health in the Prayer Book, that all true health is really a consequence of our being in a right relationship with God. Only the genuinely holy, therefore, really merit the description healthy, according to this understanding of the matter. So it is that, as we confess our sins in the daily Offices of Morning and Evening Prayer, we acknowledge that because of them 'there is no health in us'. The Psalmist puts this truth positively when he declares, 'In God is my health and my glory',[22] and the concept of mankind's salvation is also described in terms of health, when he rejoices in God's 'saving health to all nations'.[23] We ought, therefore, to consider our health in far wider terms than we usually do. As we have already reminded ourselves, Jesus was a 'perfect man' and in Scripture his health is shown as consisting of four perfections. He grew up, increasing 'in wisdom and in stature, and in favour with God and man'.[24] Health for Jesus meant what it should mean for us, health in both soul and body, through a right relationship with both God and man. We, therefore, should recognise that our health too has mental, physical, spiritual and social dimensions, and it is towards just such a fully rounded health that this Collect is guiding us. Such a health is not only one that will enable us to 'always serve', and save us 'from all infirmities', but it is one that can only be fully lived out 'in the power of [Christ's] endless life'.

So this Collect leads us to recognise the further connection between healing and the risen life. The point is this. Healing is not to be understood simply as the rediscovery of something we have lost. Rather we are to see it as something wholly positive, a discovery of something fresh and new. Then all healing becomes an entry into newness of life, an experience as essentially exciting as our awakening to a new day. John Keble caught this truth splendidly in the opening lines of his morning hymn:

> New every morning is the love
> Our wakening and uprising prove.

This is what healing, too, should be like for us! Surely it was so for St Mary Magdalen. Since she is the heroine of the Resurrection, it is particularly appropriate that her healing was for her the start of a completely new life. So for us, healing should be an experience of rising up to newness of life in God, with mental, physical, spiritual and social implications, nothing less.

If this be so, such an outcome will cast an unexpected light upon the preceding illness to the extent that we can say with the Psalmist, 'I know, O Lord...that thou of very faithfulness hast caused me to be troubled'.[25] Such a positive attitude towards sickness and healing will also enable us to endure our illnesses and disabilities in hope as well as with patience.[26] We will rightly hope for blessings to come from them more permanent than merely a temporary return to health, as happened, we know, for St Mary Magdalen.

The Collect's invocation stresses that St Mary was 'a witness to the Resurrection'. We, too, through healing, whether experienced by ourselves or by others, may become similarly 'witnesses' of new life being given by God. Here we should acknowledge that it is, perhaps, commoner for us to see this truth in the healing of others than in our own! Interestingly in the Gospels we notice that it is usually the reaction of bystanders that is remarked upon.[27] The fact is that all healing is so impressive. The healing ministry of the Church is consequently such a particularly powerful evangelistic ministry, and its neglect greatly weakens the Church's life and mission. In the longer ending of St Mark's Gospel we read how the risen Christ sent out the Apostles 'to lay hands on the sick', and he said, 'They will recover'. They then fulfilled his instructions and their ministry was 'confirmed by signs following'.[28] We have already mentioned Dorothy Kerin and Burrswood. Both she in the past and Burrswood in the present have given and are giving inspiration and encouragement to this healing ministry. She in herself was such an exceptional 'witness to the Resurrection', and worked many amazing healings 'in the power of his endless life', but it is particularly the Church, as the Body of the risen Christ, that is the constant 'witness to the Resurrection' down the ages and throughout the world, and the one that has been permanently empowered by God to minister to the needs of the sick and suffering 'in the power of his endless life'. The verdict of history is that whenever the Church does this fully and faithfully eager disciples are made for Jesus. A healing ministry should be an automatic part of every Parish, as indeed the B.C.P. makes plain, despite the fact that its section 'The Visitation of the Sick' is clearly inadequate to meet all the needs of this most important ministry today.

Yet this particular work of God is certainly not limited to his special instrument, the Church. The medical profession is of God too; and it was a desire of Dorothy Kerin to promote not only the healing ministry of the Church, but also the fullest co-operation between the Church and the medical profession. This dual aim is the correct one for both, and their common desire to heal the sick and make them whole in body, mind and spirit, is restricted without this needful co-operation. For us to be healed of 'all our infirmities' we shall need all the ways of healing that God in his providence has allowed to flourish. Being of him, all may be used in his service.

SAINT JAMES THE APOSTLE
July 25th

Grant, O merciful God, that as thine holy Apostle Saint James, leaving his father and all that he had, without delay was obedient unto the calling of thy Son Jesus Christ, and followed him; so we, forsaking all worldly and carnal affections, may be evermore ready to follow thy holy commandments; through Jesus Christ our Lord. Amen.

St James the Great, as the son of Zebedee is called to distinguish him from St James the Less, the son of Alphaeus, was one of the privileged triumvirate of St Peter, himself and his younger, but even more famous, brother St John. Only they were chosen to be witnesses of Jesus's healing of Jairus' daughter,[1] his Transfiguration,[2] and his last vigil of prayer in the garden of Gethsemane.[3] Their companionship, we may therefore presume, was especially helpful to Jesus, and what a compliment that is to them!

Besides these three occasions, and the various lists of the Apostles,[4] St James is mentioned three more times in the Gospels. It is perhaps noticeable that in each he is linked with his brother, which may indicate a particularly close relationship between them. The first of these is their call by Jesus to become, instead of fishermen, 'fishers of men'.[5] As we have already noticed in commenting on the Collects for the other three with whom he was called, St James would have met Jesus earlier, and so he would have been ready when that great day came. Nevertheless the readiness of St James, along with that of the other three, is something to admire, and Cranmer makes his call, and his ready obedience to it, the centre-piece of his new Collect. The Sarum Collect had mentioned no incident in St James's life and had referred to him only as one that now can succour and defend the people of God, presumably by his prayers, which made the Collect unacceptable to the Reformers. Here Cranmer, dwelling on his call, particularly stresses the sacrifice that was involved for St James in 'leaving his father and all that he had', as well as the eagerness with which he made it, for he 'without delay was obedient'. Perhaps we are supposed to visualise in St James a special type of man, one that was typical of the fishermen of Galilee, self-confident, independent-minded and adventurous. If so, such would have made the ideal type for Jesus to use in what was, spiritually speaking, a revolutionary mission.

The other two occasions, however, on which St James is mentioned in the Gospels, can hardly be said to enhance his memory. The first is the occasion when the two brothers asked Jesus if they might sit in the chief places of honour beside him, when at last he sat in his Kingdom on his throne of glory. Although Jesus then was sharp with, though not dismissive of, those ambitious brothers, the other Apostles were understandably outraged at their request. This, at least, is the story as told by St Mark, and since his is the earliest Gospel his version is almost certainly the true one. St Matthew, however, tells it differently; in his version the brothers' reputation is rescued by it being their mother who makes this foolish request for them.[6] Perhaps unsurprisingly Cranmer chose St Matthew's sanitised version as the Gospel for this day.

The other story tells of the ridiculous fury felt by St James and his brother at the refusal of some Samaritan villagers to welcome Jesus and his party as they made their way to Jerusalem. Again they were guilty of an outrageous request, this time that they might be given power by Jesus 'to bid fire come down from heaven and consume them'.[7] Perhaps it was this occasion that inspired Jesus's nickname for them, 'Boanerges', meaning 'sons of thunder'.[8] Much as he found their presence helpful, we cannot but notice his need for both patience and good-humour in dealing with these fiery and sometimes troublesome brothers.

It must be said that for so important a member of the Twelve these comparatively few and largely uncomplimentary stories amount to surprisingly little, and St James is mainly remembered, not for what he did, but for how and when he died. Undoubtedly his chief memorial is his martyrdom.[9] He was the first Apostle to suffer death for his faith; that is his special honour. This took place on the orders of Herod Agrippa II, the grandson of the Herod that sought to kill the infant Jesus. This dates St James's death between 41-44, the years of Herod's reign, with the implication from the account of it in Acts that it took place close to Herod's death. The Church by that time was spreading fast, and, mysteriously, it was persecution that helped this to happen.[10] We are not told why St James was singled out by Herod Agrippa, only that, in arresting and then killing him, he was currying favour with the Jewish leaders. Perhaps the impetuous St James had indeed invited trouble, for we know that the thought of martyrdom held no terrors for him.[11] That he should have made himself especially obnoxious to the Jewish leaders is therefore not surprising, but the manner of his death is. Acts tells us that he was 'killed with the sword'. To be beheaded with a sword was the characteristic, and comparatively merciful, manner in which Roman citizens were executed. This was, we know, the way St Paul met his end, but since there is no indication that St James was a Roman citizen, or that Herod Agrippa was administering Roman justice, this consideration cannot apply to St James. The most likely explanation, then, is that, like St John the Baptist at the orders of Herod Agrippa's uncle, St James also met his end by judicial murder in prison.[12]

The date of St James's death, however, has a peculiar interest. It is the ardently held tradition in Spain that it was he who brought the Gospel to that country. Chronologically this is just possible if the date of his death was 44. However we have to say that there is not only nothing in Scripture to support this belief, but also that the only mention of Spain there tends to contradict it. This comes in Romans, where we learn how St Paul wanted to preach in Spain at least fifteen years after St James's death.[13] Since it was a principle with him that he did not 'preach the Gospel...where Christ had already been named', it would seem that St Paul believed that Spain was then, as it were, still virgin soil. However St James is Spain's greatly loved Patron Saint, and his final burial place is claimed to be Santiago (St James) de Compostela. The heyday of this shrine was in the later mediaeval period, 1100-1400, and coincided with the wars fought under his banner that finally drove the Moors from Spain. We may say, therefore, that St James's posthumous reputation was very much that of 'a son of thunder', who was able to 'bring down' defeat, if not 'fire', upon the enemies of the Church. The pilgrimage to Compostela became one of the most important in the mediaeval era, and numerous monasteries were built, especially in northern Spain, to cater for the constant stream of pilgrims going there from all over Europe. A notable beneficiary of the popularity of St James was Reading Abbey, to which some bones out of his hand were brought from Compostela by the Empress Matilda, as part of her efforts to establish her position during her civil war with King Stephen. Though it is doubtful how much this acquisition strengthened the Empress, it certainly helped to establish the importance of Reading Abbey for the next 400 years. So significant was the pilgrimage to Compostela that St James's emblem in mediaeval art became the pilgrim's hat, along with the scallop-shell that typified the fishing that flourished at Compostela and that helped to feed the many pilgrims that travelled there.

Cranmer's Collect stresses the idea of sacrifice that is so essential a part of the Christian life. In the case of St James, although he died a martyr, what is especially recalled is the much simpler sacrifice of him 'leaving his father and all that he had' when he first set out to follow Jesus. This makes, however, his Collect infinitely more relevant to the way of life required of us ordinary Christians. We are not all called to martyrdom (thanks be to God), but we are all called to accept sacrifices in very ordinary, but nonetheless central and crucial, aspects and areas of our lives. Jesus says to us all, 'He who loves father or mother more then me is not worthy of me, and he who loves son or daughter more than me is not worthy of me'.[14] These words so well describe many an ordinary Christian's cross. In the case of St James it is reasonable to suppose that he had much to lose when he left his 'father Zebedee in the boat', for with him were 'hired servants',[15] which implies that the Zebedees were prosperous, successful businessmen rather than poor, simple fishermen, as is sometimes supposed. The Collect, moreover, seems to emphasise this by the phrase 'and all that he had'. No doubt St James did not come from the ranks of the very rich, but a sacrifice of 'all' that he had is descriptive of as great a sacrifice as any of us can make, even if it be only our stake in a family business. When Jesus saw the widow putting her 'mite' into the offertory box at the Temple doors, he praised her little offering in the warmest possible terms. He knew what that tiny gift meant to her; she had 'put [in] everything she had'. She could do no more.[16] Moreover, who can tell what God can do with our little sacrifices? Look what happened when a boy gave Jesus his lunch box of five small loaves and two fishes.[17]

St James's domestic sacrifice is properly, and helpfully, highlighted in the invocation of his Collect. What we are being shown is that this initial sacrifice created the essential foundation on which St James's later sacrificial life was built, which in his case did lead on to greater sacrifices still, even the greatest anyone can make. We are all called by Jesus to sacrifice, even to the 'taking up of our cross'.[18] This call will not in practice mean the same for all. It will, however, involve us all in a spiritual mortification; a dying to what is described here as 'worldly and carnal affections'. This is basic Christianity, and we are not to seek to evade such sacrifices, or to fear them. In Baptism this truth is squarely faced. We are pledged then never to be 'ashamed to confess the faith of Christ crucified, manfully to fight under his banner against sin, the world and the Devil, and to continue Christ's faithful soldier and servant unto our life's end'.[19] When these words were said over us, the Priest signed us with the sign of the Cross, and if we are 'faithful unto our life's end' we will receive even the same reward as those, like St James, who have been called by God to make the supreme sacrifice of their lives.

Special mention, as we have recognised, is made in this Collect of the need to 'forsake all worldly and carnal affections'. This phrase has the same meaning as the 'worldly and carnal lusts' that were specially commented on in our consideration of the Collect for 'The Circumcision of Christ'. Let us emphasise another aspect of this important matter here. Jesus's incarnation made him 'perfect man',[20] and that included in his make-up the full range of 'worldly and carnal affections' 'common to man'.[21] The word 'forsake' here may possibly, therefore, give a false impression. It certainly needs qualification, and to be linked to the last phrase of the petition. The truth of this matter, 'the truth as it is in Jesus',[22] is that everything we do must be in accordance with God's 'holy commandments'. His control of our lives must be total. This is what matters. What we must 'forsake' is 'all...affections' that may clash with his blessed will for us. The 'worldly and carnal affections' that do not, and are part of his will for us, not only need not be 'forsaken', but rather should be embraced in the power of his Spirit. The proper expression of 'worldly and carnal affections' is essential for a successful marriage, where 'our natural instincts and affections, implanted by God, are hallowed and directed aright'.[23] Others, however, may be called to a different kind of life, and by living celibate lives they are 'following' what is God's 'holy commandment' for them.[24]   This was the course St Paul was called to take, but even though he advocated it to others, he did so fully realising that each must follow whatever is God's will for them. 'Let everyone lead the life which the Lord has assigned to him and in which God has called him.'[25] But, in which case, 'let all that [we] do be done in love'.[26]

In following God's will, however, sacrifices of various kinds will always be required, and this truth is underlined in this Collect. These sacrifices will be, as it were, both positive and negative. Sometimes we will be required to do something different, and the acceptance of the change involved will be our difficulty, our sacrifice. Sometimes we will be called to continue as we are, and simply remaining content in our present circumstances will constitute the heart of our sacrifice. Our 'affections' must be wholly centred on God and his will. That is above all what is required of us. 'Thy will be done' lies at the heart of Jesus's prayer. For thirty years, we know, he waited, working for most of them patiently as a carpenter in Nazareth.[27] Was not that for him a sacrifice? Then, before his ministry began, he had to fight against 'worldly and carnal affections', as depicted in his special time of temptation or testing in the wilderness.[28] In the fulfilling of his vocation, he too had to forego the 'broad way', the way of 'worldly' achievement and 'carnal' prompting, for the 'narrow way' of total obedience to his Father's will.[29] Even he had to say, 'Not as I will, but as thou wilt.'[30] Even for him, therefore, there had to be a 'forsaking' of various kinds, in order that he might be 'ready to follow [God's] holy commandments.' So how much more certainly will this be the case for us? However, we are to 'have no fear of them', these required sacrifices, for in the end all will be well, even as it was for St James, so long as we never cease to 'reverence in our hearts Christ as Lord.'[31]

THE TRANSFIGURATION
August 6th

O God, who before the passion of thine only-begotten Son didst reveal his glory upon the holy mount; Grant unto us thy servants, that in faith beholding the light of his countenance, we may be strengthened to bear the cross, and be changed into his likeness from glory to glory; through the same Jesus Christ our Lord.

Although the Feast of the Transfiguration has been kept as a major Festival on August 6 from at least the beginning of the 4th century, it was omitted from the 1549 B.C.P., and in 1662 only given Black-Letter status. It was particularly enthusiastically supported by the devout and influential Empress Helena, Constantine's mother, who in 326 built a Church on Mount Tabor, one of the two sites associated with this mysterious event, Mount Hermon being the other. In the East it became ranked with the greater Festivals of Christmas, Epiphany, Ascension and Pentecost, which give precedence only to the greatest Festival of all, Easter. In the West, however, its history has been strangely different. In the Leonine Sacramentary it was linked with the theme of ordination, and featured as a part of the Lenten Embertide devotions. It was not until 1457 that it was given its own Festival Day in the western Church, but in that year by edict of Pope Callistus III it suddenly emerged from the liturgical shadows there for a most remarkable reason.

This was a time of major crisis and religious danger. Islam, having swept Christianity aside throughout the Middle East and North Africa, was, after several quiescent centuries, on the march again. Constantinople fell at last in 1453 to the Sultan of Turkey, and the drive was on once more to subjugate Europe, and with it its religion. After three years of victorious campaigning, his army was at the gates of Belgrade. On August 6th 1456, however, a Catholic army from the north, combining with Orthodox soldiers from the south, decisively defeated the Turks outside that city in the Battle of Belgrade. Defeat would certainly have opened the way into the heart of Europe, and although much fighting still lay ahead, it was a turning point and western Christendom had been saved. In thanksgiving for this deliverance, won on the day of this largely forgotten Festival, the Pope ordered that it henceforth be observed as a major Festival in the West also. What a bizarre reason, one may say, for this most mystical of Festivals to be observed at last in the West with proper devotion! Not unnaturally this link with a crucial battle has now been quite forgotten, but nonetheless on this unexpected connection some fruitful comment may yet be made. Indeed, it may help us to relate to it all the more deeply.

All the accounts of it in the Synoptic Gospels[1] confirm that the Transfiguration marks a turning point in the ministry of Jesus. He, certainly, knew himself to be engaged in the cosmic conflict that engulfs, according to Scripture, both heaven and earth.[2] We see in the Gospels Jesus, the divine warrior, marching forth, casting out and destroying the demons that oppress and enslave mankind,[3] and of his mission he said, 'I have not come to bring peace, but a sword.'[4] St Paul, especially, confirms this as being equally true of the Church's mission when he urges us to take up the 'sword of the Spirit', and, with the other elements of 'the whole armour of God,' to 'fight the good fight' as those called up by God to 'contend...against the spiritual hosts of wickedness in heavenly places'[5] that now inhabit the earth.

When Jesus 'went up on the mountain to pray' with his three chosen companions, he knew that the decisive engagement of this cosmic warfare was fast approaching. In the Lucan account we are told that when Moses and Elijah came to him 'as he prayed, they talked with him of his *exodos* which he was to accomplish at Jerusalem'.[6] This Greek word *exodos* (anglicised as 'exodus') is correctly translated 'departure' in the R.S.V. and the N.E.B., but in the A.V. it is translated 'decease'. This older rendering, however, although not a literal translation, undoubtedly gives us its real meaning in the context of that mysterious conversation, for it was Jesus's death that they were discussing, and what its results would be.

The historic overtones of this word are entirely relevant for this understanding of what was happening when Jesus was transfigured. When God saved the Israelites from Pharaoh's army at the Red Sea, and so enabled their exodus from Egypt to succeed, he wrought a crucial victory over their enemies. It is, moreover, an essential aspect of that miraculous event that it was all God's doing. 'The Lord will fight for us', said Moses to the terrified Israelites. 'You have only to be still'.[7] That first exodus, however, pointed prophetically to the second and far greater exodus that God has wrought through Jesus. This was to be 'accomplished at Jerusalem' amid the horror of his Passion and Crucifixion, and that, too, was entirely God's doing. Again unaided, 'he hath gotten himself the victory',[8] and as it was being won, the world 'had only to be still'. In this greatest of wars between the forces of God and those in rebellion against him, which, whether we perceive it or not, engulfs us all, and is the spiritual background to all our lives and the history of the world, the decisive turning point came there.

In what should be perceived as the Battle of Calvary, mankind, God's children, were saved from their age-long enemy, the Evil One. This divine victory 'accomplished at Jerusalem,' is as central to the New Testament's Gospel as the earlier divine victory that we call the Exodus, accomplished at the Red Sea, was central to the Old Testament's message. At the time of Christ's Transfiguration this second exodus still lay in the future, but on that occasion the consequences of that divinely won victory were prophetically manifested in what happened to his body. The Transfiguration, therefore, points both to the glorious victory won by Christ for all mankind upon the Cross, and also to his victorious glory in heaven, which he shares with all who join him there, now that '[his] strife is o'er, the battle done'.[9] Can we not readily acknowledge, then, that it is not in the least inappropriate that this mystical Festival should finally have come to proper liturgical prominence in the West through a crucial victory in a war against the enemies of Christendom?

––––––––––––––

The word, however, that we particularly associate with the Transfiguration is glory, rather than victory, however close these two words may be in their essential meaning, particularly in this context. There 'they saw his glory',[10] and in this Collect the word is used three times. It is fundamental to our faith that all Christ's life was glorious, for all he was and said and did revealed 'the glory that comes from the only God.'[11] However, the divine glory belongs equally to him and to the Father. He is the prophesied 'King of glory',[12] and in his miracles 'he manifested forth his [own] glory, and his disciples believed in him.'[13] Speaking for those first disciples, St John declared, 'We beheld his glory, glory as of the only Son from the Father,'[14] and those words also describe what his disciples down the centuries have seen with the eyes of faith.

It is a particular characteristic of St John's Gospel that it emphasises the theme of divine glory, and yet, although he was personally present, St John does not mention Christ's Transfiguration in it. This is all the more surprising because it is an essential element of his understanding of Christ's glory that it was not fully revealed until he endured his Passion and Crucifixion. That awful time was 'the hour' in which 'the Son of Man [was] glorified',[15] and, as we have seen, it was precisely of that 'hour', his 'decease', about which Jesus was both praying to the Father and talking with Moses and Elijah when St John saw him transfigured in glory.

St John, however, deals with this matter in his own way. He makes this truth, that Christ's glory on earth is essentially related to his Passion and Crucifixion, the subject of his last prayer in the garden of Gethsemane. It is then that we hear him speaking to the Father of that 'hour', when he 'accomplished' the 'work' of glory, that he had been sent to 'do', in his death. 'Father, the hour has come,' he prays. 'Glorify thy Son that he may glorify thee.. I have glorified thee on earth, having accomplished the work which thou gavest me to do, and now, Father, glorify thou me in thy presence with the glory which I had with thee before the world was made..[And] Father, I desire that they also, whom thou hast given me, may be with me where I am, to behold my glory which thou hast given me in thy love for me before the foundation of the world.'[16]

Can we not believe this last prayer of Jesus mirrors that which he prayed as he was transfigured? And should we not, like the three Apostles, be infinitely grateful ('Lord, it is good that we are here') even to the point of amazed wonder ('and they were filled with awe')[17] that not only may we listen to it, but we may believe that, even at that moment of personal crisis, he had us in mind?

The Collect only makes mention of Christ's heavenly glory, revealed 'upon the holy mount''before his Passion'. In his last prayer in the garden, however, we hear of 'the hour' in which he was 'glorified on earth', a reference clearly to his 'glorification' in his Passion. How strange, even repellent, this aspect of 'the truth as it is in Jesus'[18] is likely to appear to our worldly minds! It is not remotely natural for us to see a man being crucified as a glorious sight. Yet that is what the eye of faith does perceive in that cruel execution. St Paul certainly saw it as such. 'Far be it for me to glory except in the Cross of our Lord Jesus Christ,' he said.[19] So, too, did Isaac Watts 1700 years later, and his famous hymn, 'When I survey the wondrous Cross on which the Prince of glory died,'[20] describes so well what we can still see in it by faith today.

There is, and always will be, nonetheless, so much inherent mystery in this victorious 'glory'. This redeeming 'work,' 'accomplished' by Christ upon the Cross, makes many who are otherwise attracted to Jesus draw back from him because of it. This has always been the case. It is what St Paul calls 'the scandal' and 'the foolishness' of the Cross.[21] Indeed, when Jesus first spoke of the fate awaiting him to his Apostles, and of how all that was so soon to happen to him was according to God's will for him, (a conversation that took place just prior to his Transfiguration) we are told that St Peter 'took him and rebuked him.' Does this mean that St Peter actually man-handled Jesus in his indignation at what he was hearing? If so, perhaps, it is a fair indication of the vehemence with which this central element of the Gospel still offends so many. Yet that it is absolutely vital for us to accept and believe this truth is made equally clear by Jesus's uncompro-mising, even brutal, reply to St Peter. 'Get behind me, Satan. For you are not on the side of God, but of men.'[22] Nevertheless, it may also give us comfort to recognise the tone of sympathetic understanding in our Lord's reply to the equally puzzled Cleopas, 'Was it not necessary that the Christ should suffer these things and enter into his glory?' [23]

It was necessary; but why? The necessity is occasioned by the innate power of evil to prevent us from living according to God's will. This power is irresistible, humanly speaking, because it is not simply an aggressive force outside us, but an inherited interior state. It is this truth about us that afflicts all our lives in innumerable, mostly hidden, ways, throwing them off course, even when we mean well.[24] This power has its base deep within us, 'in our members...making us captive to the law of sin,' is how St Paul describes it.[25] So we are 'slaves', people controlled by a malign 'master', made 'children of wrath', living out our lives within 'a body of death' that is destined to decay and destruction.[26]   This evil power is visualised as a spiritual virus infecting that crucial part of our human nature that makes us special within God's creation and that Scripture calls our 'heart'. 'We have erred in our hearts,' confesses the Psalmist,[27] and the B.C.P. leads us to acknowledge how 'we have [disastrously] followed [their] devices and desires.'[28] 'Wretched man that I am!' exclaims St Paul (on behalf of us all). 'Who will deliver me from this body of death?'[29]

Now, the basic tenet of the Gospel is that God in Christ has acted to save us from this malign power, to do what we cannot do for ourselves, and to 'deliver us from evil.' Since the crux of our trouble is the tragic separation that evil has created between us and God, God became in Christ one of us.[30] That is how the divine process of our redemption from sin began. 'God so loved the world that he gave his only begotten Son to the end that we should not perish but have eternal life.'[31]   How very wonderful! But however much we may wonder at the sight of God in Christ taking human form in the miracle of Christ's birth in Bethlehem, it is the sight of God in Christ expiating our sinfulness on Calvary's hill that is 'yet more wonderful.'[32] The glory of divine love is only then revealed in all its 'inestimable' perfection.[33]   Its glory is in the cost. 'By this we know love, that he laid down his life for us, [for] he is the expiation for our sins, and not ours only, but also for the sins of the whole world,'[34] is how St John describes this central truth of the Gospel in his 1st Epistle.

In that redeeming sacrifice of divine love on our behalf, 'the righteous for the unrighteous',[35] we certainly perceive by faith the fullest possible revelation of divine love and power and glory, but even so there is even more to the Gospel than our redemption. There is the ultimate prospect of our sanctification too, even for us 'the hope of glory.'[36] St Paul's assessment of what the Gospel implies takes St John's words that stage further. 'God was in Christ,' he said, 'reconciling the world to himself, not counting [our] trespasses against us...For our sakes he was made man, who knew no sin, so that in him we might become the righteousness of God.'[37] The meaning of this last sentence is nothing less than this, that on the Cross God in Christ became what we are, beings separated from him by sin, so that through him we might become, in spite of sin, what is true of him, beings wholly free from sin! This is what is meant by 'the hope of glory'.

In this Collect we pray that we may 'be changed into his likeness from glory to glory.' As it was for him, so it will be for us; we, like him, are called by the Father to both an earthly glory and a heavenly glory, the one leading to the other. As the Collect teaches, the essence of our earthly glory is 'bearing the cross', whereas the nature of our heavenly glory was 'revealed upon the holy mount.' If we will follow Christ, as we are praying here we will, faithfully 'bearing the cross' of obedience to his guiding Spirit ('in faith beholding the light of his countenance'), he can bring about in us such a transformation as to 'change us into his likeness.' This has happened in the lives of the Saints, and in consequence we deem them glorious. How they lived did 'so shine before men that they...glorified God'.[38] If 'bearing the cross' should mean for us more than simply the sacrifice of daily obedience, even real suffering, we must not draw back, because then, especially, 'the spirit of glory and of God rests upon us.'[39] Indeed, should that be our calling, Jesus bids us 'rejoice and be glad' for our faithfulness in such circumstances will all the more surely be 'greatly rewarded',[40] a truth St Paul confirms like this: 'For this slight momentary affliction is preparing for us an eternal weight of glory beyond all comparison.'[41]

So, as this Collect teaches, there is a progression inherent in our calling 'from glory to glory'. If 'by bearing the cross' we reflect in our earthly life something of the glory of Christ crucified, then a sharing in his heavenly glory is 'set before us' as a 'joy' awaiting us.[42] How are we to understand

such mysterious aspects of our faith? But then, how can children understand what it will mean for them to be adults? All they can be sure of is that
the experience of adulthood does await them, and when the time comes
they will 'fully understand'.[43]   So, since God's Word is sure, such mysterious phrases as 'the hope of glory' are, says St Paul, to be understood in
terms of our ultimate 'growing up into Christ'.[44]   Indeed, he seems to go
further. He teaches that this hope includes even for us a transfiguration
experience! 'Our lowly body,' will become 'like unto his glorious body by the
power which enables him even to subject all things to himself.'[45] Such an
outcome is also, seemingly, envisaged by St John, who, although he had
himself seen Jesus transfigured in glory, is still able to say to us, 'Beloved,
we are God's children now; [however] it does not yet appear what we shall
be, but [this] we know, that, when he appears, we shall be like him'.[46]   It
does seem, therefore, that we can put no limits on 'what God has prepared
for those who love him', [47] and that we can believe that the implications of
this Festival for us are truly expressed in this Collect, not only with
devotional simplicity, but also without exaggeration.

SAINT BARTHOLOMEW THE APOSTLE
August 24th

O Almighty and everlasting God, who didst give to thine Apostle Bartholomew grace truly to believe and to preach thy Word; Grant, we beseech thee, unto thy Church to love that Word which he believed, and both to preach and receive the same; through Jesus Christ our Lord. Amen.

If we accept the generally held view of scholars that we may equate St Bartholomew with Nathanael, who plays such a prominent part in St John's opening chapter, and who is mentioned again in chapter 21, the added chapter,[1] there are several interesting and devotional things we can say about him. But if we believe that that connection is unsound, then there is almost nothing for certain known about him; and it must be admitted that no less an authority than St Augustine held this view. It is indeed mainly due to his dominant influence in the western Church that St Batholomew's mediaeval Proper was so vague, even to the point of being anonymous, for in the Sarum Missal no special Epistle and Gospel were set for his Day at all, the officiant at Mass being directed simply to use 'the Order set for an Apostle'. This was the source from which Cramner took the Epistle and Gospel in his 1549 Prayer Book, and most unfortunately they were not changed in 1662, or even in the revision of 1928. They remain, therefore, both uninspiring and inappropriate. The Collect, however, was changed, and very much for the better, in 1662. Its petition was extended to stress the important truth that 'the Word' preached had to be 'received', and the concept of it being simply something 'taught' was omitted. The 1549 Collect had prayed that we come 'both to love what he believed and to preach what he taught,' phrases taken from the Sarum

Collect. We shall have the opportunity to comment further on these changes shortly.

However, concerning the identification of St Bartholomew with Nathanael, one reason for making it arises from the way that St Bartholomew's name follows St Philip's in all the three Gospel lists of the Twelve.[2] As we have already explained (see St Philip and St James), because of St Matthew's manner of listing the Twelve in six distinct pairs, this becomes significant. It is supposed that these pairings point to the way in which Jesus sent out the Apostles 'two by two' on the evangelistic missions, about which we hear comparatively little, but which we can gather from St Luke's Gospel were quite numerous.[3] According to this reckoning, in this work, therefore, St Bartholomew and St Philip would have acted as a team. Now, in the Johannine story of Nathanael it is clear that St Philip was his special friend. Their intimacy is vividly portrayed by the way in which St Philip, having been 'found' by Jesus, immediately in his turn 'finds' Nathanael. Excitedly he argues with his friend about Jesus, although without apparently persuading him of what he himself is convinced. So he challenges him to come and meet Jesus for himself, an offer he accepts for friendship's sake, rather than eagerly. 'Can anything good come out of Nazareth?' is his cynical query. He then meets Jesus, and immediately is equally convinced, and captivated. 'You are the Son of God,' he says. 'You are the King of Israel.' It is with this scene that St John brings his first chapter to its close. In it, starting with the prologue (vv1-18) and continuing through a series of meetings and conversations, St John tells us who Jesus really is. He is 'the Word of God incarnate', 'the only Son from the Father', 'the Lamb of God who takes away the sin of the world', the one who 'baptises with the Holy Spirit', the long-awaited 'Messiah', as well as these two great titles given him by Nathanael. It is virtually inconceivable that such a person, who is so devotionally highlighted in this way by St John, should not have been one of the chosen Twelve. Indeed that he was one is surely confirmed by Nathanael being named in St John's Gospel by the unknown author of the additional Chapter 21 as one of that special group of disciples who met the risen Jesus early one morning after a night's fishing on the Sea of Galilee.[4]

If then St John establishes that Nathanael was one of the Twelve, and his special friendship with St Philip helps us to link him with St Bartholomew, there still remains the query as to why this problem over St Bartholomew ever arose. The name is a descriptive surname, meaning 'son of Tolmai' or, perhaps, 'Ptolemy.' Other such descriptive surnames are mentioned in the New Testament, and were presumably commonly used. Jesus called St Peter 'Simon Barjonah', and St Matthias's rival for a place among the Twelve was called Jospeh Barsabbas.[5] So we simply have to admit we do not know why or when St Bartholomew became no longer known by his first name; all we can say is that there is no logical reason why the synoptic Bartholomew should not be the same as the Johannine Nathanael. This connection, at all events, was made very early, Eusebius (circa 260-340) being the most famous of various proponents of this view. It would seem, therefore (*pace* St Augustine) to be eminently reasonable to accept it as true.

Let us, therefore, do so! Then we know that St Bartholomew was a Galilean from Cana where Jesus worked two miracles. Although the exact position of Cana is not known now, clearly it was near both Bethsaida and Capernaum, and therefore near the Sea. St Philip was able to go to St Bartholomew and bring him back to Jesus at Bethsaida without difficulty, and the official, whose son was cured, was able to hurry to Cana from Capernaum and back in a day, when he sought out Jesus. From that post-Resurrection fishing story we know that St Bartholomew was at least a ready fisherman, and one that was acceptable as a fishing companion by such professionals as St Peter and the Zebedee brothers. Possibly, therefore, he was a professional fisherman too. Unfortunately the one fact mentioned by St John of St Bartholomew, that he argued with St Philip 'under a fig tree',[6] tells us nothing special about him, since fig trees simply make the ideal shade for a conversation in a hot climate.

Much more significant and helpful, however, is our Lord's comment, when he first met St Bartholomew, 'Behold an Israelite indeed in whom there is no guile!' To it he reasonably answered, 'How do you know me?' Perhaps we have here an example of Jesus's psychic powers,[7] for as St John says emphatically, 'He knew all men...for he himself knew what was in man.'[8] This comment to St Bartholomew, however, was also a pun based on the story of Jacob. Jacob, Scripture stresses, was the most 'guileful' of men, but God 'knew' his spiritual heart and his potential to become a great leader of his people. So he was chosen instead of his elder, but so worldly, brother Esau. In due course the guileful Jacob became 'Israel' (God's true warrior) and the third, and arguably the greatest, of the Patriarchs.[9] Jesus here is likening St Bartholomew to Israel, so paying him an enormous compliment. And that this is what he was doing is made the more obvious by his concluding comment in that conversation, 'Truly, truly, I say to you, you will see heaven opened, and the angels of God ascending and descending upon the Son of man', for in Jacob's dream in the wilderness this is what he saw, heaven open and angels ascending and descending up and down a mystic ladder linking earth to heaven.[10] Jesus saw, perhaps, in the heart of St Bartholomew similar exciting dreams! Some commentators, consequently, have suggested that St Bartholomew was a mystic, or that he was studying the story of Jacob's dream when St Philip found him. What we know for certain is that he was going to be privileged to see many wonderful things 'that righteous men [had] longed to see and [had] not seen'.[11] The particular fulfilment of this promise, no doubt, was the Ascension of Jesus, which left the Apostles spellbound in wonder, 'looking up into heaven.'[12] However it is surely also relevant to remember here how it is 'the pure in heart who see God',[13] since it was St Bartholomew's purity of heart, his 'guilelessness', that so impressed Jesus. It is the particular reward of the pure in heart that they 'see' the divine, just as it is the characteristic of divinity to 'see' if there is purity in us. So perhaps we may say that Jesus and St Bartholomew were especially drawn to each other, each instantly recognising the truth about the other; the one saw the true Israelite, the other the true King of Israel.

Jesus and St Bartholomew had something else in common; both died horrible deaths. Tradition tells us that St Bartholomew journeyed through North India and Persia preaching the Gospel, and was finally martyred in Albanopolis in Armenia, being flayed alive and then beheaded. This appalling death established his fame and inspired the devotion paid to him, not least in England, in spite of his official anonymity, to which we have referred. Here 165 mediaeval Churches have him as their Patron and, because of the fearful manner of his martyrdom, he became, rather gruesomely perhaps, the Patron Saint of tanners, and his emblem their flaying knife.

The Collect's petition is that God's 'Church' may be both a lover and a preacher of God's Word. In speaking of God's 'Word', it refers to it as that which St Bartholomew 'believed' and 'preached', so it would seem that we are thinking here especially of the Gospel, the 'Word' of the New Testament. Between the 'Word' of the Old and the New Testament there is both a unity and a distinction. Both are the Word of God, but in the New Testament the Word is 'a Word made flesh', who 'dwelt among us'.[14] There the Word is called the 'Gospel', that is the good news of the arrival of the Messiah foretold in the Old Testament. In the Old Testament, therefore, there is that which points to the Gospel of the New Testament, the element called prophecy. Nevertheless, for all that, primarily there the 'Word' is

Law. Now Law is mainly something 'taught'; and having been taught it must be 'obeyed'. This may be contrasted with the same divine Word in the New Testament, which is Gospel, something that must be 'preached', and having been preached, must be 'believed'. In the New Testament, certainly, there is 'teaching' as well as 'preaching,' 'didache' as well as 'kergyma' (see the Conversion of St Paul), but primarily 'the Gospel of Jesus Christ, the Son of God,'[15] is something that the Church 'preaches', and if it is to 'save', it must be 'believed'[16] by those who hear it. So we may say that the primary duty of the 'Church' of the Old Testament was to 'teach' the Law and for all its members to obey it, whereas the primary duty of the 'Church' of the New Testament is to 'preach' the Gospel, and for all its members to believe in it.

In describing our right response to both the Law and the Gospel it is possible to use similar words, such as 'love' and 'believe', but a distinction does exist between them. Certainly the Old Testament Law was often taught and obeyed with a marvellous ardour, that inspired holiness in the lives of God's people before Christ came. 'O Lord, what love have I unto thy Law. All the day long is my study of it.' 'Yea, I shall keep it with my whole heart.'[17] The aspirations and prayers of the Psalmist are still an inspiration to Christians who know that Jesus came to fulfill 'both the Law and the Prophets';[18] for us, too, 'the statutes of the Lord are right and rejoice the heart.'[19] But so sadly, and perhaps so strangely, this devotion to the Word of God in the Law and the Prophets did not in fact prepare its devotees to recognise and follow with a similar devotion that same Word when it became incarnate in their midst. That God meant them to do so St Paul emphasises in Galatians.[20] The Old Testament Law was intended to act as 'a guardian or tutor', whose purpose was to prepare his people for a far fuller experience of himself than they could experience from their keeping of the Law. This fuller experience awaited the arrival of the Son, and through him the Spirit. This Spirit was 'the spirit of sonship' that would enable those who received it to say, not just 'I have promised to keep thy Law',[21] but, much more wonderfully, to cry out, '*Abba*! Father!'[22] This, however, did not happen as God desired, and this is the tragedy of the Jews, that St Paul ponders so deeply in Romans 9-11. Indeed the very opposite happened. The readers of the Prophets and the devotees of the Law, the Scribes and Pharisees, were our Lord's chief opponents. So we need to recognise a distinction, as well as a similarity, between the love and belief that is felt for the Old Testament's Law, and that which is felt for the New Testament's Gospel. Both are 'of God', part of his 'Word' to us all, with an essential unity existing between them, but yet those who love and believe in the one may yet hate and reject the other.

This distinction is particularly relevant to the way, already referred to, in which this Collect was changed by Bishop Cosin in 1662. Cranmer in 1549, as we have said, kept the petition in the mediaeval Collect unaltered, only changing the invocation. What Cosin's changes do is to reflect the difference in attitude towards the Gospel in the mediaeval Church and in the reformation Church. The mediaeval Collect prayed that 'thy Church' might 'preach what he (St Bartholomew) taught,' thereby apparently perceiving the Gospel as a thing to be 'taught'. The revised Collect of 1662, however, reads that 'thy Church' may 'both preach and receive' 'the word which he believed', reflecting clearly a different perception of the Gospel's nature. It was indeed one of the foremost criticisms of the Reformers that in the mediaeval Church the 'Gospel' had become 'Law', something to be taught, learned and obeyed, and that in consequence the general spirituality of the Church had slipped back into being similar to that of the Jewish Church, and so not at heart Christian spirituality at all. We may demur at this accusation, but nonetheless we should acknowledge that should *didache* rather than *kerygma* become the primary element in the Gospel a perversion of the Gospel has taken place. At all costs the Gospel must be kept pure,[23] for it can be corrupted. Even though one result of the

Reformation was the tragedy of disunity in the Church, if the Gospel was rescued from perversion by it, the Reformation was necessary, and so justified.

―――――――――――

If the rejection of the word 'taught' in connection with the word 'Gospel' in this Collect was significant, the inclusion of the word 'receive' was equally so. God speaks, and we must listen. 'He who has ears to hear, let him hear,' said Jesus,[24] and he said it repeatedly. But they would not. 'This people's heart has grown dull, and their ears are heavy of hearing and their eyes have closed,' he also said, quoting Isaiah.[25] The incarnate Word of God came to the people of God, and 'they received him not'.[26] They loved the Word of the Law, but they rejected the Word of the Gospel. 'They refused to hear the voice of the charmer', even though he was 'full of grace and truth'.[27] It is the 'receiving', therefore, that matters as much as the 'preaching'. So much depends on this, even our salvation. 'Receive with meekness the implanted word, which is able to save your souls,' says St James.[28] The preaching of the Gospel may be primarily a work of salvation, but it is also inevitably a work of judgement.

The word *euaggelion*, translated 'Gospel', is a special New Testament word and is not found elsewhere in Greek literature. It seems to have the meaning of 'good news', for *eu* means 'well' and *aggelion*, 'a message'. But St Mark says this: 'Now after John was arrested, Jesus came into Galilee, preaching the *euaggelion* of God, and saying, "The time is fulfilled, and the Kingdom of God is at hand; repent, and believe in the *euagellion*".'[29] The first mentioned response to the Gospel is apparently repentance, which may seem a surprising initial reaction to 'good news'. Would not 'rejoice and believe' seem more appropriate than 'repent and believe'? Consequently we must not be over-optimistic in our understanding of this essential Christian word. In the way we react to it our judgement as well as our salvation is at stake. Let us clear our minds of any shallowness, let alone hypocrisy. The Gospel is indeed the most wonderful news, but it is also a most serious matter. It is not something offered us casually by God, but rather something long and lovingly prepared for our benefit. The consequences of 'believing' and 'receiving' it are marvellous and eternal, for by so doing, we may have 'life in his name'.[30] The Gospel, however, has the power 'to bind and loose'.[31] In this awesome sense it is 'messianic'. When we 'receive' the Gospel that we hear 'preached', God enters our lives, for it is God's 'Word' we are hearing. But to reject or disobey God's Word is to keep God out of our lives, the consequences of which may also be eternal.[32]

The author of the Epistle to the Hebrews describes the coming of the Gospel into our lives like this: 'The Word of God is living and active, sharper than any two-edged sword, piercing to the division of soul and spirit...and discerning the thoughts and intentions of the heart.'[33] St Paul says, 'The Gospel...is the power of God for salvation to everyone who has faith', but 'the wrath of God' remains upon those who reject it.[34] 'To all who [receive] him, who [believe] in his name, he [gives] the power to become children of God',[35] but to reject him is to 'love darkness rather than light',[36] said St John. There is no denying, therefore, the seriousness of the Gospel message, and no exaggerating its significance for us all. To say that 'we know God', but then to reject the Gospel is something that 'blinds' those that say it. This is the teaching that comes so forcefully out of the conversation Jesus had with some Pharisees after he had healed a blind man. The Pharisees, who were such lovers of the Law, and in many cases faithful doers of it too, saw themselves as 'guides of the blind', and a 'light to those who were in darkness,'[37] but Jesus said to them, 'For judgement I came into the world, that those who do not see may see, and that those who see may become blind'. Then some of the Pharisees said, "Are we also blind?" And Jesus said to them, "if you were blind you would have no guilt, but now that you say "we see", your guilt remains." '38 We can be like that, all too easily.

So this reformation Collect guides our thoughts towards some very important truths indeed, which were not made plain by the earlier mediaeval Collects for St Bartholomew's Day. Coming to Jesus was for him, we know, a totally life-changing experience. He came to Jesus with a preconception that he was unimportant. But, having met him, he followed him, 'believing' he was none other than 'the Son of God'. Jesus is 'that Word' which St Bartholomew believed and preached, of which his Collect speaks, and which we must 'receive', and, as he did, 'love.'

SAINT MATTHEW THE APOSTLE

September 21st

O Almighty God, who by thy blessed Son didst call Matthew from the receipt of custom to be an Apostle and Evangelist; Grant us grace to forsake all covetous desires, and inordinate love of riches, and to follow the same thy Son Jesus Christ, who liveth and reigneth with thee and the Holy Ghost, one God, world without end. Amen.

St Matthew is called in this Collect both an Apostle and an Evangelist. There can be no doubt that he was the first, for all the lists of the Twelve mention him.[1] In St Matthew's list he is specifically called 'Matthew the tax collector', but a comparison between the three accounts in the Synoptic Gospels of Jesus calling a tax collector, who was 'sitting at the tax office' (all use this same phrase, so there can be no reasonable doubt that they are all referring to the same man) show us that his original name was 'Levi', and he was 'the son of Alphaeus'.[2] It is reasonable to presume that when Levi became our Lord's disciple he changed his name, as others among Christ's first disciples did. However, even though early tradition believed that he was, it is now accepted that the Apostle Matthew was not the author of the first Gospel.

There are two particularly compelling reasons for separating the Apostle from the Evangelist. The first is that the Evangelist was clearly a trained Jewish scholar. The way he handles his material is characteristic of someone from such a background, for it resembles the method of presentation we see in the books of the Pentateuch; both there and in St Matthew's Gospel (we will continue to give it that title) the teaching of Moses on the one hand and of Jesus on the other are arranged in blocks.[3] In addition, St Matthew's author knows the Old Testament Scriptures thoroughly and quotes them frequently. Like a refrain running through his Gospel we read such words as, 'All this took place to fulfil what the Lord had spoken to the prophet.'[4] In his Gospel, and only there, Jesus says, 'Think not that I have come to abolish the Law and the Prophets; I have come not to abolish them, but to fulfil them',[5] and the word 'fulfil' comes fifteen times in his Gospel. Would such a knowledge of and attitude towards the Old Testament be likely, let along typical, of one who was a tax collector?

More conclusive still, however, is the second reason for doubting that the Apostle was the Evangelist. The critical study of the Synoptic Gospels makes it clear that St Matthew's author was not an eye-witness of the events he records, and if he was the Apostle, of course, he would have been. One of the most notable features of St Matthew's Gospel is that it includes nearly everything recorded in St Mark's Gospel. Although the accounts usually differ slightly, so precise are the similarities, with several sections being verbatim the same, it is impossible to avoid the conclusion that one used the other as a written source. Who, however, used which? A comparison between the way the same event is told in each Gospel, where a difference exists, soon shows that it was St Matthew who used St Mark. Quite little changes, when studied, reveal this clearly. The vivid eye-witness quality of St Mark's narrative, of which we have already taken notice, and to which we have ascribed the presence of St Peter being behind the pen of St Mark, is almost invariably changed by St Matthew's author into a comparatively flat report. What we read there has all the appearance of an effort being made to iron out any unflattering suggestions as to what happened, and so to record what the author thinks ought to have happened rather than what did! The two accounts of Jesus stilling the storm illustrate this particularly well.[6] St Matthew begins briefly, 'When he got into the boat his disciples followed him'. Jesus here, as surely one would expect, is calm, collected and in charge. St Mark, however, makes it very clear that on this occasion that was not the case at all. Jesus was then being harassed and pursued by clamorous crowds. St Mark tells how his anxious Apostles 'took him with them in the boat, just as he was', a different scenario altogether. Both Gospels then tell of how an exhausted Jesus immediately went to sleep in the boat, but only St Mark tells us that he slept through 'the storm' with his head 'on a cushion', a charming little eye-witness detail that St Matthew typically omits.

However, simply to say that St Matthew the Apostle was not St Matthew the Evangelist begs some important questions and since we call him both in this Collect, we are bound to ask them here. For instance, how is it that this mistake was made in the first place and believed in for so long? And is there, perhaps, some hidden truth lying beneath the surface of this intriguing matter? The only reason that St Matthew was believed to have written the first Gospel is because Papias, one of the earliest Christian historians (circa 120), said, 'Matthew collected the sayings of Jesus in the Hebrew tongue'. A tax collector, though not a trained Jewish scholar, would nonetheless have been literate, and trained in and attracted to the keeping of records. It would be, therefore, very much in character if he had written down, for instance, the parables of Jesus and kept a record of what he thought were the more memorable sayings of Jesus. Such a private handbook would not have amounted to the systematic Gospel that now bears his name, but it would surely have been an invaluable source for someone who sought to write such a Gospel.

Now, New Testament scholars have established that the authors of both St Matthew's and St Luke's Gospels had behind them two documentary sources. They used them differently, but it is clear from the nature of the numerous similarities that exist in their Gospels that these shared sources were documentary, and not just hearsay. What were these two documents? One of them was undoubtedly St Mark's Gospel. The other, however, is lost, but we can gather from analysing the similarities between these two Gospels that it consisted of parables, teachings, and sayings of Jesus. Scholars have entitled this unknown source 'Q' from the German word Quelle, which means 'source'. This source, therefore, is exactly the kind of document that Papias seems to have been referring to in his brief comment, and just the kind of document that someone with St Matthew's abilities and opportunities would have been able to compile. If then St Matthew was the author of 'Q', he was at least a proto-evangelist, even if we cannot any longer consider him a true Evangelist, as tradition, and this Collect, declares. If this is the case, however, it makes the wording of this Collect far less mistaken, which is, perhaps, also a comfort.

Tradition tells us little of St Matthew the Apostle's later history. It claims he was martyred, evangelising in far away places, but as is the case with some of the other Apostles, accounts of his martyrdom differ. According to the Roman Martyrology he met his end in Ethiopia, whereas according to St Jerome's Martyrology it was in Persia. In neither are precise dates given, but we can safely surmise that he would not have lived to a ripe old age. In art, St Matthew is depicted as holding sometimes a sword, and sometimes a halberd, a kind of battle-axe, for the way he died is also reported differently, but also sometimes money bags and sometimes an inkwell.

This last choice of emblem, however, leads us to ask if we can obtain any more evidence of who was the real Evangelist. Since both Apostle and Evangelist are mentioned in our Collect, and are equally worthy of our grateful remembrance, to do so would properly assist us in the praying of this prayer. That he was a trained Jewish scholar has already been mentioned. He would have come, therefore, from that group of people we hear so much of in the Gospels, and especially in St Matthew's Gospel, 'the Scribes and Pharisees'. That they were a most important group of religious people, even in the eyes of Jesus, is emphasised by such sayings as 'the Scribes and Pharisees sit on Moses's seat, so practise and observe whatever they tell you',[7] but at the same time they were the bitterest of our Lord's opponents, and that too is emphasised especially by St Matthew the Evangelist. Perhaps like St Paul he had himself been a violent opponent of Christ's religion before converting to it, and from personal experience had learnt that his old 'righteousness' was not acceptable to God.[8]

The tenor of his writing seems to suggest a settled environment. It is revealing that St Matthew's is the only Gospel to mention the Church, which it does twice, and both these texts suggest that the Church by his time had become a more institutionalised organisation than the localised Church of the Pauline Epistles. The shadow of persecution that hung so obviously over St Mark's Gospel, had also, so it would appear, moved away, at least temporarily, at the time St Matthew's was written. We may notice that a different overriding consideration is taking its place. This is the hope of the Second Coming. St Matthew's Gospel alone tells the escatological parables of the talents, the wise and foolish virgins and the sheep and goats, and his long Chapter 24 gives a much fuller account of Jesus's apocalyptic teaching than does St Mark's Chapter 13, to which it is otherwise similar.

All this points to it being a comparatively late work, but finished before the persecution of Domitian engulfed the Church in the 80s. It would have been written in a city where there was a tradition of scholarship, and a comparatively large Jewish Christian community, and Alexandria fits this requirement admirably. This also is the city that is particularly associated with St Mark, who was its first Bishop, and we have already stressed how completely St. Matthew's Gospel is based upon St. Mark's. Antioch is, however, a reasonable alternative to Alexandria.

Beyond this, unfortunately, we cannot go. Here is one whose influence on our religion has been truly enormous, far greater than that of St Matthew the Apostle, and yet he remains entirely anonymous. How mysterious this is! Perhaps, however, we may say that the Church, because of this, has been inspired in its choice of Epistle for St Matthew's Day,[9] even though it has been mistaken in its wording of its Collect. There we read how the 'Gospel' may be 'veiled', and yet how 'the glory of Christ, who is the likeness of God' will always shine out from it. It speaks, too, of the complete unimportance of the 'preacher' of the Gospel, and of the supreme importance of its subject, Jesus Christ, who is 'Lord' of all. The Evangelist, another Pharisee turned Christian, would have surely said 'Amen' to this teaching of St Paul, and we, as we honour his anonymous memory, may surely do the same.

The Collect's invocation stresses how Jesus called St. Matthew away 'from the receipt of custom to be an Apostle'. Now, tax-collectors in the Roman Empire were everywhere despised and hated by the public.[10] No-one enjoys paying tax and the tax-man is hardly anyone's favourite person, but here at least no-one imagines that he will be in a position to overcharge the public and keep the illegal proceeds. That, however, was exactly the situation in Jesus's time. Tax-collectors in the Roman Empire were not honourable civil servants, but private citizens using the system to enrich themselves, and thick-skinned enough to bear the odium in which they would certainly be held. However, that some had religious minds and tender consciences is confirmed in the Gospels. Many were attracted to St John the Baptist as well as to Jesus, and St Luke tells us specifically that some came to St John 'to be baptised by him', something he probably emphasised for its surprise effect![11] Who would have imagined such a thing? That they came, however, in a spirit of genuine sincerity is also stressed. 'Teacher', they said, 'what shall we do?' St John did not, we should notice, tell them to give up their jobs, but rather simply 'to collect no more than is appointed you'.

This teaching of St. John is confirmed by Jesus in the case of Zacchaeus.[12] He was another tax-collector who became Christ's disciple. He, too, was uneasy in his heart about what he was doing and the way he had enriched himself. He wanted most sincerely to unburden himself to Jesus, whom he recognised as the friend of tax-collectors, and, wonderfully for him, he was able to do so. In the case of Zacchaeus Jesus did not call him away from his tax-office to follow him, as he had done with St Matthew. He left him in his job, but with the resolve that from now on he would fulfil it honestly. No doubt St Matthew's readiness to 'leave everything' and follow him gave Jesus great joy. But so, too, we know, did the eagerness with which Zacchaeus made his resolution to pay restitution to those he had defrauded and to act in future with generosity and honesty. 'Today salvation has come to this house', Jesus said with obvious heartfelt delight.

As it was for Zacchaeus, so is it likely to be for us. It is not usually what we do that matters so much as the way that we do it. This is central to our understanding of the Incarnation's significance. Jesus lived an ordinary life amid ordinary people for thirty years, although, of course, we may presume, in no ordinary way. We are told, however, that in those years he 'increased in wisdom and stature, and in favour with God and man'. As those years ended and his years of ministry began St Luke tells of the Father's voice proclaiming, 'Thou art my beloved Son; with thee I am well pleased'.[13] It is possible, therefore, we do believe, for those, who are 'in Christ', also to live holy lives without leaving the world. As it was for Jesus in Nazareth so it may be for us wherever we live. The Holy Spirit can give us too 'the spirit of sonship',[14] and then what we do will certainly 'please God'. Of the two tax-collectors, whose names are given us in the Gospels, we are only remembering St Matthew in this Collect, but Zacchaeus is also so very worthy of our remembrance and, indeed, his story may well be the one that helps us most.

Then in the petition we pray that God will 'give us grace to forsake all covetous desires and [the] inordinate love of riches'. 'Those who desire to be rich fall [inevitably] into temptation', says St Paul and 'the love of money [lies at] the root of evil [of every kind]'.[15] In this well-known passage the emphasis should be placed on the words 'desire' and 'love'. It is not money itself which is the evil; it is covetousness. Repeatedly in both Old and New Testaments God's Word warns us against it. It is expressed in both the Ten Commandments, and the Church's list of the seven Deadly Sins, yet when Jesus said, 'Woe to the rich',[16] we should interpret that as a warning, rather than a condemnation. The stakes, however, in this matter are very high. Covetousness is akin to 'idolatry', said St Paul, for wealth can so easily become an idol we worship.[17] We cannot 'serve God and Mammon', and the measure of the harm covetousness can do is to separate us from God.[18]

It is important, nonetheless, that we rescue the possession of money from the stigma of covetousness. In the petition we have the phrase 'the inordinate love of riches' to describe what we mean by covetousness. Is there then an 'ordinate' love of money that we may safely indulge? Much good has been done in the world by millionaires using their wealth under the guidance of God's Spirit. Wealth is a form of power, and with it good can be done as well as evil. The creation of such things as schools, hospitals and homes, not to mention churches, all costs money, and they cannot be created without it, at least in our society. Money is essential for job creation, and so it is for us to buy 'our daily bread'. Charitable giving is honourable, and to have money does not mean that we will inevitably misuse it. Scripture confirms this commonsensical understanding of the matter. St Paul, who warns against the misuse of riches as directly as any other apostolic writer, also gives the rich warm encouragement. '[You] are to do good, to be rich in good deeds, to be liberal and generous, thus laying up for [yourselves] a good foundation for the future, so that [you] may take hold of the life which is life indeed', is his sensible advice to them.[19]

However, unless we live 'in Christ', and God's Spirit guides our lives, the sad likelihood is that we will misuse wealth, when we possess it. So the petition hurries on, and makes us pray that at all costs we do 'follow' Christ. This Collect is by Cranmer, who rejected the Sarum Collect as unsuitable. There we prayed that, 'What we are not able of ourselves to obtain, may be bestowed on us [by God] by the intercessions of St Matthew'. We may well object to this petition, but we should notice how it points to the part prayer should play in our 'obtaining' what may be thought the necessities of life and the way we spend our money. We are not to be covetous, but equally, says Jesus, we are not to be over-anxious either. God knows our physical needs, and how real they are.[20] Without having a devotional life, however, of which prayer is the first ingredient, we are so likely to be one or the other. A proper faith and hope in God will protect us from both covetousness and anxiety. Nevertheless to follow Christ's teaching on this matter is extraordinarily hard. It is part of that narrow way that only the few apparently find.[21]

'Seek first his Kingdom and his righteousness, and all these things [for which we need money] will be yours as well',[22] are not easy words to digest, let alone live out. Do they not call for heroic faith? We are only going to understand what Jesus is saying, if we recognise in this matter, as in all others, the primacy of love. Love has a way of squaring the circles in life, and making the impossible and incomprehensible possible and sensible. It is revealed pre-eminently by Jesus on the Cross, so it will not be something that releases us from sacrifice and difficulty. But, as St Paul said, 'It is the power of God and the wisdom of God',[23] that is the only thing that makes good things happen and makes sense of our difficulties. So in this matter of money for our needs, we are taken in this Collect by the phrase 'follow the same thy Son Jesus Christ', away from the consideration of 'getting' to that of 'giving'. The maxim that sums up Christ's teaching in this matter is 'To give is to receive', or to put it more bluntly still, 'To give is to get'. 'Give and it will be given to you; good measure, pressed down, shaken together, running over, will be put into your lap. For the measure you give will be the measure you get' are his words.[24] And what a challenge is set before us by them! Greater by far, one has to say, than the demands of Stewardship with its sensible calculations and percentages.

As St Paul assures us, 'God loves a cheerful giver',[25] for God himself is the most cheerful, eager giver of all. 'Woe to the rich' then is not Scripture's last word, any more than the purpose of this Collect is only to warn against and to condemn 'covetousness'. There is a saying of Jesus that comes to us in a most unusual way. When St Paul was bidding the Church in Ephesus his last farewell he ended by quoting it; 'It is more blessed to give than to receive'.[26] These words do seem to give Scripture's final verdict on this matter, and to underline the direction in which this Collect points us. Although we must at all costs 'forsake' covetousness, there is a perfectly proper reason for obtaining wealth, and that is to 'give' it as God directs, and to seek the blessing he promises to those who do. The readiness, indeed the eagerness, to give of what we have brings not only great blessings upon others, but also upon ourselves too. The Gospel has a way of 'turning the world upside down',[27] as even its critics have readily perceived, but that means, of course, turning it the right way up!

SAINT MICHAEL AND ALL ANGELS
September 29th

O Everlasting God, who hast ordained and constituted the services of Angels and men in a wonderful order; Mercifully grant, that as thy holy Angels always do thee service in heaven, so by thy appointment they may succour and defend us on earth; through Jesus Christ our Lord. Amen.

This is one of the few Saints' Day Collects that follow closely the mediaeval Collect. Cranmer, however, altered the tense of the opening relative clause and added to it the word 'constituted'. The original Gregorian Collect used in the Sarum Missal started, 'O everlasting God, who ordains the services of angels and men in a wonderful order'. The present tense there seems to stress the continuing nature of God's purposes for 'angels and men', and perhaps we can say that Cranmer's change of tense to the perfect does not alter this emphasis. This prayer should be understood, therefore, as not just emphasising our closeness to angels, but also as stressing that what God 'ordained and constituted' in the beginning he continues to control and use at the present time. The words 'services' and 'order' in the invocation both seem to underline this truth.

In this context the word 'ordained' would seem to have special significance. In the original Collect, as we have said, it stood alone, and the word 'constituted' appears frankly to add nothing to its meaning, 'ordained' being so much the stronger word. Ordination confers Holy Order and establishes Priesthood. The angels in the Collect are called 'holy', and we notice the evocative combination of the words 'ordain', 'service' and 'order'. The Collect consequently appears to teach that God meant 'angels and men' to share in a cosmic Priesthood to all in heaven and earth.

Different as angels and men undoubtedly are, we may nonetheless, therefore, compare ourselves with them, in that context at least, as like with like. By being 'made flesh' we are told that the Son of God was 'for a little while made lower than the angels'.[1] As heavenly beings the angels take precedence over us earthly creatures, but, as Scripture stresses, the Incarnation conferred on mankind through the person of Jesus an honour that transcends any the angels may enjoy. 'For to what angel did God ever say, "Thou art my Son, today I have begotten thee", Or again, "I will be to him a Father, and he will be to me a Son"?'[2] However, since both angels and men have been 'ordained and constituted' to love and serve God freely, our fellowship together is both of the Holy Spirit and part of the Communion of Saints. Words of St John come to mind, 'You may have fellowship with us, and our fellowship is with the Father and with his Son Jesus Christ'.[3] If they do describe our fellowship with the angels then, as the Collect says, it is worthy of the description 'wonderful'.

The Festival is entitled 'St Michael and All Angels', although in the Collect St Michael himself is not mentioned, and only 'holy angels' are referred to. If we take the second point first, we should certainly stress that the ordinary perception that 'all angels' are good, let alone holy, is quite unscriptural. 2 Peter, Jude and above all Revelation all tell of evil angels in league with the Devil.[4] Indeed, Scripture teaches that the Devil himself is a fallen angel. In Revelation 12 we are warned that 'the Devil, the deceiver' of the whole world, was thrown down to the earth and his angels were thrown down with him, and from this the connection was made between the evil angels and the 'demons' or 'unclean spirits' that were the enemies of Jesus in the Gospels. These demonic spirits, we are told, immediately recognised Jesus. They are portrayed as far worse than mere agents of illness. They are rather agents of evil, whom Jesus had 'come to destroy', as indeed they feared.[5] Jesus had power to cast them out, which was something that filled both their victims and all bystanders with wonder and gratitude,[6] and it is also central to the Gospel that he has given this same power to his Church.[7]

St John's vision in Revelation, to which we have just referred, reminds us of the words of Jesus with which he gave thanks after the Seventy's successful evangelistic exercise. These early evangelists were ecstatic 'with joy' at what had happened as they ministered 'in his Name'. 'Lord', they said, 'even the demons are subject to us in your Name!' Then Jesus said to them, 'I saw Satan fall like lightning from heaven.'[8] It is from this passage particularly that the Devil has received the name Lucifer, meaning the light bearer, a name Milton has made a household word through his great poem Paradise Lost. It is not precisely scriptural. The Isaianic text, however, 'How you are fallen from heaven, O Day-Star, Son of the Dawn',[9] may have inspired our Lord's comment. Taken together these two texts have encouraged the concept, accepted particularly by Milton, that the Devil is not just a fallen angel, but was once an especially favoured angel, a fact that made his fall all the more dreadful.

This understanding of the matter is seemingly underlined in Revelation and Jude where the Devil's special protagonist is St Michael. His name means 'God's warrior', and he and the Devil, with their respective angelic forces, 'fought', and, as Revelation Chapter 12 vividly describes, St Michael and his angels 'prevailed'. In Jude we are told how St Michael disputed with the Devil over the body of Moses, for tradition has it that he, like Elijah, was assumed into heaven, but at the time this honour was fiercely opposed by the Devil.[10] St Michael is mentioned in Daniel as the special Guardian Angel of the Jewish people, 'the great prince who has charge of your people',[11] and from this reference and from that in Jude, St Michael has been especially linked with the Guardian Angels that Jesus declared we all possess. [12]

St Michael is the only angel named in our Festival, but three others are named in Scripture. The most famous of these is Gabriel, for ever famous for his role in the story of Christmas. There he is God's messenger of good news, first to Zechariah and then to the Blessed Virgin,[13] a fact that reminds us that the Greek word *aggelos* means 'messenger'. Another angel whose name is given us is Raphael.[14] The word in Hebrew means 'God heals', and consequently he has been accepted as the Patron Saint of various guilds of healing in the Church. The other angel to be named is Uriel, mentioned as Raphael also is in the Book of Enoch. His appointed task is to receive the dead on their arrival into the eternal world and take them to 'the place prepared for them'.[15]

According to the traditional teaching of the Church, gleaned from Scripture, there are nine orders of angels. These are Seraphim, Cherubim, Thrones, Dominions, Principalities, Authorities, Powers, Archangels and Angels. Although all are mentioned in Scripture,[16] no consistent pattern emerges from it to explain the significance of all these titles. This has not discouraged the speculations of theologians down the ages, whose (often wild) theories are dignified by the title of Angelology. The danger inherent in these speculations, however, is particularly emphasised in Scripture. Angelology, for instance, was a central element of Gnosticism, the pseudo-religion that was such an insidious and powerful opponent of the Gospel in the first and second centuries. St Paul was particularly concerned that the Christians in Colossae should have no dealings with those who 'insisted on the worship of angels',[17] and to the Ephesians, also, he stressed the danger of this false spirituality; 'We are not contending', he said, 'against flesh and

blood [opponents)], but [against angelic opponents], against the principalities, against the powers, against the world rulers of this present darkness,
against the spiritual hosts of wickedness in the heavenly places'.[18] The
opposition of evil angels was as real to him as it had been to Jesus.

Everywhere throughout both Testaments of Scripture angels are mentioned, and certainly for the most part they are depicted as holy creatures.
Constant reference is made throughout Scripture to their most characteristic activity and chief delight, the worship of God. 'To thee all angels cry
aloud'[19] in praise and thanksgiving is its verdict, only excepting the evil
angels, who are destined for elimination when God's Kingdom is finally
established on earth as it is in heaven.[20] However this major truth about
the 'holy angels' is muted in Cranmer's rendering of the Latin Collect.
There the word *ministrantibus* has overtones of deep yet eager reverence
that is not, perhaps, caught by the simple phrase 'do thee service'. Implicit
in that word is the repeated scriptural reference to the angels 'standing
before God' in a position of both reverence and readiness. Dean Goulbourn
suggests that it ought to be translated 'standing before thee to minister'.
'I saw the seven angels who stand before God', said St John the Divine.[21]
The angel Gabriel described himself thus, 'I am Gabriel who stands in the
presence of God'.[22] Cranmer's wording, however, would seem to owe much
to Hebrews, where the role of the 'holy angels' is discussed, and where we
read, 'Are they not all ministering spirits sent forth to serve?'[23] Yet here
we should notice that the word translated 'ministering' is *leitourgika*, a
word related to our word 'liturgy', which describes the Church's main form
of public worship. It is the angels' ministry of worship, therefore, that is
particularly being emphasised there too. Consequently we are bound to
feel that Cranmer's rendering of the mediaeval Collect does not sufficiently
preserve the emphasis on worship in 'the service' of the angels that the
Latin Collect conveyed, and which is so definitely scriptural. We should,
therefore, pray it with this truth in mind, a truth, also, to which the Church

has from earliest times given a central place in its eucharistic worship through the Sanctus, which, to give him his due, Cranmer preserved in our Prayer Book Service of Holy Communion..

However a *caveat* may be pressed here. This scriptural emphasis on worship in the lives of angels, linked as it is with the word 'standing', may give a false impression of inactivity in their lives. Although few have been privileged to see angels, the accounts of those privileged few of what they have seen are naturally intensely interesting. Dorothy Kerin, the Foundress of Burrswood, the Home of Healing near Tunbridge Wells, had the extraordinary experience of passing through the door of death and then coming back again. During that experience she saw angels, and this is her witness in her book The Living Touch: 'I seemed to drift into space, no longer conscious of my body, but my spirit was overflowing with joy and love and a transcendent feeling of supreme happiness impossible to describe... I passed on...and saw coming from every direction white robed figures...their movements making lovely music; they all looked as though they were coming and going with some definite purpose. No words of mine can express or exaggerate the exquisite beauty of the scene.' Her witness to angels here vividly reminds us of Jacob's vision of the ladder that united heaven and earth, and the busy, ordered movement of angels up and down it. 'Behold, the angels of God were ascending and descending on it',[24] he said. How mistaken, therefore, we would be if we imagined the life of angels to be purposeless or dull!

The Collect's petition is especially that the 'holy angels' may 'by God's appointment' 'succour and defend' us in the course of our lives here. For our encouragement in this regard we have seen how Scripture assures us that this has repeatedly happened to God's faithful servants in the past, and even more to the point, Jesus declared that we all have Guardian Angels assigned to us by divine appointment. In revealing that, Jesus added that 'they always behold the face of my Father who is in heaven'.[25] The fact that this is a strange comment is good reason to suppose that it is of importance. The implication clearly is that for our Guardian Angels there will always be a proper waiting upon God's will in all that they may do for us. We are not at all to imagine that they are at our bidding to do our will. They are not like Aladdin's geni! And surely this is a truth to be accepted gladly. These words, 'succour and defend', therefore, should be interpreted in the first instance spiritually as we pray them. They remind us, particularly, of the final clause of the Lord's Prayer. There we pray for 'succour' in temptation's hour, and 'defence' in the face of the Enemy. It is in God's answering of that prayer, therefore, which we so constantly pray, that we may believe our Guardian Angels are kept most busy. A text comes to mind; 'He shall give his angels charge over thee to keep thee in all thy ways'.[26]

Nevertheless, the teaching of Scripture concerning 'the services of angels' for us does not limit them to the spiritual realm. Just as the demons in the Gospels were the cause of physical suffering, so the angels are, we may believe, sometimes at least, the agents of physical protection and practical assistance. The same Psalm just quoted continues: 'They shall bear thee in their hands that thou hurt not thy foot against a stone.'[27] It should be just as we would expect, therefore, that angels have been most often seen, or experienced, where there has been injury, sickness or death, that is in hospital wards, at the scene of accidents, in the midst of some great natural calamity, and on the battlefield. That angels, for instance, were at our Lord's tomb is just as one would expect. However, when seen or experienced the first reaction to angels is likely to be that of St Peter when he was rescued from prison by his Guardian Angel; 'He did not know what was done by the angel was real'. Only later he could say, 'Now I am sure that the Lord has sent his angel to rescue me.'[28]

The Collect, as we have said, in spite of the change of tense, has the force of emphasising that what God once 'ordained and constituted' pertains still today. As confirmation of this, here is the witness of someone I know very well of an event that took place near Salisbury, now Harare, in Zimbabwe nearly forty years ago (reported as to an imaginary listener). "Most foolishly, as it turned out, I accelerated to overtake a large lorry just as we were approaching a right-hand turning that was not signed up. As I drew level with it, the lorry turned across our front into the road to our right. And what happened next is frankly a blur and a complete mystery. The facts are, however, that the lorry turned into the road and yet we ended up in the ditch beyond the turning. How we got there without hitting the lorry I cannot understand. The driver of a car that was coming towards us, however, apparently saw what happened, and said that our car seemed to leap over the turning lorry! In those days we did not use seat belts and there were two small children in the car. We were all unhurt. I am personally convinced that we were miraculously saved by our Guardian Angels. What other explanation can there be?" I particularly give thanks to God and his angels for their 'succour and defence' in that extraordinary incident, for it was the closest members of my own family in that car.

SAINT LUKE THE EVANGELIST
October 18th

Almighty God, who called Luke the Physician, whose praise is in the Gospel, to be an Evangelist, and Physician of the soul; May it please thee, that, by the wholesome medicines of the doctrine delivered by him, all the diseases of our souls may be healed; through the merits of thy Son Jesus Christ our Lord. Amen.

This Collect is by Cranmer. The Sarum Collect sought for us the intercession of St Luke, and mentioned the tradition, unconfirmed by Scripture, that he was crucified. On both of these counts the old Collect would not have pleased the Reformers. Cranmer's new Collect, however, strangely did not describe St Luke as an Evangelist, as the Sarum Collect had, and Bishop Cosin added this in 1662 to the obvious improvement of the prayer.

The invocation now emphasises the two main facts that we know about St Luke, that he was the author of the third Gospel (and of Acts), and that he was a doctor.[1] Tradition, however, largely dependent on the writings of Eusebius, who was Bishop of Caesarea in the 4th century, tells us that he was a resident of Antioch, remained unmarried and was crucified. We also learn from him that he was a painter and that he had a special relationship with the Blessed Virgin Mary. This tradition is supported by the way in which he tells the Christmas story so clearly from her point of view (just as St Matthew seems to tell it from that of St Joseph), and also by the claim that a painting of her, now in the church of Santa Maria Maggiore in Rome, is by him. (He is in consequence the Patron Saint of artists as well as of doctors and surgeons.) However, this tradition conflicts with that earliest tradition concerning the end of St Mary's life (see The Annunciation). If, according to it, she only lived three years with St John in Jerusalem, St Mary could not have met St Luke. His intimate knowledge of our Lord's conception, birth and early years, and of St Mary's actual words and behaviour at that time, could, however, have come, not from her, but from the Apostle. Indeed there is a particular reason to believe this to be the case. Those precious stories that, except for his introduction, comprise his first two chapters, are so different in style from the rest of his Gospel that they appear to be the work of another hand. To explain this commentators are divided, but one hypothesis is that behind them lies a memoir written by St John of what St Mary told him of those earliest moments, months and years of our Lord's life, which St Luke inserted, or more probably edited, to such memorable effect.

One of the most interesting features of Cranmer's Collect is the connection made in it between St Luke and the unknown 'brother' whom St Paul sent with Titus to the Corinthian Church.[2] The delightful phrase 'whose praise is in the Gospel' is taken from the A.V. version of that text, but the R.S.V. gives that passage a different interpretation. 'The brother' there is said to be 'famous among all the churches for his preaching of the Gospel', thus making him a preacher rather than a writer. And in this, one has to say, the R.S.V. is almost certainly correct. The following verse (19) then tells us that he was 'appointed by the churches to travel with St Paul', and so we may surely expect that this unknown brother, who was a famous preacher, would most likely have been one of those whom St Paul mentions in his lists of companions that end some of his Epistles. Of these the fullest come at the end of Colossians and 2 Timothy, and in both we notice that St Luke is mentioned. In the first he is called 'the beloved physician',[3] and in the second we are told that he 'alone' is with St Paul.[4] St Paul, we know, suffered from a serious physical disorder, which he famously asked God to take from him so that he might be the better able to serve him, but was told by God that 'his grace' was all he needed, and that 'the power' of that grace

was made the more 'perfect in weakness'.[5] Nonetheless, the presence of a
doctor in his band of companions would have been a most sensible provision
'by the churches'. Although there can be no certainty that this unknown
'brother' was St Luke, this identification was made by several of the early
Fathers, especially Origen, and is as reasonable as it is attractive. Why
should not a trusted companion, who is a notable preacher, be also a
beloved doctor, who becomes in the end an inspired writer?

Even if St Luke was not that 'brother' he is certainly well described as one
'whose praise is in the Gospel'. His Gospel has been called the loveliest book
in the world. It has a number of characteristics that tell us important facts
about its author and reveal, too, the kind of man he was. One warms to him
as one reads. The first is that his Gospel is clearly written for Gentiles, and
so, in that narrow sense, it may be said he is writing specially for our own
sakes. He was not a Jew. He dedicates it and Acts to a Roman Governor,
'the most excellent Theophilus', who was probably a patron, but, perhaps,
also a friend.[6] He dates the arrival of John the Baptist, which heralded the
start of our Lord's ministry, by stating first the names of the Roman
Emperor and the Roman Governor, as being for his readers, and no doubt
himself, people of special importance.[7] In his genealogy Jesus's descent is
traced from Adam, and not as in St Matthew's Gospel merely from
Abraham.[8] Jesus for St Luke is supremely 'the Saviour of the world'.

Secondly, his Gospel is also manifestly a message of good news to those
who, in the Jewish world out of which the Gospel emerged, were despised
or rejected, and the material in his Gospel that is peculiar to him especially
reflects this. The despised Samaritans, we are told, are not to be shut out
of the Kingdom,[9] and, typically, only in his Gospel do we find the parable
of the Good Samaritan.[10] Gentiles and women and outcasts, such as tax-
collectors and prostitutes, are treated with special generosity. Only in his
Gospel are found the parables of the Prodigal Son,[11] Dives and Lazarus,[12]
and the Pharisee and the Publican.[13] It is in his Gospel only that we hear

of the widow of Nain,[14] and 'the woman of the city' who anointed Jesus's feet during the supper in the house of Simon the Pharisee.[15] Only in his Gospel do we hear Jesus lauding the widow of Zeraphath and Naaman the Syrian as examples to be followed to the fury of the orthodox in the synagogue at Nazareth,[16] and of his picking out of Zacchaeus, the greedy tax-collector, as someone he particularly wanted to meet, to the equal fury of the orthodox at Jericho.[17] Two texts, perhaps, both peculiar to his Gospel, may be said to reveal this characteristic of it particularly clearly. 'Men shall come from east and west, and from north and south, and sit in the Kingdom of God',[18] and 'the poor shall have good news preached to them, and blessed is he who takes no offence at me'.[19]

This then is the universal Gospel. St Luke may or may not have been 'famous for his preaching' from the pulpit, but he certainly is, since his words still live, a preacher of the Gospel who has never been silenced. In the Collect he is said to have been 'called' to be an Evangelist. We hear nothing of his call in Scripture, but in his introduction to his Gospel he tells us how carefully he studied the life of Jesus and how concerned he was that all he wrote was only what he knew for certain was the truth about him.[20] 'Having followed all things closely', he says, (and here the Greek word *akribos* is perhaps better translated 'accurately' or 'with scrupulous care') he is now writing for his friend Theophilus 'an orderly (or historical) account' of Jesus's life so 'that he may know the truth' of what he may have heard about it. (The word translated 'truth' here is *asphaleia*, not *aletheia* as is usual in the New Testament; this word has a quasi-legal sense and so means 'something that can be totally relied upon'). There can be no doubt, therefore, from this introduction that St Luke believed completely in the veracity of all he tells us, and that he made every effort to check his sources. In our turn we may gratefully accept that God did 'call' him to perform this great work, and particularly for those who are not Jews.

St Luke, also, was a physician. We owe this knowledge to St Paul, but we might have deduced it from the internal evidence of both the Gospel and Acts. When he mentions an illness he does so using the proper medical terms, as when he described St Peter's mother-in-law as being 'ill with a high fever',[21] the father of Publius as suffering from 'fever and dysentery'[22] and, while Jesus prayed in the Garden of Gethsemane, that 'his sweat became like great drops of blood falling down upon the ground'.[23] He alone records the saying, surely full of special meaning for himself, 'Physician, heal yourself!'[24] Precisely what made St Luke a Christian is not told us, but it is perhaps reasonable to suppose that the miraculous healings brought about by St Paul, all of which were done in the name of the Lord Jesus, would have been a potent factor.[25]

It is clear from Acts that St Luke joined St Paul's band of missionaries just when God called them to take the Gospel into Europe.[26] (Suddenly the pronoun changes to first person plural as he describes what St Paul and his associates are doing.) It was therefore a critical moment in the spread of the Gospel. The evidence of St Paul's Epistles is that St Luke after that remained part of St Paul's closest circle of assistants to the end of the Apostle's life. Physical healing would, no doubt, have continued to be his special occupation, but now as a Christian he would have come to appreciate that everyone's greatest need is the healing of the soul. In the Collect he is specifically called a 'physician of the soul', and we pray there that his writings may be the means of healing 'all the diseases of our souls'. This emphatic pointing away from the physical towards the spiritual may surprise us. Such an emphasis is not at first sight born out in the ministry of Jesus, especially as portrayed in St Luke's Gospel,[27] for there Jesus is clearly shown to be both intensely concerned for the physical sufferings of the sick and the physical needs of the poor. So is Cranmer in error here?

However, by way of balance in this matter, we must recall another special characteristic of this Gospel, which is the way it emphasises the prayer life of Jesus. None of the other Evangelists stress it to the same degree. Since it is such a major element in St Luke's portraiture of Jesus it surely shows how well he realised that for Jesus the spiritual was infinitely more important than the physical. In this context a story of Jesus healing a leper is particularly relevant and revealing. It is told by all the synoptic Evangelists, but handled differently by each. St Matthew simply tells the story without recording any special reaction by anyone else to the leper's healing.[28] St Mark stresses the tremendous interest it caused, emphasising that this was something Jesus had sought to avoid.[29] St Luke, however, ends his account like this: 'Then great multitudes gathered to hear him and to be healed of their infirmities, but Jesus withdrew to the wilderness and prayed'.[30] He is recognising, and stressing, that for Jesus healing lepers of their leprosy was not all that he was sent to do. For all his natural interest in Jesus's healing ministry, St Luke clearly and passionately believed that Jesus was sent to be the Saviour of the world, not simply the healer of the sick.

Another related characteristic of St Luke's Gospel stresses the same truth. It lays a unique emphasis on the evangelistic campaigns that Jesus organised in the few years of his active ministry. It alone, for instance, mentions the 'Seventy' disciples (or perhaps it was 'seventy-two', for ancient authorities vary on this point), who helped in this evangelistic work.[31] St Matthew and St Mark only tell of the Twelve as being involved in this ministry,[32] and St John ignores it altogether. As we have already mentioned (see St Mary Magdalen), involved in this ministry were numerous women, and this too is only reported by St Luke. As part of this evangelistic ministry of Jesus both the Twelve and the Seventy were given the commission and the power to 'heal the sick', but we should notice that St Luke makes it plain that when the Seventy returned to tell Jesus excitedly of the way they had healed 'in his Name', he replied, 'Do not rejoice in this...but rejoice that your names are written in heaven'. In spite of his loving concern for all aspects of our lives, for Jesus the spiritual is of greater importance than the physical, the heavenly than the earthly. Healing is portrayed as simply part of the greater mission of establishing God's Kingdom, and as a sign of divine approval and blessing that both confirms and inspires the preaching of the Gospel.[33]

This Collect, therefore, in portraying St Luke as 'a physician of the soul' is correctly reflecting the inner convictions of the writer of both the Gospel and Acts. Although in his lifetime he presumably spent most of it being concerned for the healing of bodies, down the ages he has been to millions a physician of another sort. The real sickness of mankind, he had come to perceive, is of the soul, and in his writings he has 'delivered', or should we say 'prescribed', 'wholesome medicines' for the healing of those 'diseases' to which our 'souls' are prone. What are they? The Church in its wisdom has defined them for us as 'pride, covetousness, lust, envy, gluttony, anger and sloth', the seven deadly sins. These are man's most dangerous ailments. If they infect 'our souls' they 'defile' us, according to Jesus.[34] *Koinos* (unclean) is the Greek word for this, and is the opposite to *hagios* (holy), the latter describing those that are acceptable to God, the former, by contrast, those that are unacceptable to him. So the Church describes these sins as 'deadly', a grim description but one confirmed by Scripture and accepted by our Prayer Book. Jesus spoke of those who might 'die in their sins',[35] and the B.C.P. declares that God does not desire 'the death of a sinner'.[36] God has made us in such a way that we may rise to the height of eternal fellowship with him, be filled with his Holy Spirit, and become a Saint, or we may descend to the ultimate depth of defilement, finally to pass out of existence when the time comes for all evil to be destroyed.[37]

Do we not all need these 'wholesome medicines' of which this Collect speaks? St Luke 'delivered', or prescribed, them in his 'doctrine' in the Gospel that he was 'called' by God to write. They are now, however, the precious property of the Church, which is God's instrument in dispensing them. The Church in Scripture is often likened to a building.[38] This is seen as a place of worship only, but it could very properly be thought of as a place of healing, a hospital rather than a church. When we come to worship, we always come, even as the sick came to Jesus, conscious of our need for healing. We come seeking the 'wholesome medicines' that alone can 'heal all the diseases of our souls'. It is this innermost healing that St Luke's Gospel so wisely stresses.[39] It is what really matters for us all. It makes us not just healthy, but whole or holy, acceptable to God.

SAINT SIMON AND SAINT JUDE, APOSTLES
October 28th

Almighty God, who has built thy Church upon the foundation of the Apostles and Prophets, Jesus Christ himself being the head corner-stone; Grant us so to be joined together in unity of spirit by their doctrine, that we may be made an holy temple acceptable unto thee; through the same Jesus Christ our Lord. Amen

---

This is another Collect by Cranmer. The Sarum Collect, however, was, we may suppose, rejected more for being obscure in its meaning than for being objectionable in its theology. The petition prayed, 'Grant us, while we grow, to celebrate their eternal glory, (the two Apostles having been mentioned by name in the invocation) and also, while we celebrate, to grow'. Few can deny that Cranmer's new Collect is at least clearer in its meaning! However, it is surely most regrettable that neither of the Apostles we are remembering is now mentioned by name, as they very properly had been in the mediaeval Collect.

Cranmer also changed the theme for his Collect making it now one of Christian unity. His reason for doing this is uncertain. His choice of words is clearly inspired by Ephesians,[1] but perhaps we can also say that in choosing this theme Cranmer was responding in a general way to both the Epistle and Gospel for the day. St Jude's Epistle starts by urging his readers 'to contend for the faith which was once for all delivered to the Saints' and which was threatened by 'ungodly persons who were . . . denying our only Master and Lord, Jesus Christ',[2] and the Gospel starts with our Lord's command to us to 'love one another'.[3] However, such reasoning is hardly convincing and the theme of Christian unity does seem here to have been imposed on this Festival for Cranmer's own reasons. Perhaps this looks all the more likely when one notices that the Ephesians passage on which this Collect is so clearly based is in fact the set Epistle for St Thomas's Day. The probability is, therefore, that the theme of Christian unity was of such special concern to Cranmer that he was determined to make it the theme of one of his new Saints' Day Collects, and that he simply chose this one. That his vision, however, of Christian unity was not at all the same as ours today is another matter, which we must consider later. In 1662 Bishop Cosin made one alteration to Cranmer's Collect, changing 'thy congregation' to 'thy Church'. It is not likely that more can be made of this than to suggest it is possibly a case of the Catholic-minded Bishop upgrading the language of the more Protestant-minded Archbishop.

The reason why St Simon and St Jude have a united Festival is because they were martyred together in Persia. They go naturally together, however, for another reason. In all the lists of the Twelve they fill the last two places before Judas Iscariot; in the Lucan lists St Simon, as in the title for this Festival, precedes St Jude, whereas in the lists in St Matthew and St Mark the order is reversed. Both Saints, however, fade away from our view after Pentecost, that is if the Apostle Jude is not the author of the Epistle of St Jude.

Until comparatively recently the Church believed that he was, but in this it is now generally accepted that it was mistaken. The Epistle writer describes himself as 'the brother of James',[4] whereas the Apostle is described by St Luke as 'the son of James'.[5] Who these Jameses were is not known. There are several Jameses in the New Testament but none fits the role of either St Jude's father or brother, even though he would have been someone well known to the early Church. Then there is the question of by what name he was generally known in the Church. In both St Matthew's and St Mark's list of the Twelve his name is given as Thaddaeus, not Jude or Judas (with one ancient manuscript giving his name as Lebbaeus),[6] but this most probably was to distinguish him clearly from the traitor. The fact that he shared the traitor's name was, we know, a matter of concern, as one would expect, for in St John's Gospel, we read 'Judas (not Iscariot) said to him, "Lord how is it that you will manifest yourself to us, and not to the world?"'[7]

This question put by him to Jesus is the only time we hear of St Jude (we will continue to call him that), beyond his name appearing in the lists of the Twelve. However, it is surely an important one, and introduces the passage in which Jesus describes the effect that the Holy Spirit will have on his disciples' lives. We should, therefore, be particularly grateful to St Jude for asking it, for in it he surely speaks for all of us who converse with Jesus in the secret places of our hearts. It would seem, consequently, somewhat unfair that St Jude came later to be entitled 'the Obscure'! Rather he is one for whom we may all feel a particular respect and affection. This indeed is as it has turned out. To the faithful down the ages St Jude has enjoyed an extraordinary popularity as the Patron Saint of troubled spirits, hopeless cases and lost causes. The efficacy of prayer to him for help in all manner of desperate circumstances is regularly testified to with thanksgiving, even in the personal columns of The Times! Such testimony moves us, then, to pay tribute to him as one that Jesus specially loved and used. We have noticed the strange wording of the mediaeval Collect, but surely it was absolutely right to lay special emphasis, as was done there, on the 'eternal glory' that St Jude, with St Simon, now enjoys.

St Simon is also described differently by St Luke and the other two synoptic evangelists. In the two Lucan lists of the Twelve, he is called 'the Zealot', and in the other two lists 'the Cananaean'.[8] It may be, however, that these two descriptions mean the same thing. 'Cananaean' is the Greek transliteration of the Aramaic word that means a 'zealous man', and that may be all that is meant by the title 'the Zealot'. However, the Zealots was the title given to a party of militant Jews who sought to incite rebellion against the Romans, and Josephus stresses that they played a vital, and in the event disastrous, role in the catastrophic uprising in the 60s, as a result of which Jerusalem was totally destroyed in 70. They could, however, have been a power in the land as early as the time of Jesus, and so St Simon a member of them. This is now generally thought to be the truth of the matter, and if so, how clearly it shows that the Twelve were made up of the widest range of characters. St Matthew was a quisling tax-collector, and St Simon an ardent nationalist committed to terrorist violence! Yet both were called by Jesus to be his disciples, and so would have found reconciliation and a common cause in his service. In these days of violence in the social and political life of so many countries, not least our own United Kingdom, is this not an important witness?

Tradition, as we have said, links St Simon with St Jude as evangelists in Persia, where they were martyred together. In liturgical art St Simon is depicted with a broad curved sword as his emblem, the kind with which the heathen priests are said to have killed him. St Jude's emblem is a club, the instrument used for his execution. October 28 is not, however, the day of their martyrdom, which is unknown, but the day on which their relics were translated to St Peter's in Rome.

Cranmer's Collect prays for Christian unity, basing its appeal to God on the scriptural teaching that he laid sure foundations for unity when the Church began. These foundations were 'the Apostles and Prophets', 'Jesus

Christ himself being the head cornerstone'. The wording is taken, as we have said, from Ephesians (though 'head' has been substituted for 'chief'), and as the prayer continues other aspects of that passage are included, in particular that we may become 'joined together' to create 'an holy temple' acceptable to God.[9]

Nonetheless, despite the similarity there is one real difference. The Collect speaks of 'their doctrine' being the crucial element in the 'unity of spirit' with which we are 'joined together'. In Ephesians this concept is not only not found, but seems positively to be denied. The unity mentioned there is not one dependent on the keeping of 'commandments and ordinances', but rather it is conceived of as an unity centred essentially upon the Cross, and dependent on a shared faith in and experience of what God in Christ has done there for all mankind. The choice of the word 'doctrine', therefore, seems to put the Collect at variance with the Ephesians' passage, on which it is otherwise so clearly based.[10]   However, what most likely are being inadvertently revealed here are the particular aspirations of Cranmer regarding Christian unity. These, frankly, are not what most today would consider descriptive of Christian unity, any more than they are of the vision of it in Ephesians. There was very definitely no thought, for instance, in Cranmer's mind of reunion with Rome, nor even of any desire for unity with the other emerging national Churches of northern Europe with which the Church of England was on friendly terms. On the contrary, a basic tenet of the Reformation was that each country was free to establish in its own land the brand of Christianity of its own choice; cuios *regio, huios religio,* was the catch-phrase from the Peace of Augsburg (1555) that enshrined this as the accepted principle at that time.   What Cranmer sought, therefore, was national Christian uniformity for our country. His Prayer Book of 1549 was established in law by an Act of Uniformity, as was its revision in 1552. In his Litany, we notice, he only prayed that God would give 'to all nations unity, peace and concord', and in his two early Prayer

Books there were no prayers for Christian unity as such, if we except this one.

Following the attempt by Queen Mary to re-establish the authority of Rome, in which time Cranmer was so pitilessly martyred, the Elizabethan Settlement of 1559 was established by a third Act of Uniformity. Thereafter despite Cromwell's Puritan reign and the continuing presence of recusants and dissidents, not to mention the establishment of Presbyterianism in Scotland, the firm hold of Catholicism in Ireland and the triumph of Methodism in Wales and our own industrial cities, Cranmer's basic aspirations, as revealed in this Collect, quickly took root in England and became the established aim of our country's spiritual life throughout the next 300 years. The 1662 B.C.P., we have to admit, displays no more interest in Church unity than its predecessors. Its new prayer 'for all sorts and conditions of men' certainly prays 'for the good estate of the Catholic Church', but it seeks only that 'all who profess and call themselves Christians hold the faith in unity...peace...and righteousness', a wholly indidividualistic vision of Church unity. There is no echo here of the desire that is so evident in our Lord's prayer in the garden for the organic unity of the Church, and that has stamped itself upon the conscience of all Churches today.

The fact is that it was not until the missionary societies, following the imperial flag in the 19th century, began to lay the foundations of the present worldwide Anglican Communion that a more outward-looking attitude began to spread throughout the Church of England. Indeed it was our 19th century missionaries' providential function to sow the seeds that were to grow not only into the Anglican Communion, but also into the world-wide ecumenical movement. Today's modern, broader view of Christian unity has now quite overlaid the earlier shallower vision of national uniformity that was Cranmer's, and that continued for so long to inspire and satisfy our country and our Church.

We may be tempted, consequently, to consider such a narrow-minded view of Christian unity very reprehensible. We must not, however, judge Cranmer and his vision unfairly. It is hard today to visualise those extraordinary times. All was being made new. Our country was experiencing a new birth both politically and spiritually as the old mediaeval world began to pass away. It was, however, a time of danger as well as opportunity, as Cranmer's own martyrdom well illustrates. Though he was not destined to see it, we know that our country eventually emerged from it young, strong and united in Queen Elizabeth's long and successful reign, and we can judge now that Cranmer's contribution to this fresh flowering of our nation and its Church was of seminal importance. How greatly he contributed to the arrival of a land renewed, independent and Christian, at one with its past yet open to its future, ruled by a Christian monarch supported by a loyal, but independent-minded, Church and Parliament, with the worship of its people conducted in their own language, using throughout the land services written in inspired liturgical prose and set out in a single unifying Book of Common Prayer, such as did emerge in the halcyon years of Good Queen Bess! Further, that this legacy persisted for so long to the political and spiritual benefit of our country should be a matter of real thanksgiving, however readily we may recognise that a new era with new challenges has arrived.

The generally accepted vision of Christian unity has moved on dramatically since Cranmer's time owing to the ecumenical movement that has been such a distinctive feature of Church history in this century. It grew, as we have said, out of the missionary activity that emerged so splendidly in the last, and inspired so many heroic men and women, genuine Saints who lived and died in the highest traditions of the 'Apostles and Prophets' of the early Church. They quickly, perceived, however, how seriously the differing brands of Christianity being propagated at their adjoining mission stations undermined their converts' trust in 'the one Lord, one faith, one baptism, one God and Father of us all,'[11] that all proclaimed.

We know from the New Testament that in fact disunity has troubled the Church from its earliest times. 'I appeal to you, brethren, that you all agree,' wrote St Paul to the Corinthians. Some were saying, 'I belong to Paul...or to Apollos..or to Cephas..or to Christ'. 'Is Christ divided?' [12] was his sad and angry rebuke to them. The 19th century missionaries were only experiencing the same misery and frustration that so many other 'apostles and prophets' have felt before them, but in their case the sinfulness of Christian disunity so penetrated the hearts and minds of the several Churches involved that they all determined to do something definite about it. Suddenly it was as if the ears of the Churches were being opened afresh to 'hear the Spirit speaking to them.'[13] What they heard was no new word, but rather the old word that Jesus had spoken in the garden before his Crucifixion; 'that they may all be one, even as thou art in me and I in thee...so that the world may believe that thou has sent me.'[14] The truth these words imply, however, was suddenly being heard by all the Churches as something new and imperative, and that truth is this, that, if there is disunity in the Church, there is no clear Word and no certain Sacraments. 'Is Christ divided?' Of course not, but what if we appear to 'divide' him through our broken fellowship? Can someone really be 'baptised into Christ'[15] in a divided Church? And what of its message? In a divided Church is not 'the bugle' sure to give an 'uncertain sound'?[16] It was being perceived afresh that Christian unity was an essential element of the Christian Gospel, and however worthy the work of those saintly missionaries may have been, it was not to be believed that it was God's will to establish in unsown fields a divided Church.

Starting from the Edinburgh Conference in 1910, the ecumenical movement quickly began to excite and, in its earliest years, to involve, all the Churches in its vision and activities. However, disappointments soon arose. The two World Wars materially slowed its progress. Despite early interest, especially from influential figures like Cardinal Mercier, the Roman Catholic Church in 1928 officially withdrew from its fellowship. The later Cold War years also prevented active co-operation from the Orthodox Churches within the Soviet Empire. Nonetheless, in 1948 the World Council of Churches was formed, and the ecumenical movement has subsequently succeeded in affecting the life of all the Churches at all levels. Apart from some obvious exceptions, that stand out because they are so different from what is now generally accepted, members of other Churches are seen as Christian friends and colleagues, and certainly not any longer as religious enemies. How different the climate today is from the times of Cranmer! We do not have Christian unity yet. Indeed, fresh splits are appearing within all Churches, rather than between the Churches, caused by the new opposition of liberals to traditionalists, but, for all that, the prevasive influence of the ecumenical movement has not been halted. Its spirit, or rather its Spirit, has clearly come to stay.

Nevertheless, despite its present influence, the ecumenical movement, as now constituted, gives no indication of being equipped to deliver a genuinely united Church. We seem to be as far away from that goal as ever, and as we come to the end of this ecumenical century a feeling of impatience is growing with its limited achievements, and the hope emerging that a major advance will be made in the next. The fact that we are also entering a new millennium has, naturally, done nothing to dampen this hope. The first millennium was one of unity, the second equally one of disunity. Can the third be one of reunion, in which the Church achieves that organic unity that we know from Christ's last prayer is God's will for it?

To this question, in the context of this prayer, what may be said? Perhaps first, that the truths stated in this Collect cannot be too often repeated, too strongly believed in and too firmly confirmed in our prayers. The Church's foundations are Christ and his Apostles and Prophets. No matter how our daily lives are being changed by scientific and technological advances, and by the mixing of races and cultures in our midst, we must not seek to lay fresh foundations as we seek after Christian unity, doubting the relevance of the old. The course of Christian unity is not helped forward by religious synchronism. 'For no other foundation can anyone lay that that which is laid,' and 'let each man take care how he builds upon it.'[17] (Inter-faith respect and co-operation is another matter.) In the Collect's description of the Church's foundations, Jesus is joined by the Apostles and Prophets. The significance of this is to stress that the whole Bible must always remain essential for the Church's life. The Holy Spirit 'spake by the Prophets',[18] we believe, and so what they have said, as much as the apostolic writings in the New Testament, must be for ever reverenced as God's Word, a permanent element in the Church's foundations. It was the Apostles, however, who received from Christ his own 'authority', that was then confirmed for them on Pentecost Day.[19] So with Scripture goes Apostolic, or Episcopal, Order, and the Sacraments that depend upon it. Organic reunion in the Church can only take place if the traditional authority of Word and Order and the Sacraments is fully re-established. However, for this to happen does not mean that the Church must retrace its steps. For it reunion will be a wholly fresh experience, a positive step forward. 'All my fresh springs shall be in thee',[20] said the Psalmist with prophetic insight. Even the Church's very foundations will be appreciated and understood afresh when it takes place.

Then it would seem that one more obvious observation can be made. Nothing has frustrated the ecumenical movement more than the official coolness of the Roman Catholic Church towards it. If lasting progress is to be made this must change, but if what is by a long way the largest Church enters enthusiastically into the movement for Christian unity, all life within that movement will also change. Will not, however, a dominant friend be as intimidating as a dominant enemy once was? What changes of attitude, therefore, within all Churches would be asked of an ecumenical movement 'led' by an ecumenically-minded Roman Catholic Church! Are such thoughts realistic? Cranmer would surely not have thought so. But if Christ wills it, and his prayer in the garden confirms that he does, 'is anything too hard for the Lord?'[21]

As things are it must be accepted that several official negotiations aimed at greater unity between Rome and other Churches, notably our own, have in recent years foundered, yet for all that there are other signs of the times that give the ecumenically-committed much encouragement. In our own country, especially in Liverpool, but in other places too, close co-operation and fellowship has been encouraged at the highest level and is now 'established'. The late Cardinal Hume, who did so much to bring the Roman Church into the ecumenical arena in our country, importantly said, 'There can be pluralism of doctrine in the Church, whereas there cannot be pluralism of faith.'[22] In Europe new centres of prayer and pilgrimage, like Taize and Medjugorje, that defy party labels, are drawing millions from all denominations, so many of whom are young. Further, saintly and heroic people, like Mother Teresa of Calcutta, Edith Stein and Padre Pio, have also emerged, whose lives and deaths have influenced Christians every-where, and whose example has been profoundly ecumenical. Such places and people belong to all Christians.

Then, again, and perhaps more important still, the growth areas for all the Churches, and particularly the Roman Catholic Church, are outside Europe. These new Christians are not the heirs of the wars and persecutions that are such a tragic aspect of our European Church history in the second millennium and still linger so destructively in our memories. As Christians in the Cameroons recently said to the Pope, 'We know we are divided from other Christians, but we don't know why.'[23] The indigestible doctrine of Papal Infallibility remains, but the present Pope despite his authoritarianism within his own Church, has made himself known and available to Christians outside his own Church in a quite unprecedented way. Because of his travels and remarkable charisma, he is clearly recognised, perhaps unconsciously in the case of many Christians, but very consciously by non-Christians, as the pre-eminent Christian leader in the world. What he portrays to them, moreover, is a loving Petrine figure, and not at all a strange infallible man!

If, therefore, there is officially an ecumenical chill in the air just now, could this be like the chill of dawn before the coming of the warmth and light of new day? Could such people and events be setting the stage for that longed-for major advance towards organic reunion in the Church, God being our helper. Although this prayer for Christian unity was strangely linked with the memory of St Simon and St Jude, we must not, as we use it today, think of it as referring to a lost cause—most certainly not.

In this Collect the hope of Christian unity is summed up, as it is in Ephesians, in a vision of a holy temple filled with worshippers. In Revelation, however, this Pauline vision is taken a stage further and, as we consider this devotional Collect, let us follow the scriptural analogy to its end. The Seer sees the 'new Jerusalem' that God is preparing for us as being in its entirety a place of worship. There will be no need there for a temple constructed only for worship, for the spirit of worship will pervade the whole life of the city. 'I saw no temple there, for the Lord God Almighty and the Lamb are its temple,' he says.[24] The author of Hebrews confirms this greater vision. He too speaks of 'a city of the living God' that awaits us at the end of the age in which 'innumerable angels' live with 'the spirits of just men made perfect', and where 'Jesus, the mediator' of 'the new covenant in his blood' reigns supreme.[25] We recognise this place as 'the city' foreseen four millennia earlier by the Psalmist 'that is at unity in itself',[26] and also as the place that Jesus prayed for in the garden, where all will be 'one', even as the Father and he are 'one', and where we may live together as 'one in them'.[27]

This Collect, which prays for Christian unity, commemorates two whom, we may believe, know now the fullness of the peace and unity, the joy and power, of that 'city without a temple'. Their intercession, we may also believe, is helping us today, as we long after not only experiencing the life of that eternal place of perfect unity, but also experiencing the life of organic reunion in the Church in time. They were among its founders, and would have heard those words of Jesus in the garden that the Spirit in our time is so clearly emphasising to the Churches. We may be sure that they, as we do, long to see the Churches 'joined together' in that 'unity of spirit' that is truly 'acceptable to God', for which we are praying here.

This Collect, therefore, can be seen to be three-dimensional. It can be accepted in its original context as a reformation prayer; it can be used to help us as we search for Christian unity in our very different times from those of Cranmer; we can also stretch it to embrace the widest hopes and the ultimate promises revealed in Scripture of what unity in God will mean when his Kingdom comes on earth as it is in heaven. We may well feel impatient with those who continue to live, so it seems, as if nothing has changed since Cranmer's time, and that God is not demanding now that Christian people everywhere seek after a much fuller kind of Christian unity than was appropriate in times past. Yet we must also take care not to be impatient with each other as we, who have heard his new Word to the Churches, begin in earnest to reach out to each other in hope and love. The Christian unity to which we are being called is no easy vocation. Within it, as St Paul perceived so long ago, is, since it is an essential element of the Gospel, the presence of the Cross.[28] This unity is to be 'in him', who alone has the power to bring all 'hostility to an end' and 'to reconcile us all to God in one Body through the Cross'.[29] Christian unity, when it comes, will be for the Church a resurrection experience, following what has been a passion experience, as the parts of the Body of Christ come together again to live 'a newness of life'.[30]

This unity that we believe in and hope for, because of Christ's prayer, is something that will surely happen. It may take another millennium to materialise. Or it may come soon. God grant that it does. Its purpose, however, is to enable an even greater hope, of which Scripture also speaks, to become a reality, 'a new heaven and a new earth in which righteousness dwells',[31] a 'Kingdom on earth as it is in heaven'. He 'who has made of one blood all nations of men',[32] and who sent his Son to 'reconcile the whole world to himself'[33] will not be satisfied with Christian unity only. Beyond it lies the unity of all mankind in God, described by St Paul like this; 'when all things are subjected to him, then the Son himself will also be subjected to him who put all things under him, that God may be everything to everyone'.[34] A reunited Church is to be the means to this truly blessed and promised end.

Meanwhile, 'we must run with patience' the life that lies ahead for all the Churches, 'looking to Jesus', who is 'the author and finisher' of all our ecumenical hopes,[35] and wise words from St Jude's Epistle make a particularly appropriate ending to our consideration of them. 'You, beloved, build yourselves up on your holy faith; pray in the Holy Spirit; keep yourselves in the love of God; and wait for the mercy of our Lord Jesus Christ unto eternal life.'[36]

ALL SAINTS' DAY
November 1st

O Almighty God, who hast knit together thine elect in one communion and fellowship, in the mystical body of thy Son Christ our Lord; Grant us grace so to follow thy blessed Saints in all virtuous and godly living, that we may come to those unspeakable joys, which thou has prepared for them that unfeignedly love thee; through Jesus Christ our Lord. Amen.

The Red-letter Festivals of the Saints end with this traditional celebration of all the Saints, known and unknown to the Church on earth, but who are God's 'elect' in heaven. This Festival has had a strange history. First it was celebrated on the first Sunday after Pentecost, the day that later became Trinity Sunday. Then it was given its own day on May 13, but this was changed by Pope Gregory III (731-741) to November 1, when he dedicated a Chapel in St Peter's to 'All the Saints'. This date is kept in the B.C.P., but it was given no Proper Preface or Octave until the revision of 1928. Then, however, the following day, November 2, was designated 'All Souls' Day', on which we are to remember all the departed, and also the last day of the Octave, November 8, was designated a Festival Day in memory of the 'Saints, Martyrs and Doctors of the Church of England'.

The Collect is by Cranmer, composed in 1549. The Sarum Collect emphasised the intercessionary ministry of the Saints, and the traditional aversion of the Reformers to acknowledging this ministry made it unacceptable.

The invocation includes the attractive phrase 'knit together'. It is found twice in Colossians, but in neither place is it used in quite the way it is here. Here it is used to describe our unity in Christ within his mystical Body, whereas there St Paul has first in mind the spiritual development of his readers[1], and then their spiritual safety amid the many temptations that surrounded them.[2] It comes, however, again in Ephesians, where it does reflect the theme of unity stressed in this Collect, for through a 'knitting together' we are all 'to grow up in every way...into Christ'[3]. The Greek word *sunbibazein*, translated in the R.S.V. 'knit together', does not, of course, have anything to do with knitting! It means simply 'to bring together', but in a particularly close way; in the Ephesians passage in the A.V. it is translated 'compacted'. This close bonding together, however, is just what 'knitting' does, so it is an excellent translation. The 'needles' that create this mystical 'knitting together' are in St Paul's teaching 'love'. 'We are knit together in love'[4] "The whole body ... knit together ... upbuilds itself in love'.[5] What this prayer is stressing is the 'unfeigned love' of the Saints, and its chief concern is that our 'communion and fellowship' may equally be based on love.

Linked, however, to this attractive phrase 'knit together' is that emotive word 'elect'. The concept of divine election, linked as it is with that of predestination, has fuelled the fiercest debates among the greatest of theologians, and it is an issue that was particularly prominent at the Reformation. In particular it was central to Calvin's theology in his conflict both with Rome and with other Reformers. Who are the 'elect'? It is a compelling question, to which all too many false answers have been given. Let us, therefore, remind ourselves of the Bible's teaching on this matter. How does it perceive it?

The main truth to recognise is that 'the elect' in the Bible are thought of corporately, not individualistically. This Collect correctly portrays this insight. It is 'the people of God', conceived of as a whole, that are 'the elect'.

'The Lord your God has chosen you to be a people for his own possession',[6] says Moses. However so closely 'knit together' is this people of God in the Old Testament that they are given and usually conceived of under the single personal name of Israel.

Then, secondly, the Bible makes it plain that this election of Israel, God's chosen people, is for a purpose that involves the good of all the peoples he has created and not just that of Israel. There is no element of favouritism in the biblical doctrine of election. God 'elected' Israel to act for him as priests and teachers and witnesses to all mankind, so that 'in the fullness of time ... from the rising of the sun and from the west' all would come to know that 'there is no other God besides [him]'.[7] This, however, was a purpose that Israel perversely misunderstood, and a destiny to which they tragically refused to respond.

In the story of Israel, certainly, we hear of individuals whom God chose to guide his elected people, the patriarchs, kings, priests, prophets and scribes that make up the heroes of the Old Testament. Yet the concept of divine election in the Old Testament remains basically corporate, despite the indispensable part so many individuals play within it. To this, however, there is one vitally important exception. There is one instance in which the biblical understanding of the phrase 'the elect of God' does centre unequivocally on an individual, and that is the person of the promised Messiah,[8] which brings us to the New Testament and its distinctive concept of 'the elect'.

'When the time was fully come, God sent forth his Son', the truly Elect of God. It was to be through him, Israel's Messiah, that 'the elect' would at last understand and finally fulfil their purpose, which was that all mankind 'might receive adoption as sons', and, being filled with God's Spirit, cry out to him, 'Abba, Father'.[9] 'Thine elect' in this Collect, therefore, refers to all who have received this 'adoption' and now share in the corporate life of the 'elect', which is one with the eternal life of the Elect.

They are God's 'elect' because they are incorporated into 'the mystical body of his Son, Christ our Lord'. The New Testament understanding of election, emphasised here, remains, therefore, essentially corporate. This corporate blessing, however, is something God wishes for all, not just a few as the phrase 'the elect' may unfortunately suggest. And that all finally do fulfil God's wish and become 'elect' is this prayer's petition.

How wonderful , though mysterious, this great truth of divine election is! In Romans 9-11, St Paul teaches us the true meaning and purpose of divine election, and ends appropriately by exclaiming, 'O the depth of the riches and wisdom and knowledge of God. How unsearchable are his judgements and how inscrutable his ways!...For from him and through him and to him are all things.'[10] One consequence, however, of our election by God being essentially a spiritual incorporation into the Elect is that Christ becomes for us, as Israel became for the Jews, a corporate being as well as a single person. The new Israel, the Church, is Christ, his Body. So we are all 'baptised into Christ',[11] and we are all to live our lives 'in Christ'.[12] To the Corinthians Paul tells of the extraordinary consequences of this truth. 'From now on', he says, 'even though we once regarded Christ from an [individualistic] human point of view, we regard him thus no longer. Therefore, if anyone is in Christ he is a new creation [or 'new creature']; the old [humanity] has passed away, behold the new [humanity in Christ] has come'.[13]

Thirdly, therefore, we need to perceive, that the biblical understanding of divine election is positive, loving and hopeful. It is not threatening. It is all too often made to appear so, but when it is, it is based on a theological error. To press this point, let us consider the saying of Jesus that is almost invariably quoted when this emotive subject is brought up, 'many are called, but few are chosen'[14]. The 'many' here means, as it does in other sayings of Jesus,[15] 'everyone', for 'God desires all men to be saved and to come to the knowledge of the truth'.[16] 'All', therefore, are called. However we also know that it is central to our faith that all are sinners, children of disobedience who are unworthy of the God who is our Father. 'All men..are under the power of sin.' [17] So who are 'the few'? The truth of the matter is that just as the 'many' swells into 'all', so the eye of faith recognises that the 'few' shrinks into 'one', the Elect of God, who in the end was deserted even by his chosen disciples and left 'alone'. However, he was not, of course, alone, for the Father was with him. [18] Soon, having been raised to life again by the Father's power, his disciples were once more gathered around him in the Upper Room. There both their calling and their election were confirmed and renewed, but now it was a calling and election that was only meaningful 'in him'; their lives were to be ever linked with his. The New Testament, and then the history of the Church, continues the story. Through them, and others after them, empowered by God's Spirit, the 'elect' of God increase, becoming 'knit together' 'in the mystical body' of the Elect to form 'one communion and fellowship', into which we know by faith and hope that all, not merely 'many', are called. Then by virtue of our baptism into Christ and the gift of the Holy Spirit we know that we have been 'chosen' to live with the him and the Father and 'the blessed Saints' both now and for ever.

The Collect's petition prays that we may have 'grace' to 'follow' the Saints 'in all virtuous and godly living'. In the prayer for the Church in the Holy Communion Service we pray in similar vein that we may 'follow (the) good examples' of all God's 'servants departed this life in (his) faith and fear'. The word 'follow', however, is one we particularly associate with the basic Christian call to 'follow' Jesus. 'Follow me' was the command so frequently on Jesus's lips. [19] This 'following' of the Saints, therefore, must be seen as part of our 'following' of Jesus, something that only has value if it inspires us to that greater end. St Paul sums up this point admirably in his admonition to the Corinthians: 'Be followers of me, as I am of Christ'.[20]

The greatest service, therefore, that the Saints do us is that they inspire us to follow Jesus. They are those who by their lives, and also by their deaths, proclaim 'Christ as Lord', and in so doing have become our 'servants' for Jesus's sake.[21] This is, of course, what they most desire should happen, and therefore in our admiration of them we must not make more of them than they would wish. Equally for us to ignore their shining examples and to fail to recognise the splendour of their lives would be a serious error. We are to be followers 'of those who through faith and patience inherit the promises', says the author of Hebrews.[22] There is a balance, therefore, to be kept here between not allowing our admiration of the Saints to dim our devotion to Jesus, and our devotion of him not causing us to ignore the inspiring example of his greatest disciples. Our spiritual lives are immeasurably strengthened if this balance is properly kept, and keeping these Saints' Days faithfully, as the Church requires, greatly assists us to do so.

The Collect, as we have said, especially stresses their 'virtuous and godly living', and these adjectives too give balancing emphases. 'Virtuous' speaks to us of morality and behaviour. The word reminds us of their courage, their generosity, their simplicity, their chastity, their discipline. The memorable passage with which St Paul ends his letter to the Philippians springs to mind. 'Finally, brethren, whatever is true, whatever is honourable, whatever is just, whatever is pure, whatever is lovely, whatever is gracious, if there is any excellence, if there is anything worthy of praise, think about these things'.[23] These virtues characterise the lives of the Saints, and it is in just these things that we are 'to follow (them) in all virtuous...living'.

The word 'godly', however, yields a different picture. It speaks of their faith and hope, their prayers, their total devotion to God and their passionate love of Jesus. It was especially for similar qualities that the Saints of the

Old Covenant 'received divine approval'. Such was their faith that they did nothing without God's guidance and, like Abraham, they were always ready to move at his command, even when they did not know where they were going.[24] As Isaiah prophesied, they heard his voice saying to them, 'This is the way, walk in it'.[25] Then sometimes they would see him, as it were, 'face to face',[26] as Moses did, or as an old man once said, when asked what he did while staying so long in the Church, "I just look at him and he just looks at me". For the 'blessed Saints' Jesus and the Father, as promised, through the Holy Spirit 'made their home with them'.[27] Now they are enjoying the fullest reality of that promise in eternity, and are 'at home'[28] with God and with 'all the company of heaven'.[29]

Finally, the Collect, echoing that promise of Jesus, ends by speaking of what God 'has prepared for them that unfeignedly love him'. Love of such a kind describes what we believe is most true of the Saints and what most characterises their 'virtuous and godly' lives. They loved God 'unfeignedly', and, as the Collect goes on to stress, the reward for an unfeigned love of God is 'joy'. This little word, indeed, sums up so simply what we believe to be the character of their lives in heaven. Perhaps 'blessed' is the word more frequently used in Scripture to describe the nature of their lives, and this Collect speaks of 'thy blessed Saints'. It also starts each of the Beatitudes, which appropriately are set as the Gospel for this Festival, but let us also notice that, in Christ's summing up in the last Beatitude, he assures us that in heaven the 'blessed' 'rejoice and are exceedingly glad', especially when their passionate love of Jesus has meant for them as individuals the experience of a grim and painful passion.[30] The Greek for 'blessed', *makarios*, ordinarily means 'happy', but in Scripture it always refers to the happiness that only God can give and, therefore, such as 'no one can take from us'.[31] 'What more [then] can we say?' [32] The 'joys' of the Saints in heaven are called here 'unspeakable', or perhaps, as we would say now, indescribable. To try to say too much about them, therefore, is clearly foolish. After all, did not St Paul say, quoting Isaiah, 'No eye has seen, nor ear heard, nor the heart of man conceived, what God has prepared for those who love him'?[33] When, however, Jesus was instructing his Apostles about the Kingdom of heaven, and about who was greatest there, he took to himself a child to press home his teaching.[34] So, in this context, perhaps we can do no better than to remind ourselves of the Sunday School definition of joy: 'J is for Jesus, Y is for you, with nothing in between'. Maybe such childish teaching is as near as we can get in this matter to describing the indescribable.

EPILOGUE

Among the majestic passages with which St Paul's Epistles are studded, are there any finer, or more amazing, than the prayer with which he ends his opening chapters in Ephesians? Its climax is that 'we may have power to comprehend with all the Saints what is the breadth and length and height and depth, and to know the love of Christ that surpasses knowledge, that [we] may be filled with all the fullness of God'.[1] To postulate such an end for any human life is, we may surely say, totally ridiculous, even blasphemous, were it not for what God himself has done for us in Christ. For those, however, who are 'in Christ' nothing, not even such a fulfilment of their lives, is impossible.[2] For them every barrier to their eternal union with the all-holy and almighty God is removed. Therefore, for these Saints that we have been considering, and those who have followed them, we may believe that St Paul's words are no exaggeration, but are simply a truthful description of their state.[3]

How wonderful for them! But are we not all called to be Saints? Indeed we are! This knowledge of the 'love of Christ that surpasses knowledge', with all its ultimate consequences, is for all. When St Paul wrote those remarkable words just quoted, he did not have in mind those whom we think of now when we read them, the Saints in heaven, such as these that we have been studying. No, he had rather the likes of you and me, the ordinary baptised Christian![4] We are all called 'he assures us' to share in the Saints' comprehension of 'the truth as it is in Jesus'[5] in all its 'breadth and length and height and depth'. This truth, of course, is not to do with 'the things that all perish as they are used',[6] however valuable that kind of truth may be to us here. This truth embraces the things of heaven, the things that are more important still, the things that 'abide',[7] and surpasses all knowledge of a merely earthly kind. For this reason, paradoxically, the highly educated may find this 'comprehension of the Saints' too hard to grasp, whereas little children may find it easy.[8]

All the Prayer Book Collects emphasise this 'truth as it is in Jesus', which the Saints now fully 'comprehend'. This is their great value to us, and this naturally is particularly true of the Saints' Day Collects. As we pray them, therefore, in spite of the Reformers' unfortunate prejudices to the contrary, they do inevitably bring us into a spiritual fellowship with them. Although they certainly encourage us to find in the Saints examples to follow, they also show us that they are our spiritual friends, who are sure to be concerned to help us on our way. The Collects certainly avoid asking for the prayers of the Saints, but they nonetheless assure us by implication that they do pray for us constantly. How can it be otherwise for those who are so completely 'in Christ', who 'ever lives to make intercession for us'?[9] So we may be certain that the Saints in heaven do pray for us, as well as we with them, and this conviction adds a rich extra devotional dimension to our faith and spiritual lives. To this we can add that we may believe that our relationship with them is an ingredient in their happiness. Speaking of the relationship of the Old Testament's heroes and heroines with Christians, we are told that 'apart from us they should not be made perfect'.[10] Do not such words also apply to our relationship with the New Testament's heroes and heroines, for may we not believe that the attainment of our perfection will add greatly to the joy of theirs?

We should, therefore, seek to deepen our fellowship with the Saints in every proper way and, looking up to them, to understand their secret. 'Who are these clothed in white robes, and whence have they come?' The angel gives us the answer. 'These are they who have come out of great tribulation. They have washed their robes in the blood of the Lamb'.[11] 'The comprehension of the Saints', therefore is essentially the understanding of what it means to be 'crucified with Christ'.[12] They now enjoy the risen life with Christ, because they first died to self for love of Christ.[13] St Paul looked forward to his death 'with eager expectation and hope'[14] because, he said, he had already shared in Christ's passion 'becoming like him in his death'.[15] This is the path all the Saints have trod in their different ways, and we can tread it too. 'For if we have been united with him in a death like his, we shall certainly be united with him in a resurrection like his'.[16]

St Paul also said, so tantalisingly, 'I bear in my body the marks of the Lord Jesus'.[17] To what did he refer? Were they the scars from his frequent beatings, and the terrible ordeal of being stoned? Or were they the mysterious stigmata that some of the greatest Saints have experienced? Or had he in mind something of a purely spiritual nature? Certainly we know that such would have been what he valued most of all. 'If I deliver my body to be burned and have not love, I gain nothing', he said,[18] and when he spoke about us needing to be 'crucified with Christ' he clearly did not have in mind physical crucifixion for everyone. This, certainly, was the terrible fate of some, including some of those whom we have remembered in this commentary; they could say to their Lord, as proof of their discipleship, 'Behold my hands and my feet'.[19] So many others down the centuries have also borne in their bodies the physical marks of their discipleship. But, despite the admiration we must feel for their physical courage, it is the spiritual qualities of the Saints that mark them out most clearly from other men and women, and make them so special. It is above all their 'love, joy, peace, patience, kindness, goodness, faithfulness, gentleness and self-control'[20] that mark them so distinctively as belonging to Jesus. These, however, are the marks that we can all share with them 'because he has given us [too] of his Spirit'.[21] These are the fruits that characterise that which grows on the branches of 'the true vine',[22] into which by Baptism we have been grafted. As it was for St Paul, and all the Saints, it is the mystery of 'Christ in us' that gives us 'the hope of glory'.

We are told in Acts that the Apostles were 'uneducated common men', but that the educated, important men who interviewed them 'wondered at their boldness', and that 'they recognised that they had been with Jesus'.[23]

The lives of the Saints have often been essentially ordinary and their circumstances humble. What has made their lives so different to those of others has simply been the nature of their relationship with Jesus. 'They have been with Jesus', and it has shown. This, however, has meant much more than just that they have lived properly; it has meant that they have been truly alive, 'alive to God in Christ Jesus', is how St Paul puts it.[24] The fact of the matter is that Christian sanctity is not what we do for Jesus, but what Jesus does for and in and through us.

From the lives of the Saints we have been remembering in these Collects, none of us need feel that our lives are so ordinary as to disqualify us for a place in their company. Essentially they were not extraordinary people, however extraordinary they may have become. They were 'common men' in the sense of ordinary people, brought up to live ordinary lives, doing ordinary jobs. The greatest was a housewife. Their leader was a fisherman. The greatest missionary among them earned his living as a tentmaker. Jesus himself was a carpenter. Nor need any one feel their past too reprehensible, for one was a collaborator and another a terrorist. We know, too, of their foolishness, their self-seeking, their cowardice, and general sinfulness, for all of it has been faithfully recorded in Scripture 'for our admonition'. Jesus, we know, warns us against the folly of 'casting our pearls before swine',[25] yet is not that exactly what God has always done, and through Christ and the Gospel are we not all beneficiaries of this 'divine foolishness'? God so loves us all that he gave his Son, lest we perish.[26] Through him he has poured out his Holy Spirit upon all who put their trust in him. The Saints were all sinners like ourselves, people just as much in need of redemption and sanctification as we all are. And they gladly acknowledge this.[27] For them, however, through their faithful discipleship of Christ, the Gospel's final blessings are now theirs. 'They have washed their robes'; they comprehend the greatness of God's love; they have inherited eternal life; and they are 'filled with all the fullness of

God'. For this let us rejoice, and wholeheartedly give the Saints 'such honour' as they deserve. Let us also affirm our fellowship with them in our prayers. In our proper praise and thanksgiving to God for them and their blessedness in heaven we may also take a more self-conscious comfort. Their ultimate fulfilment may be ours too; and perhaps the greatest virtue of these Collects is they greatly assist us to believe this, and wholeheartedly to long for it.

Our heavenly Father, we rejoice in the blessed communion of all thy Saints, wherein thou givest us also to have a part. We remember before thee all who have departed this life in thy faith and love, and especially those most dear to us. We thank thee for our present fellowship with them, for our common hope, and for the promise of future joy.

Oh, let the cloud of witnesses, the innumerable company of those who have gone before, and now entered into rest, be to us for an example of godly life, and even now may we be refreshed with their joy, and be aided by their prayers for us; that so with patience we may run the race that yet remains before us, looking unto Jesus the author and finisher of our faith; and obtain an entrance into thy everlasting Kingdom among the glorious assembly of the Saints, and with them ever worship and adore thy glorious Name, world without end. Amen.

FOOTNOTES

INTRODUCTION

1	Luke: 15:7
2	Heb 12:1
3	Rev: 12:12
4	Mt 13:52
5	Lk 5:39
6	2 Cor 4:4
7	Heb 12:2 (AV)
8	1 Pet 1:8
9	Galatians, Ephesians, Colossians especially
10	Rev 19:16
11	Rom 8:21
12	22nd Article of Religion
13	1 Tim 2:5
14	Rom 1:7, 1 Cor 1:2, et al.
15	Rom 6:3
16	Jn 20:25
17	1 Pet 4:14
18	1 Tim 6:13
19	1 Tim 6:12
20	Te Deum
21	Heb 12:4
22	Rev 12:1
23	Eccles 44:7
24	Ps 149:9
25	Heb 7:25
26	Jn 3:30
27	Phil 3:20
28	2 Cor 4:17
29	Eph 3:18
30	Heb 12:2
31	Heb 12:24
32	Eph 4:21
18	Rom 10:15
19	Mk 1:17
20	1 Cor 12:4-6
21	1 Tim 4:5
22	1 Cor 12:11
23	1 Cor 9:16
24	Ps 105:2
25	Ps 116:10, 2 Cor 4:3
26	Lk 10:16, Mt 10: 40,41
27	Mk 3:2
28	Mt 5:13,14
29	1 Pet 2:12
30	Mt 5:16
31	Col 4:5,6
32	1 Cor 7:16
33	Eph 6:4
34	Col 3:3 et al
35	Lk 12:35
36	1 Cor 12:27 and St Teresa's Prayer
37	Is 6:8
38	Mt 28:19

SAINT THOMAS THE APOSTLE

1	John 11:16, 20:24, 21:2
2	John 20:28
3	John 20:31
4	Jn 3:16
5	Jas 1:12,13
6	Matt 4:1
7	Catechism
8	Jn 11:16
9	Jn 14:5
10	1 Cor:13
11	Marriage Service
12	Jn 20:31

ST ANDREW'S DAY

1	Jn 1:35-42
2	Mt 10:2, Mk 3:18, Lk 6:14, Acts 1:13, nb Mk 13:3
3	Mk 5:37, 9:2, 14:33
4	Jn 12:20-22
5	Mk 4:18,20
6	Jn 1:35-42
7	Rom 8:29,30
8	Jer 1:5
9	Ps 139:1-9
10	2 Cor 12:9
11	Lk 5:8
12	Ex 3:11
13	Is 6:5
14	Jer 1:6
15	Mt 8:8
16	Rom 8:28
17	Jn 1:41

SAINT STEPHEN'S DAY

1	Acts 6 and 7
2	Lk 1:28, 9:29
3	2 Chron 24:22, Acts 7:60
4	Jn 15:13
5	Heb 12:24, Gen 4:10
6	Jn 14:6
7	Eph 4:21
8	Jn 8:13-53
9	Acts 7:56, Mk 14:61, 62
10	Is 9:6
11	Mk 1:17
12	Mt 28:18
13	Ps 33:12 et al
14	Col 3:5, 4:6

15	Mt 5:13		32	Mk 9:2-8
16	Mk 12:17, Rom 13:7		33	Rev 1:12-20
17	Jn 17:14		34	Acts 9:1-9
18	Jn 2:25		35	Ps 8:4-5
19	Is 45:23		36	Jn 17:5, 22-24

15 Mt 5:13
16 Mk 12:17, Rom 13:7
17 Jn 17:14
18 Jn 2:25
19 Is 45:23
20 Acts 8:1-4
21 Acts 4:12
22 Mk 16:20
23 Mt 28:18
24 Mk 4:3-9
25 Acts 4:18-20
26 Heb 4:14-16
27 Heb 7:25, 9:12
28 Heb 12:2
29 1 Tim 2:5
30 Jn 20:28, 29
31 Rom 11:33
32 Jn 14: 2, 3
33 Jn 20:14-17
34 Jn 20:19-20
35 Jn 14:3
36 1 Thess 4:17-18

SAINT JOHN THE EVANGELIST

1 Mk 1:16-20; then comparing Mt 27.56 with Mk 15.40
2 Jn 1:44
3 Jn 19:25
4 Mk 5:37, 9:2, 14:33
5 Jn 13:3, 19:26, 20:2, 21:20
6 Jn 13:21-26
7 Jn 19:25-27
8 Acts 3:1, 4:3, 8:14
9 Gal 2:6-10
10 Mk 3:17
11 Acts 19:23-41
12 Mk 16:18
13 Acts 25:4
14 Rev 1:9
15 Jn 20:28
16 Rom 16:22, 1 Cor 16:21, Gal 6:11
17 Mk 10:17-22
18 2 Cor 11:16-21
19 1 Jn 1:5-7
20 Gen 1:3
21 Jn 1:5
22 Jn 8:12
23 Acts 2:3, 4
24 Ps 119:105
25 Ps 36:9
26 1 Jn 1:4
27 Matt 5:45
28 1 Jn 1:3-7
29 1 Jn 2:7-11
30 Ps 43:3
31 1 Jn 4:7-12

32 Mk 9:2-8
33 Rev 1:12-20
34 Acts 9:1-9
35 Ps 8:4-5
36 Jn 17:5, 22-24

THE INNOCENTS' DAY

1 Prayer of Consecration
2 Jn 12:23-28, 17:1-5 et al
3 Col 1:24
4 Col 1:20
5 General Thanksgiving, 2 Cor 5:19 et al.
6 Jn 10:18
7 Col 3:5
8 Rom 1:24-32,7:14-23
9 Rom 8:14-17
10 Rom 1:18-32, Gal 5:19-20, Eph 5:3-19, Col 3:5-10
11 1 Jn 2:1 et al
12 Phil 3:12-14
13 Ps 37:38
14 Matt 18:3,4
15 Matt 11:29
16 1 Pet 2:2
17 Phil 3:15
18 Eph 4:14

THE CIRCUMCISION OF CHRIST

1 Lk 2:21
2 Mt 1:25
3 1 Cor 7:18-19
4 Gal 5:2-12, also Phil 3:2,3
5 Gal 3:23-29 cf Rom 4:9-12 and Phil 3:4-11
6 Rom 5:18
7 1 Cor 15:22
8 1 Cor 15: 45
9 2 Cor 5:17
10 Eph 4:21
11 Is 61:6 et al
12 Mt 22:29
13 Gal 3:10-14, Rom 9:30-33
14 Matt 23:5
15 Gal 1:6-9
16 Gal 4:4, Rom 8:21
17 Gen 3:24, Gal 3:13,5:18
18 Acts 2:23
19 1 Pet 3:18
20 Heb 9:20
21 Heb 9:26, 1 Jn 4:10
22 Phil 2:8-12
23 Rom 2:28,29
24 Eph 4:22

25	Rev 12:9
26	Jdgs 5:15
27	Gen 1:26
28	Gen 3:7
29	Athanasian Creed
30	1 Cor 10:13
31	Mt 5:8
32	Mt 5:27-30
33	Eph 5:5
34	1 Cor 12:27 et al
35	Jn 8:1-11
36	2 Cor 3:4-6, Matt 5:17-20
37	Rom 7:12
38	Ps 19:11

CONVERSION OF ST PAUL

1	2 Cor 11:23-29
2	2 Cor 10:10
3	Acts 6:15
4	Acts 20: 37,38
5	Gal 2:20
6	2 Tim 4:8
7	Acts 9, 22 &26
8	1 Cor 15:8, Gal 1:16
9	1 Cor 9:16
10	Acts 22:3, Gal 1:14
11	1 Cor15:8-10
12	Rom 15:17-21
13	Rom 15:28
14	Acts 2:37
15	Eph 1:9,10
16	2 Cor 5:18-20
17	1 Cor 15:21, Rom 5:14
18	Rom 8:14-17
19	2 Cor 5:17
20	Col 3:11
21	Rom 6:4
22	Eph 4:21
23	2 Cor 12:2
24	Jn 3:11
25	Acts 9:15
26	Gal 2:20
27	Phil 3:12
28	2 Cor 11:23
29	Phil 3:12-24
30	1 Cor 1:3
31	Phil 3:6
32	Phil 1:21 (A.V.)

THE PRESENTATION IN THE TEMPLE

1	Jn 8:12
2	Lk 2:32
3	Jn 1:9
4	Ex 13:12
5	Num 1:49-50

6	Ex 28:1
7	Lk 2:22-24
8	Heb 4:14ff
9	Rev 7:9
10	Lk 2:39
11	Isa 6:1-8
12	Heb 4:16
13	Rom 8:1
14	Rom 12:1
15	Rom 8:15
16	Jn 5:22
17	Mt 25:31
18	2 Cor 11:2
19	Rom 8:1, Phil 3:9
20	Col 1:22, 1 Cor 15:28
21	1 Jn 1:9

SAINT MATTHIAS'S DAY

1	Acts 1:15-26
2	Lk 10:1-24
3	Mt 21:6-11
4	Mt 27:88
5	Lk 24:33-43
6	1 Jn 2:18-25
7	Jn 13:21-30
8	Jn 12:6
9	1 Tim 6:10
10	Jn 12:4, 5
11	Mt 26:14-16, Mk 14:10-11
12	Matt 27:3,4
13	Acts 1:18, 19
14	Jn 13:27
15	Lk 7:36-50
16	Matt 6:22, 23
17	1 Pet 5:8
18	Rom 8:1, 38, 39
19	Acts 1:25
20	Acts 20:17, Jas 5:14, 1 Pet 5:1
21	1 Tim 3:8-13
22	Preface to Ordinal
23	Gal 1:6-9
24	2 Cor 11:13, Rev 2:2
25	Jn 17:16
26	1 Tim 3:1
27	Lk 22:31
28	Mk 14:21
29	Eph 4:15, 16

THE ANNUNCIATION OF THE BLESSED VIRGIN MARY

1	Heb 11:5
2	The Hail Mary Prayer.
3	Lk 1: 26-38
4	Lk 1:48

5	Jn 2:1-11
6	Mk 3:31
7	Jn 19:25-27
8	Acts 1:12-14
9	Lk 1:38
10	Matt 1:18,19
11	Lk 1:36
12	Esp. Hegesippus, 2nd C. historian
13	Mk 6:3
14	Mk 3:35
15	Jn 19:26,27
16	Eccles 11:5
17	Christmas Collect
18	Matt 6:23, Jn 9:39
19	Lk 1:42
20	2 Cor 5:19
21	Eph 4:21
22	Eph 2:8
23	Acts 13:43
24	'There is a Green Hill' by Mrs C.F.Alexander
25	Jn 2:5
26	Lk 1:38
27	Lk 1:46
28	Lk 2:48
29	Lk 2:51
30	Jn 2:3
31	Jn 2:5
32	Jn 19:25
33	Prayer of St Richard
34	Lk 2:55
35	2 Cor 1:20
36	2 Cor 1: 10,11

SAINT MARK'S DAY

1	Mk 1:1
2	Jn 10:28, 1 Jn 5: 11,12, et al
3	Jn 20:21
4	Mk 16:8
5	Mk 8:33, 14:37. 66-72
6	1 Pet 5:13
7	Acts 12:12
8	Mk 14:51, 52
9	Mk 8:31-38, 9:9-12, 10:32-34, 12:1-11
10	Mk 8:33
11	Mk 8:34
12	Mk 15:33, 34
13	Mk 15:39
14	1 Cor 1:17
15	Mk 1:15
16	Acts 12:25
17	Acts 15: 36-41
18	Col 4: 10, 2 Tim 4:11, Philemon 24
19	Ez 1:10
20	Eccles 11:8
21	Gal 4:3
22	Gal 5:1

23	Mt 5:17-29
24	Mt 5: 31-32
25	Mt 5: 27-30
26	Mt 22:1-14
27	Mk 8:34, 35

SAINT PHILIP AND SAINT JAMES'S DAY

1	Jn 14: 6
2	Mt 10: 2-4, Mk 3: 16-19, Lk 6: 14-16
3	Jn 1:43-45
4	Mt 10:1 ff, Mk 6: 7ff, Lk 9: 1ff
5	Jn 1:43
6	Jn 12: 20-21
7	Jn 6: 5-7
8	Jn 14: 8-11
9	Acts 21: 8-9
10	Mk 3:17-18
11	Mk 15: 40, 47; 16:1
12	Mt 28:1, Lk 24:10
13	Acts 17:25 et al
14	Isa 7:15
15	Deut 34:10
16	Deut 30: 20
17	Deut 30: 15-18
18	Deut 8:3
19	Jer 31:34
20	Isa 28:10
21	Isa 30:18-21, Jer 31:31-34
22	Joel 2: 28-32, Acts 2: 14-21
23	Gal 2: 20
24	Rom 15: 13
25	Eph 1: 13-14
26	Jn 14:5, 16:18
27	1 Pet 2:21
28	1 Cor:18-25
29	Rom 6:4
30	Ps 25:3,4
31	Mt 16: 24,25
32	Jn 13: 34
33	Jn 15: 10,11; Ps 19:11
34	Jn 14: 8,9

SAINT BARNABAS THE APOSTLE

1	Acts 4:36
2	Acts 11:24
3	Acts 4:37
4	Acts 6:1-6
5	Jn 4:42
6	Acts 10
7	Acts 11:19-26
8	Acts 9:23-30
9	Acts 15:36-41
10	Acts 14:8-18
11	Acts 11:23-26

12	Gal 2:1, 2:13, 1 Cor 9:6
13	1 Cor 12:4
14	1 Cor 12:21-30
15	Mk 10:35, Mt 23:12
16	2 Cor 5:20
17	1 Chron 29:14
18	1 Cor 13
19	2 Tim 1:6
20	1 Cor 12:8-10
21	Gal 5:2-23
22	1 Thess 5:16-18
23	1 Cor 16:13-14
24	Phil 4:8
25	Rom 6:4, 1 Cor 12:13
26	Phil 3:14, 2 Tim 1:9, Heb 3:1, 1Jn 3:1

SAINT JOHN BAPTIST'S DAY

1	Matt 3:1-5
2	Acts 19:4
3	Mk 1:6
4	Lk 7:33
5	Lk 3:18
6	Lk 3:10-14
7	Lk 3:16
8	Lk 20:6
9	Jn 3:27-30
10	Mk 9:4-5
11	Lk 7:28
12	Mk 6:14-29
13	Jn 8:32
14	Jn 18:37
15	Ibid
16	Eph 4:21
17	Jn 16:13
18	Mt 5:11,12
19	Jn 10:41
20	Lk 1:11
21	General Thanksgiving.
22	Lk 1::15-23
23	Mk 18:10
24	Lk 1:44
25	Lk 3:16
26	Acts 2:3,4
27	Gal 5:22, Ps 21:3
28	Mk 10:30
29	Jn 3:29, Mt 11:2-6
30	Ps 139:13
31	Heb 1:3
32	Jn 16:21
33	Ps 145:9
34	Ps 119:73
35	Jn 16:13
36	Thess 5:24

SAINT PETER'S DAY

1	Jn 1: 42, Mt 16:18
2	Jn 1:44
3	Mk 1:16-20, Lk 5: 1-ll
4	1 Cor 9:5, Mk 1:30
5	Jn 20:4, 21: 7. 18: 10
6	Mk 8:31-33, Mt 14:28-33, Jn 18:10
7	Jn 18:25-27 (see also 1 Pet 5:6-8)
8	1 Pet 1:8, 2:24-25, 3:13-16 et al
9	Jn 21:18-19, Lk 22-33
10	1 Pet 1:2
11	Is 22:22
12	Rev 1:18
13	Mt 13:10-15, Mk 4:11-12, Lk 8:9-10
14	Jn 20:22-23
15	Mt 18:18
16	Jn 1:42
17	Mk 3:16, Lk 6:14
18	Mt 4:18, Lk 5:1-11 (n.b. v 8)
19	Mt 1:21
20	Jn 21:15, also Lk 22:31
21	Acts 15:14, 2 Pet 1:1
22	Rom 9:33
23	1 Cor 10:1-4
24	1 Cor 1:12
25	Eph 6:12
26	Jn 1:5
27	Mt 16:22-23
28	Acts 2:4, 4:8, 11:15, 15:28
29	Mt 7:24-27
30	Rom 10:14-17
31	1 Cor 4:2
32	Gal 1:6-7
33	Acts 5:42
34	Acts 4:12
35	1 Tim 4:1-5
36	1 Cor14:8
37	Heb 13:8
38	Rom 7, Gal 3.
39	2 Cor 3
40	1 Jn 1:8
41	Mt 16:21-23
42	Mt 26:69-75
43	Mk 8: 34-38
44	1 Cor 1:18-25
45	Jn 8:34-36
46	1 Pet 2:21-25
47	Rom 7:14-25
48	Rom 6:1-11
49	Rom 8:18-23
50	Mt 27: 27-31
51	1 Pet 5:4
52	Eph 4:21
53	Mt 9:36
54	1 Pet 1:8

SAINT MARY MAGDALEN

1   Lk 7:36-50
2   Lk 8:2, Mk 16:9, Jn 20:16
3   Mk 14:3-9, Jn 12:2-8
4   Lk 8:1-3, Mk15: 40-41
5   Lk 23:49
6   Jn 20:1
7   Lk 8:30
8   Jn 20:16
9   Matt 10:7, 8
10   Matt 11:2-6
11   Is 65:17-20
12   Matt 7:21
13   Phil 2:6
14   Ibid v 7
15   Is 55:8
16   1 Cor 1:27
17   2 Cor 12:7-10, cf Gal 4:15
18   Lk 14:21
19   *The Living Touch*, by Dorothy Kerin
20   B.C.P. Catechism
21   Mk 5:25-34. Cf Lk 13:10-17
22   Ps 62:7
23   Ps 67:2
24   Lk 2:52
25   Ps 119:75
26   Rom 8:18-28
27   Mk 7:37
28   Mk 16:18-20

SAINT JAMES THE APOSTLE

1   Mk 5:37
2   Mk 9:2 et al
3   Mk 14:33
4   Mk 3:16-19, Mt 10:2-4, Lk 6:14-16,
     Acts 1:13
5   Mk 1:16-20
6   Mt 20:20-28, Mk 10:35-45
7   Lk 9:51-56
8   Mk 3:17
9   Acts 12:2
10   Acts 8:4
11   Mk 10:39
12   Mk 6:27
13   Rom 15:20-28
14   Mt 10:37
15   Mk 1:20
16   Mk 12:44
17   Jn 6:1-13
18   Mt 10:38
19   The Service of Public Baptism
20   Athanasian Creed
21   1 Cor 10:13
22   Eph 4:21
23   Marriage Service 1928 B.C.P.
24   Mt 19:12
25   1 Cor 7:17

26   1 Cor 16:14
27   Lk 3:23
28   Luke 4:1-13
29   Mt 7:13
30   Mt 26:39
31   1 Pet 3:14, 15

THE TRANSFIGURATION

1   Mt 17:1-8, Mk 9:2-10, Lk 9:28-36
2   Rev 12:7-12
3   Mk 1:23-25, Jn 16:33
4   Mt 10:34
5   Eph 6:10-20, 1 Tim 6:12
6   Lk 9:30, 31
7   Ex 14:14
8   Ps 98:2
9   Easter Hymn (Tr. F. Potts)
10   Lk 9:32
11   Jn 5:44
12   Ps 24: 8, Is 9: 6-7,
     Zach 6:12, 13 et al, *Te Deum*.
13   Jn 2:11
14   Jn 1:14
15   Jn 12:23-25
16   Jn 17:1-5, 24
17   Mt 17:4-6
18   Eph 4:21
19   Gal 6:14
20   Passiontide Hymn (I. Watts)
21   1 Cor 1:20-25
22   Mk 9:33
23   Lk 24:26
24   Rom 3:9-18
25   Rom 7:23
26   Rom 1:18-32, Eph 2:3
27   Ps 95:10
28   Confession in Morning and
     Evening Prayer, B.C.P
29   Rom 2:17-24
30   2 Cor 5:16-19
31   Jn 3:16
32   Collect for Christmas II, added in 1928
33   cf General Thanksgiving
34   1 Jn 3:16, 2:2
35   1 Pet 3:18
36   Col 1:24-29
37   2 Cor 5:19-21
38   Mt 5:16
39   1 Pet 4:14
40   Mt 5:12
41   2 Cor 4:17
42   Heb 12:2
43   1 Cor 13:11, 12
44   Eph 4:15
45   Phil 3:20, 21
46   1 Jn 3:2
47   1 Cor 2:9

SAINT BARTHOLOMEW THE APOSTLE

1 Jn 1:43-51
2 Mt 10:2-4, Mk 3:16-19,
  Lk 6:14-16, Acts 1:13
3 Lk 8:1, 9:1-2, 10:1
4 Jn 21: 2,3
5 Mt 16:17, Acts 1:22
6 Jn 1:48
7 Lk 7:44-50, 9:47, Jn 4:17, 18,
  4:50-53, 13:21
8 Gen 32:27-28
9 Gen 32:27-28
10 Gen 28:12
11 Mt 13:17
12 Acts 1:10, 11
13 Mt 5:8
14 Jn 1:14
15 Mk 1:1
16 Mk 1:14-15
17 Ps 119:47, 19:8
18 Ps 119:47, 19:8
19 Mt 5:17
20 Gal 4:1-6
21 Ps 199:57
22 Rom 8:15
23 Gal 1:6-9
24 Mk 4:9 et al
25 Mt 13:15, Is 6:10
26 Jn 1:11
27 Ps 58:5, Jn 1:14
28 Jas 1:21
29 Mk 1:14, 15
30 Jn 20:31
31 Mt 18:18
32 Jn 8:47, Jn 5:9-12
33 Heb 4:12
34 Rom 1:16-18
35 Jn 1:12
36 Jn 3:16-19
37 Rom 2:19
38 Jn 9:38-41

SAINT MATTHEW THE APOSTLE

1 Mt 10:3, Mk 3:18, Lk 6:15, Acts 1:13
2 Mt 9:9, Mk 2:14, Lk 5:27-28
3 e,g, Mt 5-7, 10, 13, 18, 24-25
4 Mt 1:22
5 Mt 5:17
6 Mt 8:23-27, Mk 4:34-41
7 Mt 23:2
8 Mt 5:20
9 2 Cor 4:1-6
10 Mt 25
11 Lk 3:12,13
12 Lk 19:1-10

13 Lk 3:23
14 Rom 8:15
15 1 Tim 6:9, 10
16 Lk 6:24
17 Col 3:5
18 Mt 6:24
19 1 Tim 6:18,19
20 Mt 6:25-33
21 Mt 7:13, 14
22 Mt 6:33
23 1 Cor 1:24
24 Lk 6:38
25 2 Cor 9:7
26 Acts 20:35
27 Acts 17:6

SAINT MICHAEL AND ALL ANGELS

1 Heb 2:9
2 Heb 1:5
3 1 Jn 1:3
4 2 Pet 2:4, Jude 6, Rev 12:7-9
5 Mk 1:21-17 et al
6 Mk 5:13
7 Mk 16:17
8 Lk 10:17, 18
9 Isa 14:12
10 Jude 9
11 Dan 12:1, also 10:13
12 Mt 18:10
13 Lk 1:19, 26
14 The Apocryphal Books of Tobit and
  Enoch
15 Jn 14:3
16 Main references: 1 Pet 3:22, 1 Thess
  4:16, Rom 8:38, Eph 1:21, 6:12, Col
  1:16, Heb 9:5, Isa 6:2
17 Col 2:18
18 Eph 6:12
19 Te Deum
20 Mt 25:41, Rev 20:14, 15
21 Rev 8:2
22 Lk 1:19
23 Heb 1:14
24 Gen 28:12
25 Mt 18:10
26 Ps 91:10,
27 Ps 91:11
28 Acts 12:9-11

SAINT LUKE THE EVANGELIST

1   Col 4: 14
2   2 Cor 8: 16-19
3   Col 4: 14
4   2 Tim 4: 11
5   2 Cor 12: 9
6   Lk 1: 3, Acts 1: 1
7   Lk 3: 1
8   Lk 3: 23-38, Mt 1: 2-18
9   Lk 9: 51-56
10   Lk 10: 30-37
11   Lk 15:1 1-32
12   Lk 16: 19:31
13   Lk 18: 9-14
14   Lk 7: 11-17
15   Lk 7: 36-50
16   Lk 4: 25-27
17   Lk 19: 1-10
18   Lk 13: 29
19   Lk 7: 22, 23
20   Lk 1: 1-14
21   Lk 4: 38
22   Acts 28: 8
23   Lk 22: 44
24   Lk 4: 23
25   Acts 19: 11, 12, 13
26   Acts 16: 18-20
27   Lk 9: 2, 10: 8, 9
28   Matt 8: 1-14
29   Mk 1: 40-45
30   Lk 5: 12-16
31   Lk 10:1-2
32   Matt 10: 5, Mk 6: 7
33   Acts 3: 1-16
34   Mk 7: 23
35   Jn 8: 24
36   Morning and Evening Prayer
37   Rev 20:1 1-5
38   Eph 2: 19-22
39   Lk 12: 20-21

SAINT SIMON and SAINT JUDE

1   Eph 2:20-21
2   Jude v 4
3   Jn 15:17
4   Jude v 1
5   Lk 6:16
6   Mt 10:3, Mk 3:18
7   Jn 14:22
8   Lk 6:15, Acts 1:13, Mt 10:4, Mk 3:18
9   Eph 2:20-22
10   Eph 2:13-16
11   Eph 4:5,6
12   1 Cor 1:12, 13
13   Rev 2: 7 et al
14   Jn 17: 22, 23
15   Rom 6:3

16   1 Cor 14:8
17   1 Cor 3:10, 11
18   Nicene Creed
19   Mt 28:18-20, Acts 1:4
20   Ps 87:7
21   Gen 18:14
22   *Cardinal Hume* by Peter Stanford,
     p.86
23   *Crossing the threshold of hope* by
     Pope John Paul II, p.148
24   Rev 21:22
25   Heb 12:22-24
26   Ps 122:3
27   Jn 17:21-23
28   1 Cor 1:17, Col 1:20
29   Eph 2:14-17
30   Rom 6:4
31   2 Pet 3:13
32   1Acts 17:26
33   2 Cor 5:19
34   1 Cor 15:28
35   Heb 12:1-2
36   Jude v 20

ALL SAINTS' DAY

1   Col 2: 2-4
2   Col 2: 18-19
3   Eph 4: 16
4   Col   2: 2
5   Eph 4:16
6   Deut 7: 6
7   Is 45: 4-6
8   Is 9: 6,7 et al
9   Gal 4: 4-6
10   Rom 11: 33-36
11   Rom 6: 3
12   Phil 1:21 et al
13   2 Cor 5: 16,17
14   Mt 22:14
15   n.b Mk 10:45
16   1 Tim 2:4
17   Rome 3: 9
18   Jn 16:32
19   Mt 8:22, 9:9 et al
20   1 Cor 11:1 A.V.
21   2 Cor 4:5
22   Heb 6:12
23   Phil 4:8
24   Heb 11:8
25   Is 30:21
26   Deut 5:4
27   Jn 14:23
28   2 Cor 5:8
29   Heb 12:23
30   Mt 5:12 A.V.
31   Jn 16:22
32   Heb 11:32
33   1 Cor 2:9
34   Mt 18:1-5

EPILOGUE

1   Eph 3:18,19
2   2 Cor 5:16, 17 et al
3   Rom 8:1,2,31-39
4   1 Cor 1:12
5   Eph 4:21
6   Col 2:22
7   1 Cor 13:13
8   Mt 18:3, 1 Cor 1:18-31
9   Heb 7:25
10   Heb 11:40
11   Rev 7:13,14
12   Gal 2:20
13   Col 3:1-3
14   Phil 1:20
15   Phil 3:10,11
16   Rom 6:5
17   Gal 6:17
18   1 Cor 13:1-3
19   Lk 24:39
20   Gal 5:22
21   1 Jn 4:13
22   Jn 15:1-5
23   Acts 4:13
24   Rom 6:11
25   Mt 7:6
26   Jn 3:16
27   Acts 3:12, Rom 7:14,15